To Dave and Joanne,
and all of theirs, with love,

UNITED STATES OF NORTH AMERICA.

ALABAMA	ARCANSAS TERRITOR
NORTH CAROLINA	SOUTH CAROLINA
CONNEC-TICUT	FLORIDA
GEORGIA	NEW JERSEY
ILLINOIS	INDIANA
KENTUCKY	LOUISIANA
MAINE	MARILAND
MASSA-CHUSETTS	MICHIGAN TERRITOR
MISSISSIPI	MISSOURI
N. WEST TERRITORI	OHIO
OREGON	PENNSYL-VANIA
TENESSEE	VERMONT
VIRGINIA	NEW YORK

Reisebericht

der

Familie Köpfli & Suppiger

nach

St. Louis am Mississippi

und

Gründung von New Switzerland

im

Staate Illinois.

Zweite, stark vermehrte Ausgabe.

Sursee, 1833.
Gedruckt in der Schnyderschen Buchdruckerei.

NEW SWITZERLAND.

Journey to New Switzerland

TRAVEL ACCOUNT OF THE

KOEPFLI AND SUPPIGER FAMILY

TO ST. LOUIS ON THE

MISSISSIPPI AND THE

FOUNDING OF

NEW SWITZERLAND

IN THE STATE OF ILLINOIS

by Joseph Suppiger, Salomon Koepfli, and

Kaspar Koepfli

TRANSLATED BY RAYMOND J. SPAHN

With Excerpts from Jennie Latzer Kaeser's Translation
of Salomon Koepfli's *Die Geschichte der Ansiedlung
von Highland* (The Story of the Settling of Highland)

EDITED BY JOHN C. ABBOTT

Foreword by Joseph Blake Koepfli

Southern Illinois University Press

Carbondale and Edwardsville

Printed in the United States of America

Edited by Curtis L. Clark

Production supervised by Natalia Nadraga

90 89 88 87   4 3 2 1

Publication of this volume has been made possible in part by
funds furnished by Friends of Lovejoy Library, Lovejoy Library,
Southern Illinois University at Edwardsville, Edwardsville,
Illinois.

Library of Congress Cataloging-in-Publication Data

Suppiger, Joseph, 1804–1861.

Journey to New Switzerland.

Translation of: Reisebericht der Familie Köpfli &
Suppiger nach St. Louis am Mississippi und Gründung
von New-Switzerland im Staate Illinois.

Bibliography: p.

1. Swiss Americans—Illinois—History—19th century.

2. Swiss Americans—Illinois—Biography.   3. Illinois—
Description and travel—To 1865.   4. Suppiger family.
5. Koepfli family.   6. Suppiger, Joseph, 1804–1861—
Diaries.   7. Mississippi River Valley—Description and
travel.   8. United States—Description and travel—1783–
1848.   I. Köpfli, Salomon.   II. Köpfli, Kaspar.
III. Abbott, John C., 1921–   .   IV. Köpfli, Salomon.
Geschichte der Ansiedlung von Highland.   English.
Selections.   1986.   V. Title.

F550.S9S813   1986   977.3'00435   86-3885

ISBN 0-8093-1313-8

Frontispiece: Cover of the 1833 *Reisebericht*

Courtesy of New York Public Library

To the late A. P. Spencer,
Jennie Latzer Kaeser, Betty Spindler Coats,
and Joseph Blake Koepfli:
their labors, along with those of many others,
have done so much to make accessible to present and future
generations
the history of New Switzerland,
an eighty-square-mile area in southwestern Illinois
with the city of Highland as its center.

CONTENTS

Illustrations / ix

Foreword / xi
Joseph Blake Koepfli

Introduction / xv

Prologue / xxv

TRAVEL ACCOUNT

Foreword / 1
Dr. Kaspar Mauris Koepfli

Part One: Journey from Sursee to Havre / 3
Joseph Suppiger

Part Two: Journey by Sea to New York / 29
Joseph Suppiger

Part Three: River Journey from New York to St. Louis
on the Mississippi / 85
Joseph Suppiger

Part Four: Letters from New Switzerland / 133
Salomon Koepfli (December 11, 1831) / 135
Joseph Suppiger (March 19, 1832) / 160
Salomon Koepfli (March 21, 1832) / 165
Joseph Suppiger (September, 1832) / 167

Part Five: Advantages and Disadvantages of the Area
We Chose to Settle / 173
Dr. Kaspar Koepfli

Epilogue / 211

Appendix: Units of Currency, Measure, and Weight / 213

Bibliography / 215

Index / 223

ILLUSTRATIONS

Cover of the 1833 *Reisebericht*
frontispiece

Dreimaster (Three-Master) from the 1833 *Reisebericht*
30

Map of Illinois from the 1833 *Reisebericht*
134

FOREWORD

The *Reisebericht*, first published in 1833, was compiled from the writings of three members of a party that left Switzerland in 1831 to found a settlement for compatriots in the midwestern United States.

A day-to-day diary of the Swiss party's journey from Sursee in the canton of Lucerne to St. Louis, Missouri, comprises the first three parts of the five-part work. The diary was kept by twenty-six-year-old *Joseph* Kaspar Thomas Suppiger, charged with the logistics of the undertaking by his uncle, Dr. Johannes Sebastian *Kaspar* Koepfli, the fifty-seven-year-old leader of the group. Suppiger, eldest son of a successful textile manufacturer in Sursee, had attended a lyceum in Lucerne as well as Jesuit schools in Sion (canton of Valais) and Fribourg before enrolling in an educational institute in Aarau in the canton of Aargau. At the institute he came under the influence of teachers such as the esteemed liberal historian, novelist, and writer of religious works Heinrich Zschokke (1771–1848) and Ignaz Paul Vital Troxler (1780–1866), a close friend and political associate of Dr. Koepfli's, who had lost his post at the lyceum in Lucerne because of his severe criticism of the faculty and the government. (Suppiger's class notes from his two winters at the institute are preserved at Harvard University's Widener Library, where they are labeled "Journal.")

Part 4 of the *Reisebericht* consists of letters written to relatives back in Sursee during the Swiss party's first year in America. Two of the letters are from my grandfather Joseph *Salomon* Julius Koepfli—then eighteen—to his eldest brother Kaspar Mauris, a physician, who had attended the lyceum in Lucerne and then followed his teacher Troxler to the institute in Aarau. Salomon audited classes at the institute during the winter of 1829–30 while enrolled at the vocational school in Aarau. The two other letters comprising part 4 are by Suppiger to relatives in Sursee who did not emigrate until two years after the founding of New Switzerland in Illinois.

Part 5, designed primarily as a guide for prospective emigrants, was written by my great-grandfather, Dr. Kaspar Koepfli. It also contains a third letter by Salomon Koepfli, which is preceded by an introduction by the recipient, his physician brother, who did not emigrate until 1839 and who took charge of the publication of the *Reisebericht* in Sursee in 1833.

The political situation of the time in Switzerland was described later by

Salomon Koepfli in his 1859 *Geschichte der Ansiedlung von Highland.*
There, he tells how his father, a subprefect in the pro-French government
installed in 1798, fell into disfavor after the fall of Napoleon, as did the
Suppigers. When the hopes of liberals for a more democratic form of
government did not materialize, the two families made tentative plans to
emigrate to America. Though the elder Koepfli was dissuaded from making the move at that time, the thought of emigrating did not die. When, in
early 1831, members of the Koepfli and Suppiger families were at last
preparing to leave for the central United States, the senior Dr. Koepfli set
forth his reasons for leaving in a "Farewell Letter" distributed to relatives
and politcally associated friends.[1] In brief, members of the group were
motivated by the desire for religious, political, and personal freedom, all of
which they were to find in America.

The descendants of the founding group, although living in widely
scattered parts of the country a century and a half later, have retained an
active interest in New Switzerland in Illinois and in the publication of
English-language versions of the nineteenth-century writings about it.

As the great-grandson of New Switzerland's founder, I take great pleasure in emphasizing the following individuals' contributions in making
pioneer Swiss writings available to present-day readers.

First is Jennie Latzer Kaeser, who splendidly translated Salomon
Koepfli's 1859 *Geschichte* as *The Story of the Settling of Highland*
(Edwardsville, 1970). This was followed by her translation of the senior
Dr. Koepfli's *Spiegel von Amerika* as "Mirror of America," which com-
prises book 1 of *New Switzerland in Illinois* (Edwardsville, 1977). Com-
prising book 2 of *New Switzerland* is Manfred Driesner's translation of
Jacob Eggen's *Aufzeichnungen aus Highlands Gruendungszeit,* under the
title "Chronicles of Early Highland."

Then came *The Swiss on Looking Glass Prairie: A Century and a Half,
1831–1981* (Edwardsville, 1983), compiled by Betty Spindler Coats,
whose brother Julius Spindler had made translations of early Swiss writings about Highland for the *Highland News Leader.* Finally we have this
definitive translation of the *Reisebericht.*

Throughout this period during which so much historical material has
been made available, there has been a continuity of scholarship and

---

1. Dr. Koepfli's "Farewell Letter" has been appended to the present volume's
Prologue.

devoted interest without which I do not believe we could have these four volumes to enjoy. For this we can be grateful to John C. Abbott, long director of Lovejoy Library, and to Raymond J. Spahn, emeritus professor of German, both of Southern Illinois University at Edwardsville, as well as to Betty Alderton Spahn.

JOSEPH BLAKE KOEPFLI
Santa Barbara, California

INTRODUCTION

I

Elsewhere I have described in some detail the five German language works written by the early settlers of New Switzerland.[1] Some further words are appropriate to describe how I came to learn about these rare accounts and the role several individuals played in making four of them, including now the *Reisebericht* (Travel Account), available in modern translations in book form.[2]

Dr. Kaspar Koepfli, his son Salomon Koepfli, and his favorite nephew Joseph Suppiger—all of whom set out with other family members from Sursee on April 21, 1831—ultimately produced four books describing their travels and early days in New Switzerland, the four-township area in southwestern Illinois surrounding what is now the city of Highland. In 1833, they were joined by Jacob Eggen, who was to publish a fifth pioneer account, also in German, describing the Swiss colony's history to about 1859. (Eggen married Dr. Koepfli's daughter, Rosa, in 1836.) The history of few communities has been as ably chronicled by its founders. However, many years were to pass before any of these five pioneer works were to become available in book form in modern translations.

Since this area contained the most important and largest Swiss community established in the United States in the nineteenth century and since all but one of the five accounts are of considerable interest and merit, their almost complete neglect deserves some explanation.

One obvious reason for such neglect is that the foreign language literature of immigration has not received nearly as much attention by translators as it deserves. A notable instance is Gottfried Duden's enormously influential and well-known *Report on a Journey to the Western States of North America,* which did not become fully available in translation until 1980, (when it was published by the State Historical Society of Missouri

1. "The Pioneer Writings about Highland," foreword to *New Switzerland in Illinois,* ed. Betty A. Spahn and Raymond J. Spahn (Edwardsville, Ill.: Friends of Lovejoy Library, 1977), pp. xi–xiv.
2. For description of serial translations of the *Reisebericht,* see the Bibliography.

and the University of Missouri Press, Columbia). Also despite its importance, the Swiss settlement in Illinois lacked the glamour which tends to become attached to altruistic colonies, better yet communal ones. The founders of New Switzerland had the more prosaic aim of establishing a settlement which would attract their compatriots to follow in their footsteps. In this they were outstandingly successful. Books about communities such as New Switzerland tend to be considered merely "local history," whereas more eccentric experiments have a greater likelihood of receiving attention, scholarly and popular.

That more was not done until recently about translating the pioneer accounts may be partly due to the fact that Swiss emigration to the United States was never large compared with that of other countries. While important studies have been published describing individual Swiss communities, the most thorough survey of Swiss immigration in the nineteenth century is still Guy S. Metraux's unpublished 1949 Yale University doctoral dissertation, "Social and Cultural Aspects of Swiss Immigration into the United States in the Nineteenth Century."

One reason, however, stands out among all others for the little attention which these five works have until recently received: their rarity, in some instances amounting to complete, or almost complete, lack of any record of their existence.

In 1968, my Carbondale, Illinois colleague Dr. Ralph McCoy called my attention to two early Highland books which were to be auctioned at the Thomas W. Streeter sale. They were Salomon Koepfli's *Neu Schweizerland in den Jahren 1831 und 1841* (Lucerne, 1842) and Kaspar Koepfli's *Die Licht- & Schattenseite von New Switzerland in Nordamerika* (Sursee, 1833). Through the generosity of Jennie Latzer Kaeser of Highland, Lovejoy Library purchased these two small volumes which, with good reason, I had never heard of. The first was recorded as being held in this country only by the New York Public Library; for the second there was no record of any library holding in this country.[3]

By 1968 I had become aware of but had not seen the *Reisebericht,* merely excessively rare, but cited fairly frequently. I was aware from Wright Howes's *USiana* that there had been two editions printed in Sursee in 1833, one of 235 pages and another of 296 pages. Shortly after the two Streeter sale acquisitions I had a chance to examine the copy of the 296-page edition of the *Reisebericht* owned by the Belleville Public Li-

---

3. Except for Lovejoy's copies, this situation apparently has not changed.

brary. I had with me a photo copy of Kaspar Koepfli's *Die Licht- &
Schattenseite,* and much to my surprise I discovered that its contents
matched part 5 of the *Reisebericht.* Therefore, though it adds to our
knowledge of the publishing history of the *Reisebericht,* this pamphlet is
not reckoned as one of the five separate pioneer works.

By this time, I had become aware also of two other works, Jacob Eggen's
Aufzeichnungen aus Highlands Gruendungszeit (Chronicles of Early
Highland), published in Highland in 1888, and Salomon Koepfli's *Geschichte der Ansiedlung von Highland* (The Story of the Settling of Highland), published in Highland in 1859. The former was recorded as being
held only by the New York Public Library, and the latter was not recorded
as being held by any library.[4]

Though a great many people have been deeply involved in the several
projects to publish translations of such pioneer writings about Highland,
the original impetus came from Jenny Latzer Kaeser. In notifying me of her
decision to provide Lovejoy Library funds to purchase Henry Lewis's *Das
illustrirte Mississippithal* (Duesseldorf, 1854–58), she wrote, "I would,
however, appreciate a translation of this book into English when obtainable." For her it was not enough that we had the text—and its pictures—
available for scholars. She was properly aware that its contents would not,
for practical purposes, be accessible to students and the general public
until it was available in English.[5] I should then perhaps not have been too
surprised when I received in the fall of 1969 a letter from Mrs. Kaeser
notifying us that she would soon be bringing us a copy of her translation of
Salomon Koepfli's *Geschichte,* undertaken in her ninetieth year. A year
later, it was published as *The Story of the Settling of Highland.*

In January of 1971, we received another pleasant surprise. Writing to
Mrs. Kaeser, Dr. Joseph Blake Koepfli, the grandson of Salomon Koepfli
and great-grandson of Kaspar Koepfli, told of an unbound pamphlet in his
possession, entitled *Spiegel von Amerika,* by Dr. Kaspar Koepfli, published in Lucerne in 1849. Of this small book there was no record of any

4. The Louis Latzer Memorial Public Library in Highland owned copies of both
the Eggen and Salomon Koepfli works, copies of which subsequently were donated
to Lovejoy Library. Lovejoy Library later received a second copy of Koepfli's
Geschichte through the generosity of Betty Spindler Coats.
5. Kaeser was assured that a translation would soon appear. It was published in
1967 by the Minnesota Historical Society (St. Paul) under the title *The Valley of the
Mississippi Illustrated,* trans. A. Hermina Poatgieter and ed. Bertha L. Heilbron.

library holding in this country.[6] We now at last knew of the existence of all five of the pioneer works.

In April of 1974, Mrs. Kaeser, now ninety-six, wrote me that she was mailing her translation of Kaspar Koepfli's *Spiegel von Amerika,* adding "I think it adds considerable information to our early history." In 1977 her translation was to become book 1, under the title "Mirror of America," of *New Switzerland in Illinois* (Edwardsville, Friends of Lovejoy Library, Southern Illinois University at Edwardsville). Book 2 of *New Switzerland* consisted of Manfred Driesner's translation, under the title "Chronicles of Early Highland," of Jacob Eggen's *Aufzeichnungen aus Highlands Gruendungszeit.* Thus three of the five pioneer writings became available in book form in modern translations. The fourth is now in front of the reader. But for the fifth, there are at least for now no plans. Salomon Koepfli's *Neu-Schweizerland in den Jahren 1831 und 1841* was written in flowery language by the homesick young man during his return trip to Switzerland. Even the chapter on New Switzerland in 1841 adds little of significance.

The prodigious energy and translating skill of one person, not previously mentioned, runs throughout all these enterprises as a connecting and absolutely indispensable link, that of Raymond Jurgen Spahn, now Professor of German Emeritus, Southern Illinois University at Edwardsville. He edited and annotated *The Story of the Settling of Highland* and—with his wife, Betty Alderton Spahn—*New Switzerland in Illinois,* as well as the invaluable *The Swiss on Looking Glass Prairie: A Century and a Half, 1831–1981* (compiled by Betty Spindler Coats for the Friends of Lovejoy Library and the Highland Historical Society, 1983.) Though many others could be named as well, some of whose contributions can be found in the Bibliography, the untiring efforts and support, extending over many years, in locating and publishing the pioneer writings and otherwise illuminating the history of their ancestral New Switzerland, of Betty Spindler Coats and Dr. Joseph Blake Koepfli have also been of inestimable value.

II

Why, and for whom was the *Reisebericht* written? And what was the effect of its publication?

6. It later turned out that a copy was owned by the Zentralbibliothek, Lucerne.

Dr. Kaspar Mauris Koepfli, the only Koepfli son not to emigrate in 1831, states in his foreword to the *Reisebericht* that the contents of the book "were not intended by their authors to be published, but were written solely for family members who remained behind." This is probably a reasonably accurate statement of the authors' original intent. They expected that Joseph Suppiger, Sr., and Kaspar Mauris Koepfli—with their families—would follow the original group to the New World (as indeed did occur, in 1833 and 1839 respectively). They were certainly aware also that family friends and associates would see, or at least hear about, their reports. From the beginning a written record was planned, Dr. Koepfli, Sr., having instructed his nephew, Joseph Suppiger, Jr., to keep the diary and write the other material which constitute parts 1 through 3. Clearly the principal, but not necessarily the only, purpose of these three parts and of part 4, which consists of two letters each by Suppiger and Salomon Koepfli, is edification of family, and to a lesser extent friends and associates, who planned to or might emigrate. But Dr. Koepfli, certainly not a reticent person, was also keenly aware of the value to him and his party of Gottfried Duden's 1829 *Report on a Journey to the Western States of North America* and must have considered the possibility of making their account more widely available through publication. In order to enhance the success of their settlement they wanted other Swiss and, perhaps to a lesser extent, Germans to follow. They were well aware that New Switzerland needed a substantial number of persons of diverse talents and occupations who must, however, have adequate financial resources to make the journey and still have enough capital to get themselves established. Yet despite the cautionary words expressed in parts 1 through 4, it soon became evident that there was a strong inclination for those who remained behind to neglect the warnings and to fantasize upon what they had read or heard.

We do not know just when in 1833 the first edition of the *Reisebericht* containing parts 1 through 4, appeared, or, for that matter the date in 1833 of the five-part second edition (the text of parts 1 through 4 of the first edition remained unchanged in the second). The main body of the added part 5, by Dr. Kaspar Koepfli, is dated March 1833, and the appended excerpt of a letter from Salomon Koepfli is dated May 13, 1833.

Dr. Koepfli subsequently donated his copy to the Louis Latzer Memorial Public Library, Highland.

Allowing for the time required to carry out the processes of publication, the second edition probably did not appear earlier than the late summer of 1833. In any event, the contents of the expanded five-part edition show considerable concern over misconceptions back home regarding emigration to America which had arisen in the minds of many, including the junior Dr. Koepfli, as a result of reading the first edition of the *Reisebericht,* and doubtless Duden's *Report,* with too little attention to the hardships and difficulties of emigration.

The urgent need to state these less positive or limiting factors is further indicated by the publication of part 5 in 1833 as a separate pamphlet. The pamphlet form provided a convenient, quick, and emphatic way to publish the facts concerning the "Advantages and Disadvantages" encountered, and it enabled those who already owned the first edition to have the contents of the second without purchasing the new edition.

In his introductory paragraph to his brother Salomon's letter of May 13, 1833, published in part 5 of the new edition, Dr. Kaspar Mauris Koepfli expressed with some alarm the fallacious thoughts which he himself had entertained earlier: "Although many of my efforts and many a beautiful hope of mine have come to nothing, I cannot withhold from the public those well-meant, and doubtless well-founded, warnings expressed by my dear brother, for from day to day I am more convinced of the truth of what he writes me."

One of the junior Kaspar's misconceptions had to do with the idea of establishing a cooperative colony in the New World. On this point Salomon took a strongly negative stand:

> We could not read without misgivings your recent letters which dealt so enthusiastically with the question of joint emigration and settlements and which extolled the central issue of Swiss emigration, the beckoning star of the emigrants, New Switzerland. But we had pictured things the same way and formed the same unrealistic ideas before we left Old Switzerland. We, too, dreamed of large group emigrations of the cream of Switzerland hither, building cities, designing community schools and churches, and even holding property in common.[7]

7. In 1831, apparently before crossing from St. Louis to Illinois, the Koepflis and Suppigers drew up a 31-article "Company Acts of the Family Koepfli and Suppiger Brothers." It was apparently never implemented. The text, in both German and

But we ask ourselves: "What has become of all this?" Only too clearly we are beginning to see that realization of such a commune is something bordering on the impossible. Only our experience and arrival here make it possible to understand this. Such joint ventures usually are already completely disintegrating, and the initial goals rejected by most of the members, long before they land in this country.

Further on Salomon warns:

You may accept as *valid* anything we have written, but *do not* pass lightly over what we have described as *difficult,* for it would be unfortunate if you were to imagine conditions to be *any more favorable* than we actually have described them.

The senior Dr. Koepfli in his contribution to part 5 was very explicit as to what kind of persons would and would not succeed in "the area we chose to settle":

By far the greater part of Swiss emigrants have not been farm workers or laborers, but students, former schoolteachers, business apprentices, frustrated speculators, or impoverished aristocrats, in short, individuals least suited for the kind of life to be found here. . . . Education and elegant manners are of little help to immigrants, especially if they do not know English. Mechanics, laborers, or farm workers will do much better. Families with children accustomed to work can improve their lot very much here, but they should be primarily moved to come here by a realization of the steadily deteriorating conditions in Europe and the growing advantages of life in America, especially in the United States. Emigration is particularly recommended for carpenters, blacksmiths, and wagon makers, and especially for persons who combine blacksmithing with wagon mak-

English, appears in Guy Serge Metraux's 1949 Yale University dissertation, "Social and Cultural Aspects of Swiss Immigration into the United States in the Nineteenth Century" (pp. 315–23). The German text appears in Max Schweizer's Zurich University dissertation published under the title *Neu-Schweizerland 1831– 1880: Genese und Funktion einer schweizerischen Siedlung in den USA* (Zug, 1980), pp. 337–41.

ing. Also needed here are tailors, tanners, and harness makers. Opportunities for other workers depend on circumstances.

It is noteworthy that throughout the *Reisebericht* political and religious matters are treated objectively and in a manner not likely to offend its readers. The focus is upon what the immigrants experienced and saw; the intent is to instruct those who were to follow, to warn them of pitfalls, and to provide practical information of all kinds. Since they did not want unduly to discourage their readers from emigrating, they did sometimes underplay or omit some experiences which might have had a negative effect. Mother Koepfli's illness in the late fall or early winter of 1831 is mentioned, but its apparent near-fatal character denied. A spectacular and dangerous prairie fire is not mentioned at all. But taken as a whole the account represents the keen and generally accurate observations of three well-educated, intelligent, and observant upper-middle-class Swiss who were well aware that their own best interests were served by providing accurate, useful, and interesting information for the types of emigrants most suitable for the development of a properous and progressive New Switzerland.

In judging the *Reisebericht*, the reader of today should keep in mind that its authors assumed of their audience a prior, thorough acquaintance with Duden's work, which they repeatedly cited. After all, fifteen hundred copies of it were circulating throughout Europe, and there had been a Swiss reprint. Therefore, to a large extent the *Reisebericht* can be taken as supplementary, and as deemed necessary, a correcting and updating of Duden's pioneering guide. The descriptions of what the authors saw and heard were, of course, limited by the circumstances that they were, until near the end, reporting as travelers in an entirely unfamiliar environment. Also, while almost certainly fluent in French, they were still just beginning to learn to speak and to understand spoken English. But their curiosity was great and, given their limitations, they made few and usually unimportant errors of fact, Their judgments of what they saw and learned are, while tinged with the biases inherent to their background, generally judicious and fair. It is of interest to note that conditions of life in the United States are described as being much superior to those in France. Predisposition or accurate reporting? Let the reader decide. In sum, they have provided for posterity an absorbing odyssey which will transport the reader back to another world in a way that the synthesizing efforts of a modern historian could never displace.

III

As I have said, the *Reisebericht,* or as we have chosen to call it, *Journey to New Switzerland,* appeared in two editions in Sursee in 1833, one of four parts and one of five. We have, of course, used the latter edition, which except for the addition of part 5 does not differ from the first. A "quotation" from George Washington, which precedes the text of the *Reisebericht* editions, also comes at the beginning of the "Farewell Letter" we have included in our Prologue. It only appears in the present book in connection with the letter.

As indicated by the title page a substantial amount of text has been inserted from Jennie Latzer Kaeser's translation of Salomon Koepfli's *Geschichte der Ansiedlung von Highland* (*The Story of the Settling of Highland*). Her translation was privately published in 1970 in an edition of 150 copies, with two small subsequent printings issued by Lovejoy Library. Because this charming and valuable account, which takes the story through 1831, had such limited distribution, mainly in the Highland area and the rest of Illinois, and includes much material which supplements the *Reisebericht,* extensive extracts have been incorporated into Salomon Koepfli's December 11 letter in part 4.

Throughout, umlauts are transcribed as "ae," "ue," or "oe," e.g. Köpfli becomes Koepfli. Occasionally material is transposed to nearby text in order to bring obviously related material together.

In preparing and editing this work for publication the translator and editor have leaned heavily upon two other publications, *New Switzerland in Illinois,* edited by Betty A. Spahn and Raymond J. Spahn, and *The Swiss on Looking Glass Prairie: A Century and a Half, 1831–1981,* compiled by Betty Spindler Coats. Therein are acknowledged the contributions of several dozen individuals and institutions, to all of whom we wish again to extend our heartfelt thanks. Special thanks are again due to the New York Public Library, this time for permission to reproduce the 1833 map of Illinois and the cover from their copy of the second edition of the *Reisebericht.* Finally must be mentioned the indispensable support over a decade and a half of the Friends of Lovejoy Library, Southern Illinois University at Edwardsville.

PROLOGUE

On April 21, 1831, members of the Koepfli and Suppiger families, German Swiss, set out from the town of Sursee, canton of Lucerne, with the object of establishing a new home in America in the state of Missouri. Led by the fifty-seven-year-old Dr. Kaspar Koepfli and his favorite and extremely capable nephew, Joseph Suppiger, these prosperous, well-educated, and decidedly liberal Swiss were not typical of the great majority of their compatriot emigrants. They had quite definite and relatively well-informed views as to what they hoped to accomplish in the New World and adequate financial means to carry out their plans. While their objectives were primarily political, members of the party were highly sensible to economic and social considerations. Not only were other family members, both Koepflis and Suppigers, expected to join them later; the original group undoubtedly intended that other Swiss would learn of their venture, emigrate to New Switzerland, and contribute to the success of the settlement they planned to establish.

As early as 1817, members of the Koepfli family and their liberal friends had considered the idea of removing to America.

> It was resolved among friends and relatives that some one of the number should come to America, see the country, and report whether or not it would be a desirable place to live in, and whether it would be a wise policy to leave Switzerland and take up their abode in the new world; and to decide who was to go. Lots were drawn, the choice fell upon Dr. Koepfli. It was agreed among them that the most desirable and suitable place for settlement was somewhere in the great Mississippi Valley above the junction of the Ohio and Mississippi Rivers.[1]

Dr. Koepfli's wife, Elisabeth, persuaded the strong-minded physician against making the move at that time, her main argument being that their children had not yet finished their educations. Indeed, the oldest son,

---

1. From an article in the *Highland Herald,* December 1, 1881, signed by "A. S.," presumably Anton Suppiger, quoted in *Koepfli: A Partial Family History* by Joseph Blake Koepfli (Santa Barbara, Calif.: privately printed, 1981), p. 3. In writing this Prologue, I am heavily indebted to Dr. Koepfli's research.

Kaspar Mauris (born October 1799), had not yet finished his medical training, and a younger son, David, was still learning English, of obvious importance to the success of the venture. Probably of weight also was the fact that the other four children—Bernard (born January 1804), Joseph (born December 1804), Rosa (born 1810), and Salomon (born April 1814)—were too young to be much assistance. Later the project received a serious setback when David, upon whose knowledge of English so much depended, died (about 1819). However, the objective of removing to America was not forgotten.

For many years before 1817, Dr. Koepfli had already had an interesting and turbulent career. He had been born in the early spring of 1774, in the small village of Lippenruetti (near Neuenkirch, canton of Lucerne). Salomon Koepfli, writing many years later, provides an account of his father's early years:

> He lost his father through death at an early age. At that time, school instruction was difficult to obtain, and the mother showed no interest in sending young Kaspar, who was too frail for farm work, to distant schools, as this would lessen her small income. His desire to learn, which could not be satisfied at home, drove the boy, while still very young, to strangers. His father, as well as his grandfather, had been rural doctors [sic], so he directed his aim in the direction of obtaining the necessary knowledge to follow that profession.
>
> In Solothurn he developed a great liking for hospital work, and rendered such good service there that he was able to get books in his field, which he studied eagerly. He continued to work in this position for several years. With his earnings and savings, it became possible for him to attend the University of Freiburg. Towards the end of the last century, he established himself as a physician in his home community of Neuenkirch. He married [Elisabeth Widmer], and both as a citizen and as a physician he was respected by his fellow men.[2]

In 1797 Napoleon's troops invaded Switzerland, and a French-dictated centralized Helvetic Republic, with a bicameral legislature, replaced the ancient league of largely independent cantons. A new constitution guaranteed the rights of the individual citizen, including freedom of worship, of assembly, of petition, and of the press. Most of the vestiges of feudalism

2. *The Story of the Settling of Highland,* trans. Jennie Latzer Kaeser and ed. Raymond J. Spahn (privately printed, 1970), pp. 1–2.

and arbitrary ecclesiastical authority were abolished. Local governments were put under the control of centrally appointed prefects, who in turn appointed district subprefects.

These were tumultuous times, during which, despite the plundering and despotic acts of the French, the liberating principles for which their revolution ostensibly stood were seized upon by many reform-minded Swiss. Among them was the young Dr. Koepfli, who in 1798 was appointed by the French-dominated regime as a subprefect for the district around Neuenkirch. In the midst of political turmoil he married Elisabeth Widmer on November 11, 1798, and began to raise a family.

There were uprisings. Koepfli's home was attacked in 1799, and he had to hide in a small boat on Lake Sempach for several days and nights. A similar attack took place about nine miles north of Neuenkirch where peasants threatened to burn the house of the elderly Dr. Johannes Suppiger (1730–1805) with the family inside. According to family tradition, the old doctor persuaded the attackers to pray, which gave time for one of the sons to ride off and return with French-led troops.

Doubtless the Koepflis and Suppigers, sharing similar political views and a common profession and living so close to each other, were already well-acquainted. In any event the two families were brought together by marriage when, in January 1804, Koepfli's sister Katharina (1772–1806) married the elderly Dr. Suppiger's son, Jacob Joseph Aloys (1770–1833). On December 22, 1804, was born their only child, Joseph Kaspar Thomas Suppiger, who in 1831 was to become his uncle Kaspar Koepfli's chief assistant when members of the two families left Sursee to go to America.

Dr. Koepfli's strong political and religious views, which set him in opposition to many of his compatriots, were to be constant themes throughout his long life.

Although the canton of Lucerne was Catholic, and Kaspar was undoubtedly brought up in that faith, at some point, perhaps as early as his twenties, he ceased to practice that faith. He early became a Freemason, and was greatly influenced by Jean Jacques Rousseau, whose writings did so much to prepare the climate of thought of the leaders of the French Revolution. Friendships with prominent liberal intellectuals Heinrich Zschokke (1771–1848) and Ignaz Paul Vital Troxler (1780–1866) probably date from his student days and were to be life-long influences upon Koepfli and members of his family. Following the restoration of a conservative government in 1814, Koepfli and Troxler circulated a petition calling for a liberal constitution, for which action they were jailed in

Lucerne and held for more than a month as political prisoners. This experience undoubtedly influenced Koepfli to consider in 1817, as previously noted, emigrating to America, a country which was looked up to by many Swiss liberals as a fulfilled embodiment of the principles they espoused for a regenerated Switzerland. Later, Koepfli's nephew, Joseph Suppiger, and at least one of Koepfli's sons, Kaspar Mauris, were to become students of Zschokke and Troxler.

It is worthy of note that Zschokke was a prolific and popular writer of histories, novels, and religious works, whose history of the Swiss people went through, in Switzerland alone, at least eight editions in German and half a dozen in French. In fact, it has been argued that the "liberal belief in progress found its most skillful interpreter in Heinrich Zschokke, an immigrant from Prussia, and a faithful adherent of German idealism. A most fertile and industrious writer, he helped to educate people in liberal ideas. . . . His work for popular education had very great influence."[3] Zschokke's almost utopian views of the United States are reflected in an article published in 1818, which concluded with the words: "From now on America shall be the home of human culture and the beacon of the globe, towards which the sages of all countries will look with longing in grateful blessings."[4]

Particularly admired by such as Zschokke and Koepfli were the free institutions of the United States, a central but federal government, and the embodiment of the concept of citizenship in the nation, a particular goal of Swiss liberals. Such ideas were not mere abstractions, but were fraught with vital economic and social consequences. As middle-class Swiss, they realized the manifest absurdity of a loose confederation of twenty-two cantons, each with its own militia, currency, and economic regulations, all stifling to commerce, industry, and agriculture, which increasingly had to be competitive with countries where such reforms had been achieved.

Following the decision in 1817 not to emigrate at that time, Dr. Koepfli moved his family, in 1821, from the village of Neuenkirch to the much larger community of Sursee, where lived members of the Suppiger family who were also to come to America. Koepfli built a house and prospered, but, along with several of his friends, failed in his efforts to be accepted as a

3. Edgar Bonjour, H. S. Offler, and G. R. Potter, *A Short History of Switzerland* (Oxford, 1965), pp. 255–56.
4. Quoted by Hans Kohn, *Nationalism and Liberty: The Swiss Example* (London, 1956), p. 74.

citizen. As a non-Catholic in the predominantly Catholic—and rural—canton of Lucerne, and as an outspoken liberal, his views were not popular with the more conservative element.[5]

The July Revolution of 1830 in France encouraged Swiss liberals to press for constitutional reforms.Troxler's appeal for a restoration of rights provided in the 1798 constitution was submitted as a petition by Dr. Koepfli at a meeting in Sursee on November 8, 1830, following which signatures were collected. In January 1831 liberal modifications to Lucerne's cantonal constitution were adopted. But by then Dr. Koepfli may well have made the decision to emigrate. Political conditions were still quite unsettled, and Koepfli's gloomy prognosis for the future of Switzerland, as revealed in his "Farewell Letter" of April 22, 1831, (appended to this Prologue) was in large measure corroborated when in July 1833 the conservatives returned to power in Lucerne, which became known as the capital for both Catholicism and conservatism in Switzerland.

The "Farewell Letter" represents the passionately held convictions of a follower of Heinrich Zschokke from whose "Founding of Maryland" Koepfli quotes at length. But in addition, there is a new influence reflected in the "Farewell Letter" which was undoubtedly decisive in convincing Koepfli, and most likely Joseph Suppiger and other family members, to remove to Missouri.

In 1830 they had come into the possession of Duden's *Report*, published the year before. In this work, which was tremendously influential in promoting German emigration, they found a comprehensive, detailed, and idyllic exposition regarding pioneer farming in Missouri which accorded perfectly with their preconceived notions of the advantages of life in the United States, Missouri in particular. Although they were to come to disagree with Duden regarding Missouri—and Illinois, which Duden did not favor—they used his work as a guidebook throughout their journey. Duden's *Report* is cited sixteen times in the *Reisebericht* and, except for disagreement regarding the merits of settling in Missouri, almost invariably found reliable and useful. There can be little doubt but that Duden's book was decisive in persuading the founders of New Switzerland to emigrate.[6]

5. In 1837 the canton of Lucerne was 95.6% Catholic (Carol L. Schmid, *Conflict and Consensus in Switzerland* [Berkeley, 1981], p. 23).
6. Sometime before their departure, Dr. Koepfli corresponded with Duden, apparently asking him whether to go to Missouri by way of New York or New

Duden's *Report* dealt much more with the economic attractions which America offered than with political and religious questions. We can be certain that Dr. Koepfli, and the Suppigers especially, would not have emigrated unless they felt that by doing so they would improve themselves financially. This consideration probably applied most strongly to the Suppigers, whose textile business had suffered from the lower prices offered by the English mills. Virtually everything Duden wrote reinforced their high expectations for a prosperous future in America. Since the *Reisebericht* tells its own story and the history of New Switzerland has already been well told elsewhere, only a few brief further facts will be recounted here.

In addition to Dr. Koepfli (57), Salomon Koepfli (17), and Joseph Suppiger (26), the party of fourteen included two other Koepfli sons, Bernard (27) and Joseph (23); a daughter, Rosa (21); a maid, Catherine Huger; Joseph Suppiger's half-brother, Anton (15, not a blood relative of the Koepflis); Joseph Vonarx; and four other men who were to assist the party during their journey as far as Havre. Of the latter four, only Sebastian Keller was eventually to join the settlers in New Switzerland. Koepfli family members left behind were Dr. Kaspar Mauris Koepfli (31), his wife, two daughters, and a son.

In the spring of 1833 arrived Joseph Suppiger, Sr.; a third son, Melchior; and Joseph Sr.'s brother, Johann, with three sons and two daughters. (Joseph, Sr., died in August 1833, the first of the Swiss to be buried in New Switzerland.) In 1834 came four other Johann Suppiger daughters and a male cousin. In 1839, with the arrival of Dr. Kaspar Mauris Koepfli, his wife, two daughters, and one son, the Koepfli-Suppiger component of New Switzerland was virtually complete.

KASPAR KOEPFLI'S "FAREWELL LETTER"

Take Note, You Elders. Here Speak the Young (At-Heart)

A confederation of republics in which true freedom,
justice, and harmony are to prevail, requires a well-ordered

Orleans (Gottfried Duden, *Report on a Journey to the Western States of North America* . . . , ed. and trans. George H. Kellner and others [Columbia: State Historical Society of Missouri and Univ. of Missouri Press, 1980], p. 273).

central administration in which authority is invested in wise, honest executives.

[George] Washington[7]

It would break our hearts to take leave of you personally, possibly forever. Allow us to write you our last farewell. The thought of shaking hands for the last time is hard enough, but to leave these well-known surroundings, to leave our dear friends behind forever, never to see those again who have favored us with their kindness and for the trust placed in us! May God, the father of human destiny, bless you in this life and in the hereafter. We shall ask him, that we be reunited at last when we part from this life. With a contrite heart we plead for your forgiveness in case we have ever hurt you in any way knowingly or unintentionally. Please continue your feelings of friendship towards us and remember us as your friends even though distance may part us. Our intentions to leave may seem very strange to many of our friends. Some might even judge us to be insane. We are human beings and as such we cannot claim to be perfect. But allow us to quote a passage from Mr. Zschokke's "Founding of Maryland." May these lines written many years ago serve to justify our action. Zschokke has Harford say:

> The history of the world is the history of mankind. From time to time, like life itself, there is renewal on the part of enlightened individuals through whom God's own providence manifests itself. For that very reason the New World was not to be discovered until two hundred years ago, not sooner or later. Mankind in Europe had to reach a degree of civilization which turned against itself. When India's, Egypt's and Persia's civilizations began to crumble, Greece appeared ready to become the sanctuary of the muses. When the barbaric invasion threatened Greece's intellectual leadership, the legacy of the human spirt was to be rekindled in the house of the Medici of Florence, and from there it was to set the entire West marvelously ablaze. And now that the European orient lies in darkness and the occident witnesses the impending setting of its sun, the same sun

7. This "quotation" from Washington also appears at the beginning of the German language editions of the *Reisebericht*. Not found in Washington's writings, it is an apt expression of the ideals of Swiss liberals, such as Koepfli and Zschokke. It may well have been a statement attributed to Washington, perhaps in a novel by Zschokke, in a German-language publication.

setting here will rise for us in America. I can foresee it now, the war raging over our continent will continue for centuries. The wheat has to be separated from the chaff.

America or Europe! What man of strength and vitality will hesitate in the choice between the two? Here to be a witness of the final and difficult struggle between old orders, old ideas, old empires; There to be a founder of new orders, new states; Here derangement, religious wars, civil wars, revolutions, at courts and among people; There peace, the plow, the pursuit of knowledge, estblishment of new cities and laws; Here subjection to temporal and spiritual despotism, enslaved beliefs, thoughts, hearts, the growing influence of oriental tyranny, oriental caste feeling, oriental barbarity of the mind, oriental injustice in the courts, oriental poverty of the masses; There a human being in his own right, free to believe and express opinions without a master-servant relationship, the ability to become as rich as his diligence and as great as his worth deserve, conqueror with the spade, proclaimer of divine thought among savages, while here the noble savages punish God-given thoughts with prison and exile; Here tedious, bloody, vain striving, disorder, prejudice, chains, and other relics of the barbaric past, and displacement of healthy common sense by abnormality; There plain reason and nature above all, and a better life not stymied by courts, ministers, priests, censorship, inquisition.

Is the choice really difficult? Off to America! I have three sons whom I want to give a fatherland. All they have here is a spacious prison. I want them to become citizens with royal documents guaranteeing their rights to their own property. Here they never will be more than slaves with titles and will have no higher advantage than to decorate their shackles with the fancy ribbon of some order or other.[8]

You may judge how suitable this [material from Zschokke's "Maryland"] is for our day and age. We sincerely believe to have come to this serious decision [to emigrate] with open minds and would not have embarked on such a seemingly daring venture without preponderate reasons. The triple motivation for our decision is the longing for religious, political, and personal freedom. To live in the country where everyone is free to pursue his faith and worship according to his conscience and his

8. The passage cited can be found in Heinrich Zschokke, "Die Gruendung von Maryland," in *Werke*, 12 vols., ed. Hans Bodmer (Berlin, n.d.), 8:167–68.

beliefs without the slightest interference; where the education of the young is actively supported by the state itself; where all citizens enjoy the same rights and privileges; where everyone can freely develop his spiritual and physical power regardless of background; where trades are flourishing and there is no pressure to become a member of the guild in order to ply one's trade; where commerce in the interior is facilitated by connecting canals and railroads, and the marketing of products is not hampered by restrictions or borders; where everything grows luxuriantly under friendly skies in soil marvelously enriched by flora-moldering of a thousand years which will result in the richest harvest without any fertilizer for the next fifty to a hundred years; where neither beggars nor thieves presently are found; where anyone possessing any diligence at all can make a good living, not troubled by shortage of food, taxes, or payment of tribute; where in recent times there have been neither wars nor revolutions; in order to achieve all this everyone concerned about his future and that of his family can unhesitantly undertake an onerous journey of three to four months, especially if he has the necessary means to make the journey as comfortable as possible and can afford the time to select his future home site at leisure.

It is difficult indeed to leave one's homeland, but what have we to look forward to here in Switzerland or in Europe generally? Scholars may preach otherwise, but it remains a fact that the Old World is suffering from an ill from which it can recuperate only by promoting colonization. This ill is called over-population. Much has been said about lives wasted in attempts to maintain a viable population. I prefer not to comment on this, but I will call attention to Horace's observation that a surfeit of anything can become unhealthy.

If the population does indeed reach such proportions that it creates poverty; that it robs the arts and sciences of their value; that it slows down the trades so that all classes are affected by unemployment and the heads of the families are troubled by worries in the face of an uncertain future; that lies and deceit, artifice and frustration are the order of the day; that decency is suppressed and denied and people advance by cruelty and lack of consideration of one another—when all of these things become part of our existence, who can refrain from cursing a population creating so many ills!

However, these are not the only ills we are hoping to escape. It is not the promise of a happier homeland and a better future alone that propels us toward our goal. Higher, nobler intentions underlie our decision.

According to confirmed reports which you can read yourself in Mr. Gottfried Duden's travel account, the particular area on the Missouri where we hope to settle is the most fruitful of all land discovered to date. Thousands of acres are yet awaiting buyers. For only two taler or five gulden plenty of fine land can be had which should yield a profit of about 80 to 140 percent without the need for fetilizer. The climate is so favorable that everyone can keep as much livestock as he can buy, for plenty of feed is available year round. For two or three thousand gulden a settler can buy a farm of eighty to a hundred acres with plenty of woods and the necessary buildings, implements, and cattle to permit a large family to live comfortably without qualms about the future. How many family heads own twice as much property here in Switzerland, possibly even three times as much, but are forced to work much harder reaping similar benefits? Often the estate is so cut up after the father dies, that the children end up poor, and without any fault of their own become dependent and a burden to the community. This is how many a prosperous community has been weakened. This very ill is also responsible for the unfortunate law to hinder marriages, which has resulted (shamefully!) in the murder of so many children in attempts to prevent the estate from being split too many ways.

Such degenerate actions surely must revolt every well-meaning citizen concerned about the lot of his fellowmen, and should alert him to seek a solution.

It was this noble intention that gave us strength in our search, and hope that we might show many an active but presently starving and troubled family head the way to a better future for his family. May the oppressed understand our mission. May the governments help promote their welfare, and may the Almighty guide us toward our goal. God be with us.

DR. CASPAR [KASPAR] KOEPFLI

Travel Account

FOREWORD [1 8 3 3]

This travel account and the supplementary letters were not intended by the writers to be published but were written solely for family members who remained behind. Only after repeated requests was it decided not to withhold them from the public, and they are published here as they were written, with only personal family items deleted.

So let the reader—if he objects to the style—keep in mind that the account is the rough draft of a traveler and that the letters were intended only to tell the relatives about the welfare and the experiences of the emigrants; in reading it, let him concentrate on the value of the information provided.

The only purpose in making the writings public is to acquaint the emigrants' many friends with the circumstances of their emigration, including its dangers, to share with them the benefit of their experience, and to correct commonly held misconceptions concerning emigration, colonization, and agriculture.

The writers of this account and of the letters have given the new settlement the same general name as their fatherland. When we [who have remained behind in old Switzerland] consider the conditions here and weigh the wisdom of emigration, it becomes readily apparent that New Switzerland holds forth much promise for the immediate future.

All of the Swiss emigrants whom the writers met in various parts of the United States of America considered themselves quite fortunate except that they were not surrounded by their compatriots. It was not the same old familiar mountain surroundings that they missed so much as the language of their forefathers, the customs of their homeland, and the intimate life to which they were accustomed.

Messrs. Koepfli and Suppiger set about establishing a colony of the type espoused by the Swiss Emigrants Society, in which the emigrants would not live isolated from their compatriots. After a great deal of traveling, in the course of which they made many inquiries, they decided to settle in a region where the climate and other conditions met their approval. What with thousands and thousands of acres of land in the state of Illinois still available for farming, they felt it would be especially appropriate for the Swiss, after the long journey from their homeland, to settle in a beautiful, healthful area with ideal farming conditions, where—in addition to the freedom of the new country available to all immigrants—there would be the language, religion, schools, and customs of their distant homeland. Settling in an area where other Swiss were building this type of community in the immense new world would ensure their welfare as citizens of a regenerated Switzerland.

The original travel account and the letters are available for examination. Joseph Suppiger, Jr., kept the diary [and he and members of the Koepfli family wrote the letters and other text]. The travel group included Dr. Kaspar Koepfli, Sr., his wife, three [of his] sons, a daughter, and a maid; Joseph Suppiger, Jr., and his half brother Anton; Joseph Vonarx of Stuesslingen in the canton of Solothurn; Sebastian Keller and Kaspar Helfenstein of Neuenkirch; Moritz Geisshuesler of Hildesrieden; and Alois Kappeler, a Sursee carpenter [the three last-named places all located in the canton of Lucerne].

[KASPAR MAURIS KOEPFLI]

PART ONE

Journey from Sursee to Havre

FRIDAY, APRIL 22, 1831

On the day of our departure [April 21] we set out with a carriage,[1] a freight wagon, and seven horses for Sissach in the canton of Basel [our first night's stopping place], the horses changed from one vehicle to the other as we crossed the Hauenstein Mountains.

For me the leave-taking had been no harder than for a trip of six to eight weeks. I was convinced that I would see you, my loved ones, again, and this—combined with the abruptness of our departure—helped me keep my emotions in check. I have nothing against the shedding of tears by friends at parting, but I am grateful when displays of emotion are held in check. Furthermore, since I intend to visit home again as soon as possible, it was for me no permanent leave-taking.

SATURDAY, APRIL 23

By noon we reached the French border at St. Louis, the old Bourglibre. The canton tolls were high, and they impeded our progress. If all of France were divided proportionately into as many small parts as those in Switzerland that one traverses between Sursee and Basel, the entrance and exit tolls, bridge, road, and escort fees—and whatever else these impositions are called—would cost more than the maintenance of our seven horses.

If traffic through Switzerland is to flourish, the collecting of these myriads of unnecessary and burdensome fees must cease. It is not only costly, but it actually serves to inhibit rather than promote commerce. Surely these irksome toll stations between cantons could be abolished and a general Swiss tax established to maintain all roads. But it is not likely that we will see this happen in antiquated Europe, where the old prerogatives of the cantons are as set as those of individual families.

In the afternoon our effects were to be examined at the French border,

---

1. Salomon Koepfli elsewhere tells how the coach, richly gilded and painted and said to have belonged to Marie Louise, had to make its way through masses of people, even beyond the city gates. Some of the people had walked long distances to see what they considered one of the happiest of families depart for America, and many of them stood with tears in their eyes and outstretched hands to bid the party farewell (*The Story of the Settling of Highland,* trans. Jennie Latzer Kaeser and ed. Raymond J. Spahn [privately printed, 1970], p. 4).

so we unpacked the freight wagon, placing our chests, unlocked, in rows on the road. The inspector appeared, and the first chest he looked at had many new boots and shoes right on top. Tearing the paper from the items, he glanced at them and decreed: "These are new goods, away with them, they cannot pass!" With that he hurried off without looking further, leaving us stand there somewhat nonplussed. But then I remembered assurances given me that very morning by the friendly underinspector in charge of this checkpoint, who was not at hand just then.

When he appeared after 3:00 P.M. and found our effects still unexamined—although he had left orders to take care of us—he set matters in motion. A customs man was ordered to check whether merely clothing and no other new goods were involved. This man examined our things very superficially, not requiring us to do any unpacking. Several chests, the keys to which were not readily available, were not opened, and in a few minutes the inspection was finished. Not only were we permitted free passage with no customs fees imposed on provisions, but the underinspector supplied us with a written recommendation to the next checkpoint to pass us through without delay. He said, "I can readily see that you are not smugglers but are carrying only your own effects, and I am authorized to give you free passage."

This was the first person I had found in such a position who deserved the respect of his fellow men. He understood the intent of the law and did not have to interpret it to the letter. He understood that it served France to have American colonists make their way through the country. No doubt such transit will become more general before long. There are men at the top in France who know how to appraise the interests of their country properly. Also, the press is free again, and one may surely expect that many voices will make themselves heard.[2]

The next problem was our freight wagon. We had learned in Basel that a wagon like ours did not meet the regulations in France. Its wheels were too narrow even for a two-horse wagon. I ran ahead and obtained permission in the weigh station to drive the wagon as far as the customs station. The French regulations governing wagons are oppressive even for the rare person who understands them, and we never were able to obtain satisfactory information about them.

2. The July 1830 Revolution, resulting in the overthrow of the Bourbon, Charles X, brought Louis Philippe to the throne, reestablished a free press and implemented other reforms applauded by liberals in Switzerland.

French law demands that on freight wagons, but not on two-wheeled carriages or wagonettes and the like, the fellies be at least two inches wide. But wagons of this width may be drawn by only one horse, although no limit is placed on the weight of the load, so everyone loads as much as his horse can pull, the French often piling on 2500–3000 pounds. If drawn by more than one horse the wagon must have fellies 4.2 French inches wide, and it is the load which is checked, for excessively heavy loads ruin the roads. The French maintain that a load which a single horse can draw (over hill and dale) will not damage the roads. They set no limit on the number of horses beyond one, since they hold that the road will not suffer more whether two or twenty horses are used. This is certainly a proper view, and the French provide means of weighing the loads so that drivers are delayed scarcely five minutes.

A wagon with fellies 4.2 inches in width may carry 8500 pounds, with no limit to the number of horses drawing it. Only overloading is unlawful. (The two-tenths of an inch allows for possible wear on the felly.) With each tenth of an inch increase in the width of a felly a certain number of hundredweight can be added, as long as the width of the felly is adequate for the load. This regulation is obviously a beneficent one.

For a time there had been abuses, small wagons being fitted with axles so wide that wagons could not pass one another on narrow streets, thus causing many mishaps. The regulations now finally provide that the axles may not project more than four French inches over the felly guards. That this does not impair the solidity of the wagon is demonstrated by French wagons with wheels eight to twelve inches wide, on which comparatively huge loads can be carried.

Our freight wagon did not have the prescribed wheels, and no old wagon with such wheels was to be found because the axle law had been in effect for only two years. All new wagons are reinforced with iron, and the core of each wheel hub is of cast iron. Furthermore, they cost eighteen to twenty louis d'or.

While we scurried around trying to find a solution but coming to no firm decision, our carriage also arrived. There were conveyances we could have hired to haul the freight to Paris or Havre, but they were designed for larger loads than ours, and the cartage would have come too high. Moreover, unless we stayed with our effects, they could not be brought through the country without having all of the new goods eliminated. Acting on the advice of the members of our party who had just arrived in the carriage, we commissioned Lehmann the blacksmith to fit some available post wheels to our wagon, a costly procedure involving work with the axles. It was agreed that the wagon would be ready by Monday noon.

SUNDAY, APRIL 24

Because the money exchanges in Basel were closed on Sunday, we had to delay changing our money until the next day. We used the time to compute our travel expenses and write our farewell letters. In the evening Alois Kappeler arrived to join the group. Joseph Vonarx, who was also to travel with us, had arrived the evening before. Accompanying him to see us off was Jakob Dommann, Sr., landlord of the Stag Inn in Sursee. We all greatly appreciate his interest in our venture.

MONDAY, APRIL 25

Our first chore was to change our money. The time-tested integrity and goodwill of the Iselin Brothers' Basel commercial establishment continued to stand us in good stead. By 3:00 P.M. everything had been arranged. I exchanged everything except my gold, and my companions did the same. We obtained New York bills of exchange payable on presentation at the commercial house of [Henry C.] DeRham, [Isaac] Iselin and Moore. The American dollar was calculated for us at 36 batzen, the Brabant taler at 38½, the French taler at 39, and the five-livre taler at 33¾.[3] Depending on the rate of exchange, one received an *agio* on the Brabant taler which at this time amounted to three-fourths of 1 percent with one-half of 1 percent *courtage*, which is considerable on large amounts. (*Agio* is what one receives in changing one's currency into the kind one wants, and *courtage* is the commission the exchange house deducts from the *agio*.) This exchange is carried on in Basel mostly by old, well-known Jews. The transactions often are made directly between commercial establishments.

Before one buys a bill of exchange one should inquire at the exchange house as to the exact rate of exchange. This can be determined quite accurately some weeks in advance, and one can earn hundreds of francs when large sums of different kinds of money are involved. Had we known that the old French taler would be accepted at 39 batzen and the Brabant

3. See Appendix: Units of Currency, Measure, and Weight.

taler at only 38½, we could have saved much on this kind of money, since we would have been able to exchange it at home at the rate of 39 batzen. Had we known that three-fourths of 1 percent *agio* would be given on the Brabant taler, we would have taken Brabant taler instead of the French five-livre currency.

We could have saved five centimes on the dollar by taking sixty-day bills of exchange, but we wanted to be able to pick up our money in New York as soon as we arrived there, at the commercial house of DeRham, Iselin and Moore. Letters will reach me most quickly if sent c/o Iselin Brothers in Basel. All overseas letters must be postpaid, so you should inquire c/o the Iselin Brothers as to charges. My reports will be sent through the same channel later.

In the afternoon we called on Professor Troxler, who received us most hospitably and reproached us for not having visited him before, which we had not done because we had wanted to avoid delay in the exchange transactions. Late in the evening we took leave of this fine old friend. His spouse indicated her readiness to follow us to America at the first possible moment.

When we returned to Bourglibre we found our freight wagon reloaded, the repairs having been completed. The tolls for our horses were paid, and our departure was set for early the next morning. Up to this afternoon the weather had been quite favorable, but in the evening a heavy rain set in.

TUESDAY, APRIL 26

Our itinerary from St. Louis to Havre is shown on the following table from a French guidebook. It gives the number of *poststunden* [leagues, about three miles] between towns, as well as the cumulative number of *poststunden* as one progresses from St. Louis, or Bourglibre, to Havre.

From St. Louis, or Bourglibre, to:

Les-trois-Maisons ...		4	Vesoul	3	32½
Altkirch	5	9	Pont-sur-Saône	3	35½
Chavanne-sur-l'Étang	4	13	Combeau-Fontaine ..	3	38½
Belfort	4	17	Cintrey	3	41½
Champagney	4	21	Fay-Billor	3	44½
Lure	4½	25½	Les Griffonotes	3	47½
Calmoutiers	4	29½	Langres	3	50½

Vesaignes	4	54½	Gros-Bois	2	111½
Chaumont-en-Bassigny	4	58½	Charenton	3	114½
			PARIS	2	116½
Suzenecourt	4	62½	Courbevoie	2	118½
Colombey-les-2-églises	2	64½	Herblay	3	121½
			Pontoise	2	123½
Bar-sur-Aube	3½	68	Bordeau-de-Vigny	4	127½
Vandeuvre	5	73	Magny	3	130½
Montieramé	3	76	Tilliers	4	134½
Troyes	4½	80½	Éconis	4	138½
Les Grez	3	83½	Bourg-Boudoin	3½	142
Les Granges	2	85½	La-Forge-Foret	2	144
Pont-sur-Seine	3	88½	Rouen	3	147
Nogent-sur-Seine	2	90½	Barentin	4	151
Provins	4	94½	Yvelot	4½	155½
La maison rouge	3	97½	Alliquerville	3	158½
Nangis	3	100½	Bolbee	2½	161
Mormonet	3	103½	La Rotte	3	164
Guignes	2	105½	Le HAVRE	4	168
Brie-Comte-Robert	4	109½			

(The 14 *poststunden* from Sursee to Basel must be added to this total.)

We set out from St. Louis in the morning without breakfast and in the face of a steady rain. The depressing departure had such a distressing effect on the doctor's wife, already suffering from a sore finger, that we feared she was going to be ill. However, the comfort of a good breakfast brought everything back into balance. Today we reached Chavanne-sur-l'Étang from where we sent you the documents respecting business transactions Dr. Koepfli wanted carried out. We could proceed now without hindrance, but here and there we were required to pay the so-called post charges (*droit de poste*).

Strictly enforced post regulations exist in France. Every postmaster must at all times—no matter what the hour—have enough horses ready for the regular post coaches as well as for extra post vehicles and carriages of foreign and domestic travelers, in order to enable them to proceed without delay. Everything moves speedily from one station to another. These stations are leased from the government. For the reimbursement of these postmasters, who under penalty of the law cannot demand more than the established fees for services, the law provides that no hired coachman can carry foreign or domestic travelers through France without paying the postmaster seven sols per horse at every station (two short leagues apart). Anyone can travel where he wishes with his own conveyance. Therefore as soon as we proved ourselves to be owners of the horses and vehicles, we were permitted to pass. This is quite irksome for travelers, but it is the law. An ordinary vehicle would not have given rise to so many questions. But we were recognized immediately as emigrants, partly because of the baggage on the carriage and partly because a good many colonists have been traveling through the country this spring.

Do not expect descriptions of French towns and regions. Printed brochures will give you a much better idea of France than would be possible for someone passing through the land as hastily as we. I will say merely that France has not turned out to be the wealthy country we had expected. The peasant seems much poorer, living in worse hovels and in greater squalor than in our country, although the rich property owner may be better off than ours.

One travels long distances without seeing a single house, and the few one sees rarely have outbuildings, so it is hard to imagine where they store the harvest from the many fields under cultivation. The soil we have seen so far seems good, fertile, and easy to work. Except in several small areas the plowing we have observed usually was done with a pair of miserable oxen, and sometimes with one horse, the man guiding the plow also serving as the driver. Even if one could adjust to this country and these surroundings, one would find it difficult to make progress as a farmer. Our opinion of the advanced state of French civilization gradually has been lowered, and we have become more and more convinced that the French rate their civilized state much too highly, seeing beauty and liberty where an impartial eye does not see them.

WEDNESDAY, APRIL 27

We left our lodgings quite early today and soon reached the fortress of Belfort, which is being restored. Martial activity was very much in evidence. Here we were provided with a certificate attesting to our ownership of our two vehicles, so that we could be saved long delays at the post stations. The letter of recommendation we had brought from the underinspector at St. Louis was producing the intended results. We were being permitted to pass along freely without delay. At night we reached Lure, a fairly important old city.

Nothing to report but bad weather. Land usage much the same as we moved along. The earth everywhere reddish from the iron content. Everywhere the same poverty and lack of cleanliness among the common people.

THURSDAY, APRIL 28

Rainy weather now for the past three days has made the roads miserable, with ruts that make progress difficult. The road is generally broad but apparently constructed of poor material, mostly white limestone, the ground-up particles of which quickly become slime in rainy weather, and in dry weather turn just as quickly to clouds of dust.

Toward 4:00 P.M. we reached Pont-sur-Saône, a small town on both banks of the Saône, connected by a beautiful bridge. Since the rain had slackened somewhat, we drove on without difficulty. Beyond the town the road began to climb noticeably.

After an interval of some ten minutes a young boy came running after us, calling out loudly that we were to pay post tolls. We tried to explain to him that as owners of the vehicles and horses we had nothing to pay. He fell back, and we set out again, considering the matter closed. But we had gone scarcely twenty paces when the boy reappeared with a post employee who seized the reins and forcibly prevented us from moving forward. All of our attempts to explain were fruitless. Tempers on both sides became heated, and soon it would have come to violence between our coachman Helfenstein and the post employee.

Next to come on the scene was the postmaster's daughter, who subjected us to loud outcries. Before long a crowd of spectators was surrounding our wagon. Even the postmaster came, and he proved to be no more reasonable. Either he was a stupid oaf and did not understand the meaning of the law, or he did not want to go unpaid and see himself shamed before the people standing around. In short, we had no choice but to return and appear before the magistrate or pay. Since we were nearly a fourth of a league from the village with night approaching, and faced with the possiblity of having more charges levied by the judge (for a native's part is always taken in preference to a foreigner's), we decided to pay the trifle and put an end to the troublesome scene, especially since heavy rain had set in again. The malicious smiles of the postmaster and the onlookers convinced us that he was conscious of his injustice.

This adventure delayed us so long that we did not reach the village of Combeau-Fontaine until after 10:00 P.M. I ran ahead to find a place to stop for the night. The night watchman, who probably regarded me as a vagabond, coming at such a late hour, treated me quite roughly. However, the arrival of the entire travel group and the presentation of the letters satisfied him immediately.

Because no one demanded passports during the daytime, we adopted the practice of traveling no more than necessary at night. Our quarters here, like those at the last place, were fairly good. It was only with the meals that we had fault to find, since we consistently avoided the large hotels, and the smaller guest houses nearly everywhere left much to be desired, with the result that we rarely found a place to our taste.

FRIDAY, APRIL 29

We saw two men from Zurich taking a large flock of sheep to be sold in the Paris market. Otherwise very few friendly faces on this day. When evening brought heavy squalls of rain, it began to seem that we were to meet every possible inconvenience in Europe, killing any love we might have for it. The ruts resembled ditches, so the carriage suffered badly, and it was late evening before we reached Langres, where again we had tolerable but not choice food. With the same ingredients we could have done far better in Switzerland.

SATURDAY, APRIL 30

Because the constant rainy weather had given our doctor a cold, he stayed in bed longer on this day to sweat it out, and we let the freight wagon take off by itself, so that it could travel at a slower rate on the extremely bad road. At 9:00 A.M. we followed rapidly with the carriage and soon overtook it. Between Chaumont-en-Bassigny and Suzenecourt we stopped in a village for the night.

The sun shone today as if God wished, with a little better weather, to honor the festival of the new king Louis Philippe I, celebrated throughout

France. Everywhere we heard the drums of the national guard. In one miserable village, where the guards could afford no uniforms, they nevertheless took part in a procession during the morning church service, with old rusted guns and swords. In Bar-sur-Aube, an attractive little town, the festival was celebrated more lavishly, and everyone seemed to be happy. In the evening there were public amusements such as dancing and fireworks. Tri-colored flags[4] were displayed before every house. Toward night it began to rain when we stopped in Vandeuvre, where we found tolerable lodging.

MONDAY, MAY 2

Today the wagon again started a little in advance of our carriage. Scarcely two hundred paces outside Vandeuvre we were met by Keller returning with bad news. Because of the deep ruts, the wagon had dropped an axle pin, the rear right wheel had fallen off, and the axle had shattered. It was obvious that the bad road, not the driver, had caused the accident. The carriage was ordered ahead to the next place. Buehlmann, Kappeler, and I stayed behind with the three drivers and the wagon. The blacksmith and wagonmaker immediately were brought out from Vandeuvre. Fortunately it was possible to remove the axle without unloading our effects and exposing them to the weather. The wagon was guarded while repairs were made in Vandeuvre. Late at night, amidst lightning and rain, the new axle was attached to the wagon, and it was all done at a cost that probably would have been much greater in a hundred other places. At 11:00 P.M. we set out at full speed, and a league beyond Vandeuvre we caught up with the carriage, in the next town. Not many miles this day!

TUESDAY, MAY 3

We examined the axle and found a broken place on the same end off which the wheel had fallen the day before, and it was decided that Geisshuesler and I would accompany it back to the smithy to have the necessary repairs made. Although the road was good and we were careful to move slowly,

4. The tricolor of the French revolution, replaced 1815–30 by the fleur-de-lis of the Bourbons, was restored by the 1830 Revolution.

the wheel slid off after only five hundred paces or so, and the wagon collapsed. The shaft was broken, but the damage to the axle was less severe this time. By 1:00 P.M. all was in order again, but not without the expenditure of a good deal of effort. Today's workers had never heard of a screw jack, the miserable smith had not a piece of new iron, and no proper piece of wood could be found. But today's lesser work cost us more than what we'd had done the day before! We were becoming noticeably depressed.

We set out, and a few leagues before Troyes, in a place where we stopped for a drink, we met a man who identified himself as the landlord in the little village closest to Troyes. He invited us to stop at his place for the night at a reasonable price and promised us good service. We had advanced little in the past two days, but it was as though heaven had intervened to spare our horses. We should have had to stop for a day's rest in any case, and the lodgings were inexpensive albeit miserable. There was no meat to be had, and if we had not already stabled our horses and unpacked our luggage from the carriage, we would have gone on to Troyes.

Our landlord finally produced some potatoes he had found at a neighbor's, but our people had to prepare them. We also received a little bread and butter. The sleeping quarters were bad. The doctor and his wife occupied a bed in the kitchen, common practice in France. Geisshuesler and Vonarx kept watch for a while and then lay down in the dank hall with the rest of the party. Only the landlord's maid remained awake.

After midnight the village guards appeared, finished the leftovers despite the maid's protest, and finally went away. The doctor and his wife, awakened by the noise, did not know what had happened. Hardly had the guards left than we were awakened and told of the incident. Dr. Koepfli's cold had not let up, and the kitchen fumes and disturbance were aggravating it. We opened the doors to air the place, when the drunken oafs appeared again. According to the law these guards have the right to enter any house where light is noticed and the doors are not locked. Insolently they demanded to see our papers, but I refused at first to show them, protesting the improper conduct. To get rid of the brutes I finally produced our passports, but unfortunately the oafs could not read. They acted as if the passports contained strange, suspicious names and places, and they brought in their captain from his sleep. This man, like an old village magistrate, wore a blue denim smock, which was more of a uniform than the guards wore. With the help of his pince-nez the captain finally found our papers in order, but he passed over my complaint about the conduct of his subordinates as quickly as possible. In the meantime the landlord, having heard what was happening, arrived and forced the unbidden guests out with hard kicks. That passes for police! national guards! night watchmen! O, dear freedom, whence are you leading your lesser sons?

WEDNESDAY, MAY 4

We lost no time vacating our strange quarters, happy to get out into the fresh air. We began walking to Troyes, and from afar we could see huge letters, five to ten feet high, proclaiming it as an important center for hosiery manufacture. We found some genuine champagne and spent several hours in the place. The doctor soon recovered. The weather was good for once.

From Troyes to Paris we will have a paved road. The highways in France, although generally forty feet wide, are on the whole twice as bad as our Swiss roads. Lack of road-building material may be the principal reason. The fact that all roads leading out of Paris are paved—including the Paris-Troyes highway—is not due to French love of grandeur but to necessity, paving being absolutely essential because of the tremendous quantities of supplies constantly being brought into Paris from the country to feed the populace. With such heavy use ordinary roads would become so damaged after a week of bad weather that no freight wagons could come through safely. This could lead to a dearth of supplies which—even if temporary—could raise the spectre of famine quickly in a city like Paris.

The paving stones are not large, as one would expect, but white limestone cubes about eight inches square, unhewn, but dressed to size with a hammer so that they are quite regular, and they are kept in good repair. Although the highway is forty feet wide, only a strip in the middle, varying in width from eight to ten feet, is paved with these stones. This means that two wagons barely can pass one another, and generally one turns out onto the unpaved part, which is poorly maintained, being nothing but the natural soil. Horses can pull vehicles readily on this paving, but wagons must be strongly built to withstand the constant jolting.

Expensive as the maintenance of these roads leading out of Paris must be, I believe that the total length of streets in Paris paved with these same stones must be even greater, and it must require an incredibly large number of hand-shaped stones.

Today we progressed no farther than Les Granges. We were surprised to find some excellent flints among the heaps of broken limestone alongside the road. As we moved along we passed a number of buildings constructed entirely of a chalk-like stone. It is used principally for stables and outbuildings because of its softness, its inability to bear much weight, and its propensity to crack easily in wet weather. In Les Grez the stable of the inn is built entirely of this chalk, which is white and soft enough to write with.

This day remained pleasant, our lodgings at Les Granges where we stopped for the night were not bad, and there were no unpleasant incidents.

THURSDAY, MAY 5

Today we wanted to wait until after 10:00 A.M. before setting out with the carriage, so that our leader would be completely recovered. As paymaster I went ahead with the freight wagon, with the understanding that I was to advance as far as possible without waiting for the others. But at 4:00 P.M. the coach passed us, and it reached La maison rouge, our good but expensive lodging for the night, in time to miss a heavy rain which soaked us through at the very end of the day's journey.

FRIDAY, MAY 6

Today we repeated the procedure of the day before, except that Mr. Vonarx was sent along as paymaster. Here I could make some remarks about the royal hunting lodges, but I will restrain myself.

SATURDAY, MAY 7

We reached Paris in good time in the afternoon. In order to avoid the inspection to which all carriages and wagons entering the city must submit, we drove all the way around the city and managed to evade the so-called *barrieres* [custom gates]. After some two leagues we reached the Barriere la Chapelle St. Denis, through which suburb the road to Havre leads. Here we stopped at La Ville Damiens to decide whether we should leave Paris on this day. Because the lodging appeared to be satisfactory and inexpensive, we decided to stay here while we tried to sell our horses in Paris. Sending someone to meet the freight wagon, I took a hackney coach to the post office in the city to see whether there was a letter from Havre, and I also called on Mr. N. Wuest, from whom I learned that one could take a steamboat to Havre. He and I went to St. Nicholas, where these boats stop, and found that one was scheduled to leave in two days, the fare being twelve French francs per person and twenty-five sols per hundred pounds for the effects.

I had found no letter at the post office, but everyone back at our lodging was glad to hear my news about the steamboats, and we agreed to leave on the first one. They take roughly four days to get to Havre. Designed to transport goods rather than people, they have no cabins but only a fairly high hold and an open deck, and they stop at night where the passengers can find lodgings.

Our freight wagon arrived in good shape at 4:00 P.M. I inquired whether anything could enter the city without examination and learned that all provisions and merchandise are assessed duty, so one can find better wine and cheaper living in the suburbs. Passage through the city is under seal and with an escort. Anything unloaded in the city, such as our effects, cannot be considered as being in transit. But we received assurance that our effects would be treated as transit goods, which would involve having them sealed and escorted to where the steamboats left for Havre. There is always a guard on duty who watches to see that nothing is added or removed.

SUNDAY, MAY 8

Our first order of business was to come to terms about the shipping costs and to load our effects. This last was difficult, but finally the wagon was sealed in the city customs, and we were escorted to the Port of St. Nicholas. There we came upon a good many German emigrants, mostly of a kind that inspired little respect. On the way to Paris we often had met emigrant families with their covered wagons, but it had not occurred to us that there would be such a throng of them.

Most of them had left their fatherland with no definite destination in mind, and with inadequate leadership. To many of them the name America seemed to be the only name they knew in the entire new world. Few of them I thought had much chance for happiness there unless conditions were such that anyone could succeed.

They were mostly from [the kingdom of] Wuerttemberg and [the grand duchy of] Baden, with some from [the kingdom of] Bavaria. We did not learn of any Swiss except for a district bailiff from Graubuenden of whom we had heard in St. Louis [at the Swiss border], and he had set out for Havre by land, according to [Picoli] a young man from Graubuenden who was going there by steamboat.

Our party was advised to bring everything aboard on the chance that the steamboat would depart before the end of the day. Mr. Joseph Koepfli and I were to remain behind to sell the horses and vehicles, Geisshuesler having been appointed to take care of them in the meantime, after driving the freight wagon the two leagues back to our quarters.

Our people had no more than boarded at 6:00 P.M. when the steamboat prepared to leave. A second vessel, just as large, was attached to it, both loaded with emigrants bound for America, more than two hundred in number. We took leave of the members of our party who were going on ahead, planning to join them in Havre shortly. Keller and Helfenstein, whose passage already had been paid, were missing.

MONDAY, MAY 9

Troubled as I was about our lost associates, I felt they were learning an excellent lesson. They now had a good opportunity to learn about the vastness of Paris. Since I had to go to the printing house to have a sales announcement printed for the *petits affiches* that appeared daily, I sent Geisshuesler to look for the men in the general area in which he had lost sight of them the day before. However, they had disappeared, and since they were not to be found in the morgue, we decided to let matters take their course.

We have little hope of a good sale. Because of the banishment of Charles X so many horses and vehicles have been available for almost nothing that there is no possibility of making an advantageous sale. It is very discouraging and the situation is worsened because of a fixed price of four hundred francs, for which amount it does not pay to bring horses to Paris. Furthermore the wholesalers of the city have taken advantage of the fact that nearly all of the Carlists—who had been the ones with the most money to spend—sold their horses and vehicles, dismissed their servants, and left the city with the king. Since that time business has been very depressed in Paris, and one hears complaints everywhere of scarcity and lack of income. People feel that present conditions cannot last very long, and they fear that another revolution would destroy everything they own. All this and more gives us cause to worry that our horse business will yield no 100 percent profit.

In the afternoon our lost ones were found by a native of Biel in the canton of Bern who had come here thirteen years before as a master tailor. They had been able to tell him that we were staying outside the city in the direction of Switzerland, and he had guided them up and down the streets of several suburbs until—after five or six hours—they finally found our lodgings. Since another steamboat was scheduled to leave for Havre the following Thursday a reservation was made on it for them. They probably will not wander too far afield again.

TUESDAY, MAY 10

Soon buyers for our horses appeared. Because we feared that they would pick out the best ones if we sold them separately, we resolved to sell them in one lot. One horse dealer, considered to be the biggest of those present, offered us 110 Napoleons for all seven horses, but we held this to be too low and decided to wait. No one showed any interest in the wagon and carriage. The wagon had a wretched appearance and no style, and potential buyers for a family carriage had disappeared with the old king. It was lucky that the horses looked so good, for all seven were in better condition than when we had left home. Apparently other emigrants were finding it even harder to sell their horses.

WEDNESDAY, MAY 11

The situation is becoming monotonous. Our expenses—what with maintaining the horses—are mounting each day, so this morning we looked up our buyer again. But he had bought only about half of the forty horses offered him the day before, and he was not in a good humor. Again a damned piece of business for us. Nevertheless he came and had the horses paraded before him again, but he found so many defects in them that we regretted not having given in to him the day before. He no longer wanted the little red one at all, and he offered us only 100 Napoleons for the other six, which had to satisfy us. We had engaged two brokers, who received their percentage of the sale. They advised us to take the last horse to market the next day.

We visited the Museum of Arts and Crafts and in the evening the royal palace. Several months would not be long enough to see all the products of the many artists, mechanics, and artisans brought together in the museum, in some instances in miniature. The huge royal palace, the home of King [Louis] Philippe I, might be mistaken on the outside for houses on other Paris streets, but inside it is a long rectangle with a double court, built with lavish magnificence. The rooms on the ground floors and arcades are occupied by merchants, artists, bankers, and confectioners, and contain every imaginable kind of wares and valuable objects. It offers everything, be it pleasure or goods, that one is seeking. The king derives nearly eight million francs annually in rent from this building, in which also roulette games are located.

THURSDAY, MAY 12

While Joseph Koepfli busied himself with the sale of the remaining horse, I had our carriage brought to the dock, but no one offered to buy it. I had entered into an agreement the day before to have the boat carry it to Havre for fifteen francs, but today the man in charge would not accept it. With the help of Mr. Wuest, who charged the boatmaster outright with not holding to his agreement, I finally managed to get it taken aboard for thirty francs. Geisshuesler, who was no longer needed in Paris, and the two men who had got lost in the city were to leave on the boat carrying the carriage.

I made reservations on the stagecoach to Havre for Mr. Joseph Koepfli and myself for the following evening. When I arrived at our lodgings at noon I had to listen to discouraging news about our vehicle and our last horse. It seemed that at the market even fine horses were worth less than 10 Napoleons, and no buyer had appeared for the freight wagon. We went to several cartwrights and blacksmiths to offer it as firewood and scrap iron, but to no avail. Then we noticed that our horse was beginning to limp.

FRIDAY, MAY 13

We were due to leave in the evening, and we had several duties to perform in the city, and still nothing sold. When I came into the stable, one of the brokers was there. I did not trust the fellow, and I suspected that this cheat might have injured our horse. Its hind feet were badly swollen, and we feared they might become stiff. Another broker showed up, and we let the horse go for 140 francs and the wagon for 80, paid the landlord, collected our luggage, bought some necessities, and hurried from the place as fast as we could, happy to have done as well as we had. With Mr. Wuest we visited the Louvre, the Tuileries, the library, Notre Dame Cathedral, the zoo and botanical garden, and the museum. But we moved so fast that we scarcely had time to look at anything, and now we regretted that we had to leave Paris, although we realized that it would take years to become acquainted with all of the city's wonders. When we reluctantly finished our excursion we boarded the stage coach for Havre.

Some observations about the present events in Paris that may be of more interest at this stage than a description of the city's points of interest, about which volumes have been written: nearly all of the Carlists have left the city, dismissed their servants, sold their horses and wagons, and either hidden on their country estates or left France. The household property of Charles X that was left behind is said to have been auctioned off at ridiculous prices for the payment of his debts. Because of the withdrawal of the old nobility many persons have become unemployed, and they deplore the overthrow of the old king. The common people are of various minds as to whether the present order can be maintained. Three parties oppose one another, and each has its followers:

First, the Carlists, who still have strong adherents, especially among the clergy. Screaming and crying in support of them are those who have become unemployed through the fall of the Carlists and who wish only for the return of the good old times.

Second, the followers of Louis Philippe, who include especially the more moderate republicans. Their supporters are principally adventurers who benefited from the revolution and workers in factories that began operating again as a result of it.

Third, the Napoleonists, who want the young duke of Reichstadt [Napoleon's son] on the throne of France. They seem to have a great number of followers under pay as singers, actors, mountebanks, and picture and song merchants whose only objective is to immortalize the name of Napoleon and to bring the son the love and honor of the people.

Everywhere they try to force their propaganda on one. Usually they give away their writings and pictures, and occasionally they request a small payment for them. They are to be found principally at the Place Vendome near the bronze column of Napoleon, the base of which is covered with so many wreaths that one cannot see the illustrated work on it. There one hears freedom songs sung with fanatic fervor and explanations of the column, on which the deeds of Napoleon are delineated. We even heard the duke of Reichstadt proclaimed king of France there, and the tumult became so strong the day before yesterday that the police had to intervene forcibly to disperse the crowd, remove the admirers' ornamentation from the column, and place a watch to bar access to the enclosure.

Presently there is fear in Paris for the stability of Louis Philippe's throne and concern that if the out-of-power Carlists join with the Napoleonists it will be all over for Philippe as quickly as it was with Charles X.

Forming a fourth element are the democrats, who wish France to become a representative republic and who would readily unite with the followers of Napoleon.

The population of France seems to be capable of anything. The exercise of authority can ensure law and order for the time being, but business and trade must be stimulated to provide employment for the idle and hungry in Paris, who will side with anyone who offers them livelihood. Louis Philippe's reign seems to me quite mild and wisely calculated to win the confidence of the French people. Next Sunday he will review the national guard. He also wants to travel about in the kingdom. His appearance will win him the adherence of many.

Here is an anecdote that illustrates how individuals in France seek to influence others and how fanatic they can become: In meandering through the streets of Paris I saw an aged man, dressed in part in the uniform of an old soldier. Kneeling on the ground with his hands supporting his head, he was leaning against the corner of a house and weeping. On the pavement before him lay a rough woodcut of the dictator Napoleon, spread out for sale. This dealer showed such emotion over the loss of his fatherland's hero that from pure greed he was producing tears and in this manner trying to sell his wares. A respectably dressed man who passed just then smiled, and so did I. I continue with my diary.

SATURDAY, MAY 14

The stagecoach rolled on all night at tremendous speed. It was to arrive in

Havre the following evening. The fare was thirty francs per person. The dust was terrible, for there has been no rain since our arrival in Paris. Quick stops were made at the stations to change horses until we reached La-Forge-Foret where we had breakfast. We reached Rouen by 8:00 A.M., where we had time to wander around the city for an hour. The area facing the river is beautiful, with mostly new buildings, but the other city streets are narrow and grim. Along the river bank lay countless boats of all kinds, for Rouen is one of the most important commercial centers of France, and fairly large ocean ships can come this far up the Seine. An old pontoon bridge and a magnificent stone bridge of Napoleon's time connect the principal part of the city and the sparsely populated opposite bank.

When we set out again at 9:00 A.M. the road led through level terrain with houses on both sides. Beyond the last house it took an abrupt turn to the right, and here we were asked to get out and walk up a steep elevation which lay before us. This is customary procedure in France, and it is a welcome change from sitting for hours on end in a moving box.

Now the countryside began to look better, and there were fruit trees, which may account for the fact that much cider is drunk. It is inexpensive and not bad.

At 6:00 P.M. we entered Havre, where our passes were inspected briefly. At the posthouse we joined those of our party who had left Paris before us. We inquired whether it would be possible for us to leave the following day and were astonished to learn that Mr. R., whom we had considered reliable, had made no arrangements for our ship reservations or for lodging. A mail ship was scheduled to depart in two days, but it was completely sold out, and we were going to have to wait until June 1 for the next packet ship to leave. The passage was 150 francs per head, and 300 francs had been paid for us in advance. We minded the delay less when we came to realize that we would need several days to buy provisions for the voyage.

We had much difficulty finding lodgings because of the crush of travelers. Mr. [Hans] Hitz, the bailiff, who had been with our people on the steamboat, had a friend called Jenny, a native of Glarus, a brewer and cloth manufacturer, who had rented a lodging here for him. This good man—of whom I will tell more later—permitted our people to lodge with him although he had a good many members of his own family with him. Our group had been drawn to this family because the other boat passengers had been mostly people that in Switzerland would be considered outcasts of humanity. Because the captain of the boat had been a sensible man and because the weather had been beautiful, it had been unnecessary [for the two families] to be with the dirty, repulsive, uncouth people in the boat's hold, where the pestilential stink would have made them ill.

We managed as well as it was possible in view of the fact that twenty-four persons were crowded together in lodgings consisting of a kitchen, a living room, two little adjoining rooms, and a garret. Space was found for our largest effects in a warehouse, and the individuals were packed into the living quarters as follows: Three persons occupied the smallest adjoining room, the door of which could be opened only halfway because my travel bed had been placed there for Dr. Koepfli, who had the greatest need for rest. His wife and daughter slept on a mattress placed diagonally on the floor behind the door, their feet stretched underneath his bed. In the adjoining room which was half again as large, slept Mr. Hitz and his wife [Christina] and their son [Johann][5] and his wife [Anna] with two of their small children. In the living room, which was cleared during the day, slept four daughters of the older Mr. Hitz and two daughters of the younger Mr. Hitz, besides the doctor's maid [Catherine Huger] and Mrs. Meuli (a member of Mr. Hitz's group). In the garret, which was just two feet wider than our mattresses and long enough so that one could place four mattresses side by side, slept the three sons of the doctor, our Vonarx, a Dr. Luethy who was traveling with Mr. Hitz, my brother, and my humble self; also, in a corner slept a miner, Abraham Ambuel from Graubuenden, and in another corner an Italian called Toscan.[6] Ambuel was in the company of the bailiff, and Toscan in that of Mr. Meuli, who was staying in another lodging. Kappeler, Keller, Helfenstein, and Geisshuesler also had to stay in another lodging. Our straw sacks and mattresses all lay on the floor.

SUNDAY, MAY 15

Part of our travel company was now dissolved and the accounts settled. Messrs. Kappeler, Keller, Helfenstein, and Geisshuesler, who had deposited their money with Dr. Koepfli, were given the balance due them (the

5. Johann Hitz, 1800–64, served as Swiss consul general in Washington, D.C., the last eleven years of his life (*Highland Bote*, Feb. 3, 1864; see also *National Cyclopedia of American Biography*, 57 vols. [New York: James T. White, 1892–1977], 33:300.
6. Later—in the May 28 diary entry—the Italian's name is spelled *Toscar*.

two last-named got theirs when they embarked), and from now on each of them managed his own subsistence as well and as inexpensively as he could.

The expenses per person up to now came to 133 French francs and 89 centimes. For those responsible for the equipment it came to much more because of the loss incurred in the sale of the horses and wagons and their upkeep, which amounted to 19.96 francs per person. Including the customs charges in St. Louis this came to 74.94 francs per person, or a total of 226.89 French francs.

REPORT ON THIS KIND OF TRAVEL

Although I do not consider the total cost excessive, I believe that the journey through France could be made more quickly if not more pleasant. It might be possible to find a more favorable time for the sale of horses and wagons and even make a profit thereby. However, having one's own conveyances always makes for complications and unpleasantness. For my part, I would prefer the following method of travel, which may become possible in the future with the opening of transit through France.

Without doubt, in the future freight will be transported from Havre to Basel on a regular basis, because traffic to North America demands it, and this is the shortest and best route. Then the baggage of emigrants going from St. Louis to Havre would be carried on these conveyances. Since these would be round trips originating in Havre, a hundred pounds could be taken from Basel to Havre at 6—or at most—100 French francs. In Havre a forwarding agent would assume responsibility for the shipment. The emigrants, traveling by coach, would then have with them for the short time involved only the most necessary articles of clothing, which in the diligence would be free of duty. Thus they would arrive in Paris in three days and in another one and a half days in Havre.

In order that the trip would not be too strenuous and would permit time for relaxation, I would divide it into three parts, with stopovers in Troyes and Paris for as many days as one wished. The coach fare, including gratuities for the postilions, would come to approximately 70 to 72 francs per person. On the travel days the sustenance (for four and a half days) would be 18 French francs. Six to eight days' stopover in Troyes and Paris would cost at most 40 francs. Approximately three pounds of luggage at 8 francs would cost 24 francs, making a total of 154 French francs. With this amount of money one could get along fairly well. Living costs might possibly come to less, but not much less.

If one nevertheless preferred one's own conveyances, I would advise acquiring serviceable but quite inexpensive horses so that at the very worst little could be lost on them, but that does not mean using nags. The equipage would at best be constructed in the style of Dutch travel wagons, namely a kind of covered chariot. With that kind of vehicle one would not have to worry about wheel width because with only one horse one could get through anywhere without being delayed. The load would have to be adjusted for just one horse, so that the vehicle would not be damaged. If at the same time one wished to carry along some cooking equipment in order to prepare one's own food at the miserable French inns, one could manage quite inexpensively. Such vehicles could be transported overseas without great cost, and if they were well-built they would find a ready sale in America, because they cost much more there. Travelers probably would not have to pay shipping costs for such wagons because they would take up so little space when disassembled.

PART TWO

Journey by Sea to New York

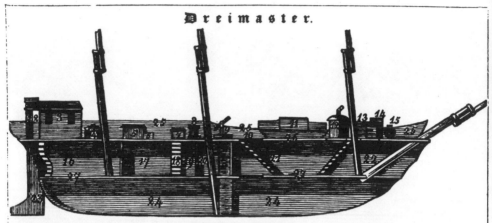

Dreimaster.

1. Zwei Abtritte der Cajütenpaſſagiere.	7. Eingang zur Cajütentreppe.	18. Cajütentreppe.
2. Zugang zu vorigen und Raum zum Rad des Steuerruders.	8. Windſtock zum Ein= und Ausladen.	19. Bereitungsort der Speiſen ꝛc.
3. Zimmer des Capitäns und der Cajüt= Reiſenden mit einer Treppe hinab.	9. Doppelte Waſſerpumpe.	20. Unſer Raum.
	10. Oeffnung zum Einladen der Waaren.	21. Raum der übrigen Reiſenden.
4. Licht gebendes Gehäus z. untern Caj.	11. Schweine=, Küh= und Hühnerſtälle.	22. Matroſenhöhle. 23. Steuerruder.
5. Ein gleiches zur zweiten Cajüte.	12. Cajütenküche. 13. Küche d. Reiſenden.	24. Keller worin die Waaren verpackt.
6. Kiſte zu Aufbewahrung nothwendiger Matroſenwerkzeuge.	14. Eingang in das Matroſenloch.	25. Höhe des Geländers oder Bordes.
	15. Windſtock um die Anker zu lichten.	26. Verdeckboden.
	16. Männer=Cajüte. 17. Damen=Cajüte.	27. Zwiſchendeckboden.

Dreimaster (Three-Master) from the 1833 *Reisebericht*

The original legend can be translated as (1) Two toilets for cabin passengers; (2) Entry to toilets and housing for rudder wheel; (3) Captain's and cabin passengers' quarters with steps to lower deck; (4) Skylight for men's salon; (5) The same for women's salon; (6) Storage chest for sailors' tools; (7) Entry to salon steps; (8) Windlass for loading and unloading; (9) Double water pump; (10) Hatch; (11) Hog, cow, and chicken pens; (12) Cabin passengers' galley; (13) Galley for other passengers; (14) Entry to forecastle; (15) Windlass for weighing anchor; (16) Men's salon; (17) Ladies' salon; (18) Salon steps; (19) Place for preparation of meals; (20) Our quarters; (21) Quarters for the other passengers; (22) Forecastle; (23) Rudder; (24) Hold; (25) Ship's rail; (26) Upper deck; (27) Between deck.

Courtesy of Elijah P. Lovejoy Memorial Library, Southern Illinois University–Edwardsville

MONDAY, MAY 16

The mail ship was scheduled to leave today, but it is customary for the departure to be delayed several days. While the ship was being loaded I utilized the time to view the harbor and the ships lying there. Havre's excellent harbor, a work of the Napoleonic period, is so constructed that even at ebb tide ships can remain afloat. It has been extended into the center of the city, making the greater part of the municipality an island surrounded by masts and sail booms resembling a dead forest. Locks hold the water back as in canals, permitting the ships inside the harbor to remain afloat at ebb tide.

For a long time I walked around looking for the large ocean ships, or floating cities, as I pictured them: several-storied structures capable of lodging two or three hundred people. I made a complete tour of the harbor, but among the countless ships I could find none that to my mind qualified as an ocean-going vessel. And when I inquired about the mail ships or about the New York packet ships that, I had heard, surpassed all others in size and beauty, someone pointed out two ships like the ones near our lodging house, except that they were more neatly painted. Actually there were many vessels there that seemed even smaller and lighter and, like these three [sic], had only two masts, and in some instances only one. I regarded these as ordinary riverboats and could not believe that one would venture onto the high seas in such vessels. Living so far inland I was of course unfamiliar with ocean ships, and reading many tales about floating palaces with many sails had caused me to form ideas not in agreement with reality. Since I will have opportunity later to speak of the various kinds of ships, I will use this space for other subjects.

TUESDAY, MAY 17

There is probably no better place to observe the ebb and flow of tides than a French harbor. Depending on the position of the moon, which is considered the cause of this phenomenon, the tide rises here from twelve to eighteen French feet, so that ships can pass over places that at ebb tide stand six to eight feet out of the water.

I have found it best to take my meals at a restaurant. In that way one can live very inexpensively here. I pay thirty sols a day or ten sols per meal. Many foodstuffs are considerably cheaper here than in the rest of France, especially milk, butter, and bread. Meat is quite expensive. A well-stocked vegetable market provides the inhabitants daily with all kinds of food-stuffs.

The city of Havre seems very secure. It has double, and in many places triple, entrenchments that are always filled with water. The earthworks are well-maintained. Actually there are no troops here. The national guard manages the watches and maintains fairly good order. The streets are laid out quite regularly, and there are provisions for widening them. However, as in most of France, this self-proclaimed arbiter of fashions, one finds no toilets except for the great outdoors, or at most a chamber pot. *O tempora, O mores!*

With good times Havre would soon double in size. The town lies on completely level land, and farther inland the terrain suddenly becomes hilly. Almost adjoining Havre is Engoville, the site of an educational institution. The heights provide a surprisingly beautiful view of the city, its environs, and the adjacent ocean in the background. The first time one stands on the shore of the boundless sea, one is certain to feel the greatness of God in his infinite creation.

WEDNESDAY, MAY 18

Because the mail ship *Francois I* was due to leave today, it is readily understandable that we went there to see it off so as to get an idea of what we would be going through when our turn came to leave. But we could not endure the horrible sight very long. The ship was crammed full, and the travelers seemed to be treated no better than slaves we had been told about. The fact that they had not been dragged forcibly from their home-land like slaves presumably could only make them feel more embittered about their treatment. The ship's hold in which these emigrants were packed measured some twenty-two to twenty-four feet in width, and forty-four to fifty feet in length. Along the windowless walls were tiered bunks about five feet wide and five and a half feet long, one above the other. In height the room measured more than six feet. Beneath the lower bunk, or board bench, was a space less than two feet high for the storing of the travelers' chests. Even the center was built up with two-tier bunks, leaving a passageway of less than three feet.

Picture this room, filled with 160 passengers and their baggage and provisions for sixty days, with no light or fresh air entering except through two hatches for merchandise! Boards that were nailed together were attached to these hatches, and one could see that in rainy weather the hatches would be closed, and the occupants would have to provide their own light with a lantern, as in a cave. When one considers the uncleanliness of the children and the many adults and the continual evil of seasickness, it cannot but make one's skin crawl to see such a ship sail away.

A number of persons who had booked passage were so disheartened that they offered to sell their places, some of them for as little as half price, but most emigrants found this too great a sacrifice. To make matters worse the fares had been increased this year, and many family heads who had counted on paying no more than 70 to 80 francs were forced to pay 150 francs, and they found themselves stripped of funds even before leaving Europe. At noon the ship left the harbor. At the same time a smaller vessel left for New York, and a third ship, larger, left for New Orleans.

Thus in a Christian country of Europe, and in the land that cries the loudest about the preservation and maintenance of humanity, human beings are packed together in this manner for gain. O France, O humanity! Such exploitation not only sickened us but frightened us. I am sure that we all swore silently before God not to let ourselves be packed together in this manner at the risk of our lives. To be sure, the 300 francs we had deposited bound us to board the next ship, but divided among the thirty-two people concerned it came to less than 10 francs each, and we preferred forfeiting this to putting our lives in jeopardy. Not only silently but openly the decision was made to find better passage.

As to the availability of better accommodations, they were to be had on packets but for more money. Cabins, with meals like the captain's without which no such passage is to be had, cost now not less then 750 francs, in addition to the gratuities which the crew expect. The cost for the Koepfli family would have been tremendous. For the head of a family and for people who have no money to waste these cabins were too expensive. Nothing reasonably comfortable for less money was to be had, for there was a surplus of emigrants and a shortage of available vessels.

We went immediately to Mr. Barbe,[1] who charters the packets and

1. A "Barbe" was still concerned with shipping at Havre 16 years later. In Dr. Koepfli's 1847 *Spiegel von Amerika* the name "J. Barbe, Quai Casimir-Delavergne No. 23," occurs in connection with shipping instructions for that year (See *New Switzerland in Illinois*, ed. Betty A. Spahn and Raymond J. Spahn and trans. Jennie Latzer Kaeser [Edwardsville, Ill.: Friends of Lovejoy Library, 1977], p. 64).

explained to him that we would not let ourselves be packed together in such a way, and we asked to see the space intended for us. We indicated that we would gladly pay 1000 [Swiss] francs or 1500 French francs more if we could only have the rear cabin and some sleeping places there and the rest of the space in the between-deck. He answered smoothly that he would treat us fairly and clear the space next to the cabins. He said that he himself had no authority in this matter, and the captain was in Paris. If it developed that there would be few cabin passengers, as now seemed probable, the captain possibly would be willing to come to some kind of agreement. But this did not comfort us very much. He would not even give us the dimensions of the space that would be assigned to us, so we were no further along than before.

We did not care to remain longer in such uncertainty. Our agreement with Mr. Barbe provided nothing more than had been received by the emigrants we had watched depart. And we did not feel that we could rely on the flattering words of a man who was not ashamed to cram a ship full and then state smilingly that these people were satisfied with their lot. We not only made up our minds about this dealer in souls (he deserves no better appellation), but we also went to the firm that took care of the freight for this ship. Here, too, we were told that there was nothing to be done but wait for the arrival of the captian. And so the day passed.

THURSDAY, MAY 19

Today we again besieged Mr. Barbe, asking for at least written assurance of the promised space beside the cabin and the determination of its size. We received nothing but evasive answers, so we began to look for another ship. Nowhere did we find anything. Some French ships offered to take us for 140 to 150 francs per person, but most of these vessels were much worse and did not attract us at all since they had no cabin class and were in part already occupied by passengers ready to depart. The crowd of emigrants was too great, and more arrived every day, some coming overland and some down the Seine. The ships' fares climbed ever higher, and the French firms took advantage of the situation, having old ships repaired and sending them out loaded with people. A month before, one could have chartered the finest ship for 6000 francs, or at most 10,000; now they were not offered at any price. We even thought of shipping over to England on one of the steamers bound for there, and then continuing to America on a Liverpool packet.

While we were running uncertainly around the harbor, we met Messrs. Picoli and Joller,[2] who told us there was a ship to be had. Picoli was the young man from Anders in the canton of Graubuenden and Joller was a young merchant's clerk to whom he had been referred. The ship offered was the *Henriette,* and it lay all ready to sail. It was scheduled to depart on May 26 at the latest and was chartered by André Guillot & Company to go to New York, then to Guadeloupe, and to return from there with a cargo of sugar. It could be had for the extremely low price of 18,000 francs, but since someone else was considering it, we would have to decide immediately, we were told. To do this before giving the matter proper consideration would have been unwise in our estimation, so we promised to make a decision by the next morning. We inspected the ship, examined the space, and went back and examined it again. We learned that it was not a packet but a French vessel that was being held by customs because the owners recently had gone bankrupt and had not paid the entry tax.

The between-deck, for which we would have to pay 18,000 francs, was twenty-two feet by seventy-five feet long, of which two-thirds was five feet high and rising two feet higher from there to the rear. No large man could stand upright in the front part, and the vessel lacked the elegance of a packet. However, this three-master was the largest French ship in the harbor at this time. We sought the advice of qualified persons because we were exceedingly worried. In general it was indicated that the *Henriette* was the best sailer, a fast new ship, but because it had lain unused for some time under detention, it did not have a neat appearance. This, however, could be taken care of by cleaning. The man who would be in command, Captain Fritz, was said to be an outstanding French seaman who thoroughly understood his business. He had made several discoveries and corrections of a geographical and statistical nature having to do with the West Indies Islands, for which he had been decorated by the Parisian Society. We could discover nothing detrimental about the firm of Guillot & Company, and the plan seemed feasible to us.

2. The spelling of these two names varies greatly in the journal entries of May 19–29, the spelling *Picoli* and *Piccoli* occuring 9 times each; *Joller* 4 times, and *Soller* 6.

FRIDAY, MAY 20

It appeared to us that the greatest risk lay in the ship's having been detained. However, Guillot & Company had promised to pay the customs, so this problem was resolved. We remained undecided all day long, although we received one message after another asking whether we wanted the ship. But this pressure made us suspicious. We wondered why this firm did not charter the ship itself and take the profit, if indeed any was to be had. However, since Messrs. Picoli and Joller also importuned us and said there was someone else who would pay five hundred francs more, we held council, that is, the Koepfli family, Hitz, and I, and decided to close the deal.

There were many things to consider: the sad spectacle of the overcrowded *Francois I,* the uncertainty in which we found ourselves, and the poor prospects of getting anything better. We could have arranged passage on an English steamer or schooner to Southampton or Portsmouth, the first for a guinea a person and the other for twice that amount, but we had no assurance that we would be more humanely treated in England. We decided in the end that getting to America was worth putting up with excessive costs and inadequate accomodations. Furthermore, the information we had gleaned concerning both the ship and the captain sounded favorable, and we finally resolved to take the ship. I was to serve as business manager, and I promised to do my best. The agreement was put in writing in the afternoon.

First I assured myself of the honesty of the younger Mr. Guillot, inasmuch as it was he who was accepting all of the safeguards I was proposing for inclusion in the contract. Then the agreement was edited and duplicate copies made. It stipulated in brief:

> That the undersigned have rented from Guillot & Company the between-deck of the three-master *Henriette* of 400 tons for the transport of 160 persons to New York for the sum of 18,000 French francs; that the passengers not be required to pay embarkation or debarkation fees but that they be ready to leave the ship immediately upon its arrival in America (because it was to sail on at once for Guadeloupe); furthermore, that the ship, under the command of Captain Fritz, leave not later than May 28, and in case of delay, the party causing it pay the other party to the contract 100 francs per day (except in the case of unfavorable winds); that the merchant be

responsible for sufficient (and potable) water and wood for the passengers (as provided by law), as well as for a galley, and that he have berths prepared according to specifications from good, dry lumber; that 3000 francs be deposited at once and the remainder of the 18,000 be paid upon departure.

To indicate satisfaction with the terms of the contract, the signatures of both parties were affixed to it. No sooner had Mr. Hitz, Dr. Koepfli, and I signed it than Mr. Picoli, for reasons unknown to us, arrived on the scene. We had made no previous private agreement or understanding, being concerned only with procuring adequate passage for ourselves and our families. Since we felt obligated to Mr. Picoli, we did not want to exclude him, and we invited him to enjoy the same advantages. In order that he might be sure of this we urged him in as many words to ratify the contract, but this he seemed, through evasive answers, to want to avoid. We felt that common courtesy demanded that he lend us his confidence since we were not denying him any of the advantages we were to enjoy.

The three thousand-franc deposit was made at once and work on the ship begun. Since the vessel had no cabins, we chose the space at the stern for ourselves, which we could close off from the rest of the deck with a board wall. But in order not to be faithless to the purpose of our plans and our reasons for not going with the other ship, it was agreed in advance to take only as many passengers as could be cared for humanely, and that this number could be reduced but not increased. American law specifies not more than two passengers per five tons. I measured the entire space, drew a plan of it on paper, and divided the berths so that there would be three persons per bed, as against the four to six who had to share a bed on the *Francois I*. Also, there would be no double-deck berths. According to this design all of the berths were to be built with the ends against the wall in the style of barrack bunks, with the center part of the between-deck left clear.

SATURDAY, MAY 21

The plan would enable us to carry some 122 persons besides our own families. The fare was set at only 140 francs per person, but it was to be paid immediately. Although we avoided as far as possible taking families with many children, we had our full count by evening and the money in hand for all of the fares. Of 122 persons there were 6½ places not paid for in full because there were 13 children for whom we asked only half price. The families Hitz, Koepfli, Picoli, with my brother and me, totaled 29 so that the passenger list comprised 151 souls. In our cabin we would have had room for a few more, but we preferred being comfortable to taking 9 more passengers.

The reason we could carry 151 passengers comfortably when a large packet, although fifteen to twenty feet longer, had to pack its passengers in like herring in order to carry 160 was that packets had cabins in the stern taking up more than fifty feet of space for persons who were not included in compiling the head count. In our *Henriette* we could occupy the cabin ourselves and comprise part of the total count. Moreover the hold, normally reserved for the transport of merchandise, was to be left free for the storing of passengers' effects.

SUNDAY, MAY 22

Today when we visited the ship with the representative of Guillot & Company and the captain to decide on the arrangement of the bunks, my plan was rejected by our experienced seaman, who pointed out that in the rolling of the ship during an unfavorable wind the sleepers' heads and feet alternately would be too high or too low. Furthermore, the sleepers would have nothing to brace themselves against and would easily be thrown from their bunks. He preferred building double-deck bunks to make it possible to carry the desired number of passengers, with only two to a bunk.

So the plan for the bunks was changed. The lower one was built only three inches above the floor, and the upper was halfway between this and the ceiling, so there was more space than in the packets where much space was left underneath for passengers' effects. In order to carry the number of passengers we wanted, we also had to have bunks in the center of the space in three places. But since these were only three and a half feet wide, designed for double occupancy, there remained a passageway of more than five feet. This change was shown immediately to our passengers, along with the choice of withdrawing, but most of them quickly recognized the advantage, and no one wished to desert our ship, although every effort was being made in Havre to pass judgment on it. Because there was such a rush to the Swiss ship, as they now called the *Henriette,* we had to refuse a good many people. It would easily have been possible for us to fill several ships in the course of three days, while other brokers needed three weeks.

A good number of travelers had so much confidence in us that they left other ships and forfeited their deposits. The French brokers understandably began to hate us, and they refused to return the passports to their deserting passengers. They also spread various rumors in order to cast suspicion on us, for example, that we German Swiss were thieves and that passengers would be well-advised to be on guard against us, for when we got their passage money we would abscond with it immediately, taking their baggage as well. Furthermore, they said, the *Henriette* was not headed for America but would carry the passengers to Africa and Algiers, where there were French colonies, and more of the same nonsense. All of this slander accomplished nothing, but it was a nuisance to have to refute it.

MONDAY, MAY 23

In the meantime the equipping of our ship was speeded up. The joiner with whom the merchant had contracted for the work had brought the lumber for the bunks in ample time. However, Captain Fritz, on examining it, found it old, wet, and unusable, and rejected it. Another workman was hired, who then furnished sound material.

TUESDAY, MAY 24

The water casks for the *Henriette* stood ready at the pumps. They usually are filled, allowed to stand two days, then emptied and freshly filled. Our efficient captain examined also this extremely important procedure. He found that most of the casks had not been charred out, although red wine previously had been stored in them. He observed to us that in two or three days' time the water would be spoiled, and refilling would not help.

We were beginning to think there was reason to doubt the honesty of Guillot & Company, for it seemed due to the firm's parsimony that the first shipment of lumber had been bad, and we were beginning to regret having paid five-thousand additional francs on May 21. However, the outstanding five thousand francs seemed to us enough security. We immediately demanded that other water casks be supplied or that those on hand be properly charred. The latter was immediately arranged.

WEDNESDAY, MAY 25

We were not entirely sorry about the delay, for several of our passengers did not have their papers in order, and I had this to take care of also. Because Baden and Wuerttemberg do not favor emigration, most of the emigrants from there had taken out passports only to France. In addition to this, many women merely had birth and residence certificates. These were rejected forthwith by the police (actually by the petty police clerk, due partly to the angry brokers' having incited him against us, and partly due to Guillot & Company's having urged him to delay so that more time would be gained to get the water casks in order). Most of our passengers understood not a word of French, and I had to drag them from pillar to post, and for a long time I got nowhere.

The Prussian consul, who took care of such affairs for all Germans, was quite surprised that we sought his visa for various travel documents and passports. He is a very good and efficient man, but at first he turned us down. Finally he gave us a letter to the police in which he expressed himself as follows: "I wonder why these passports are not honored, since hundreds of Germans have embarked here for New York, and my visa never has been requested before."

But this did not help, and we had to go to the head of the police. Finally the consul helped us. He not only entered visas in the passports but prepared new passports for several families that had come with only residence and birth certificates. I now had to prepare a register listing these papers for the third time. After the papers were cleared by the police, all of the passengers had to go to police and sign the register. Since they were not all together the first time, and I had to make several trips to the police, it made interpreting somewhat irksome.

THURSDAY, MAY 26

In the midst of this activity Mr. Barbe informed us of the arrival of Captain Funk of *La France*.[3] We had asked him earlier for Mr. Hitz's passport, which had been deposited with him and which he refused to surrender. We now explained to him that we had chartered our own ship and did not

---

3. *La France,* a 411-ton packet of the Havre Line, was in service 1827–37 (William Armstrong Fairburn, *Merchant Sail,* 6 vols. [Center Lovell, Maine, 1945–55], 5:1779).

intend to sail on *La France* and asked that he return our deposit of 300 francs. We also offered to find other travelers for our places, for there were enough to be had. But Mr. Barbe answered us very curtly that not only was this unacceptable, but that if we did not sail on his ship he had the right to the three hundred francs, and according to the law, to half the fares as well. This explanation understandably caused us considerable consternation for it meant losing twenty-six thousand francs (which this indemnification would come to) or being packed like sardines on his ship.

This, now, was the first effect of the travel agents' revenge. Barbe suggested that we could arrive at a satisfactory accomodation with Captain Funk, but we felt we could not agree to this. However, Barbe insisted that we abide by our contract. Thus we had no alternative but to start a lawsuit, pay half the passage money, or go on *La France,* filling our places on the *Henriette* with other passengers. The choice was difficult, and we had no time to lose for the *Henriette* was due to leave in two days, and matters could not be settled so quickly. We decided to sail on *La France,* and we went to the captain to make what arrangements we could concerning comfortable quarters.

There was no possibility of getting a cabin without paying the cabin rate. What we could get was the privilege of having our own space closed off from the rest [of the between-deck] with a board partition. For this we were to pay twenty-five francs more per person. We also were given an exit through the rear cabin stairs which was of the greatest value to us.

FRIDAY, MAY 27

When we told our story to Mr. Guillot and he saw our predicament, he could well have brought up the matter of the hundred-franc-per-day penalty, but he told us pleasantly that he would see to it that our passports, already in the hands of the port authorities, were returned. But he added that we must see to filling our places this very day, since the police and the port authorities did not always take the time to dispatch ships at the owners' convenience. Also, he had to pay the police one franc for every pass in order to have everything arranged speedily. We would have to reimburse him for this and collect from the passengers. We really did not have time to inquire into everything to see whether it was correct or not. We hurriedly looked for enough new passengers to make a full complement of 160, using double bunks.

By midday we had the full number together. Because of the repeated revision of the register and the confusion of the irregular papers, I ended up with one passenger too many. (Often several persons had only one passport, and one of these had been entered in two places.) Fortunately one person had contracted smallpox, which gave us cause to reject him, and we were freed from the difficulty of eliminating someone indiscriminately.

But there was still another problem to cope with, and it was due to Picoli, our fellow Swiss. At the instigation of Mr. Joller he informed us that as underwriter of the contract for the *Henriette* he was entitled to a fourth of the profit. When the fares of our company members were reckoned at 140 francs like those of the other passengers, the total exceeded 18,000 francs, and he demanded a fourth of this excess. This demand not only astonished us but seemed most unfair, for of course we were not engaged in a business speculation but only wished to procure inexpensive and comfortable transportation for ourselves and our families. We were not even considering demanding 140 francs from Mr. Picoli and his comrades. We intended having our company members make up any deficit in the 18,000 francs we had contracted to pay Guillot & Company. According to the first reckoning we had been paid 16,170 francs by 122 passengers, of whom thirteen had paid only the half fares charged children. With two additional passengers taken on later there was a sum of only 1550 francs to be made up by the 29 company members, namely 53 francs, 45 centimes each.

But Mr. Picoli was not satisfied with this. Mr. Joller even had the effrontery to present us with a bill for 350 francs for chartering the *Henriette*, and he specified the time and place of payment. We only laughed at this and gave no answer. But Mr. Picoli was able to win support from members of the company, namely Mr. and Mrs. Meuli, who had arrived here earlier with Mr. Hitz, and of course the Italian Toscan sided with them.

SUNDAY, MAY 29

Because of contrary wind that had been blowing for several days, the ship could not leave yesterday, which was better for Guillot & Company than for us, because there was still water to be loaded. Mr. Hitz, who had a letter of recommendation to Wanner, Langer & Company, had not gone to see them until yesterday. It was really fortunate for us to get to know

this firm, especially Mr. Wanner, a Swiss from Nidau in the canton of
Bern. Through the courtesy of Mr. Iselin we too had received a letter of
recommendation to this firm from Mr. Bettin of Basel, but Mr. Wanner
had not been in when we presented it, and we had not tried it again. It took
us a long time to recount all of our adventures to Mr. Wanner, and he too
was amazed at the outrageous demand of Mr. Joller. He promised to give
us all possible help and to accompany us this afternoon to the Swiss
consul, from whom we had just received a summons that Mr. Picoli had
instigated. It read as follows:

> The undersigned consul of the Swiss Confederation invites Messrs.
> Hitz, Koepfli, Suppiger, and Picoli to present themselves at his place,
> Rue de la Couderie No. 45, today at noon for important matters that
> concern them. Havre, May 29, 1931.
>
> (signed) B. Mandrot de Luze.
> to Mr. Picoli, to be shared with Messrs. Koepfli, Hitz, and Suppiger.
> en Ville [down town][4]

Mr. Wanner expressed his regret at not having met us sooner, and we
told him we were sorry to have to present him so abruptly with unpleasant
requests. Shortly after noon we arrived at the consulate, Mr. Picoli with his
henchman and interpreter, Mr. Joller with his comrades Toscan and
Meuli, and we with Mr. Wanner. A certified copy of the agreement which
had been signed in regard to the *Henriette* lay ready in the hands of our
consul. All of Mr. Wanner's efforts were fruitless. Mr. Joller literally
shouted him down ten times. Consul Mandrot regarded the matter fac-
tually as it lay before him, and we saw very soon how it was going to be
decided, so we declared then and there that although the demand was
unjust, we would pay Mr. Picoli the fourth part he demanded. But Mr.
Joller withdrew his own demand, rather shamefacedly it seemed to us, and
I believe that if we had not had his demand in writing, he would have
denied having made it. It really had been most unconscionable of him
arbitrarily to present a bill of 350 francs for having come to us with his
friend Mr. Picoli to tell us that we could rent a ship from the Guillot
brothers. We are convinced, but cannot prove, that Messrs. Joller and
Picoli received their reward from the Guillot brothers when they got them
18,000 francs [from us] for their ship. And when they saw that we were

---

4. In his diary, Suppiger reproduced the summons in the Swiss consul's French.

not going to lose money but come out ahead, they became envious and tried through this chicanery to rob us.

In the afternoon I delivered to the consul the following statement of our ship's account as it stood after we had filled our places: 155 fares—20,310 francs—plus 700 francs still owed by Mr. Picoli for five places, came to a total of 21,010 francs. According to the agreement 18,000 francs were to be paid for the chartering. There remained therefore 3010 francs, of which one fourth, or 752 francs and 50 centimes must be paid Mr. Picoli as his share. Since he still owed 700 francs to the treasury, there was due him the sum of 52 francs and 50 centimes, which was paid immediately, Mr. Picoli having to acknowledge receipt in writing.

Thus again a lesson that one should never trust strangers too quickly. Without Mr. Joller's counsel, Picoli would not have attempted this base extortion. We had perceived that the man had some scheme in mind when he held back his payment and those of Mr. and Mrs. Meuli, Toscan, and another Italian comrade. He was not satisfied to have found better and cheaper accomodations for himself and his family, but he wanted profit, unfair profit.

Now we were happy not to have to leave on the *Henriette,* for the sight of this scoundrel would have embittered many hours. We did not replace Kappeler, Geisshuesler, and Helfenstein with other passengers, and we also permitted Sebastian Keller to go with them because we had loaded the chaise and harness on the *Henriette—La France* having refused to take these things (that is, without charge)—and they could thus be sent in his care. All were satisfied, because the fare on *La France* cost 175 francs, and the accomodations would not have been so comfortable as on the *Henriette.*

MONDAY, MAY 30

There continued to be a contrary wind, and the passengers were becoming impatient and beginning to complain, although they could see it was impossible to leave the harbor. We made a call on Captain Fritz with a gift of six bottles of champagne, charged to our ship's account. He received us most courteously, and we all deplored the fact that we would not be making the trip together. We especially commended our countryman Keller to him.

TUESDAY, MAY 31

No sooner had the wind become more favorable than Captain Fritz unfurled his sails. At midday the *Henriette* left, and with her our anxiety and concern. She was followed by a three-master, [the *New Orleans,*] also loaded with emigrants.

WEDNESDAY, JUNE 1

Today *La France* was scheduled to leave, but departure was delayed again because the loading had not been completed. In the confusion of attending to our business matters, I had been unable to provide for our food aboard the ship, so I had arranged with Mr. Hitz to take care of the matter. We boarded the ship this day, for we wanted to discontinue paying for our accomodations ashore as soon as possible. Our landlord had been complaining since our first week there that he had rented our rooms to one family and not to an entire regiment. The agreement that had been made with Mr. Jenny was for two francs per day, and now a demand for eight francs was being made, which we considered exhorbitant. It was not merely double the amount of the original agreement, but four times as much, and this was outrageous. What difference could it make to him whether fourteen or twenty-four people were living in his rooms? They were surely the more uncomfortable for it! O, you Christian-Jewish French! To live in Havre in a kitchen, a living room, and a small room for twenty days cost 160 francs instead of the 40 originally agreed upon.[5] This night we finally slept on the ship, although our larger chests and our provisions were still not on board.

THURSDAY, JUNE 2

Water, wood, and merchandise were loaded all afternoon. With great difficulty we loaded our own effects. We thought they would be placed in the hold, but despite all of our arguments we had to take them into our own enclosure. Several friends came to visit us on the ship and thought we were royally situated. Even Mr. Wanner said we seemed to be faring far

5. Suppiger neglects to mention their occupancy of the attic in the dwelling.

better than any other emigrants he had seen depart. Perhaps we looked fairly comfortable, but we were too crowded because of our baggage.

Mr. Wanner is the best man we have met in Havre, and we have chosen him to act as our correspondent. Nothing better reconciles one to a place where one has suffered a good deal of unpleasantness than when among the multitude one finds one sympathetic heart, one man who with counsel and deed seeks to help his fellow men. He furnished us with letters of introduction to be used in New York.

We left the harbor at 1:15 P.M. Two other ships (French) sailed with emigrants for the same destination: the *Antonin,* a miserable two-master which had been forbidden the high seas, and the *Martiniquaise,* a three-master.

A naval official was on board, as there was on each departing ship. He turns over his record of the passengers to the captain and holds a review from which no one is exempted. All passengers must be on deck while the official and the captain search every nook and cranny to ensure that there are no stowaways. If one is found, the official takes him back with him. This search takes place at some distance from land on the open sea. A sloop with a sailor in it is tied fast to the large ship, and he takes the official back after the inspection. In our case the official was finished after about two hours. Everything was in order except that a young journeyman baker who could not pay his passage and had helped the sailors for several days, thought that the captain would take him along to do sailor's work at sea, but the captain would not hear of it. The boy was paid for the work he had done and was forced to go back with the official.

Mr. Barbe the accountant also cheered us with his presence and had the pleasure of being greeted by the other passengers he had cheated, with the same charm and courtesy accorded him by us. He tried to comfort us with the boast that this packet would arrive in New York a week ahead of the *Henriette,* since it was better fitted with sails. This ship had to be in New York by July 1 in order to return in mid-July. He wanted to bet our entire belongings aboard that we would get there in twenty-six days at the most. We let him chatter and treated him with contempt. More about him later.

FRIDAY, JUNE 3

Beautiful weather but little progress because of light wind. The French coast always in sight on our left. Splendid sunrise and even more beautiful sunset. On this day we still were sighting some sea birds, just as yesterday we still had seen some leaping porpoises.

The space on this ship for our twenty-four-person association was twenty-four feet wide and eleven feet long. Since we did not have room enough in its open space to stand upright, we would shove some bunks to the side in the daytime so that we could have a place to sit. Many casks with biscuits and other provisions, as well as wine casks were stored outside our board wall, where—as a great favor—space has been assigned for them, even though it narrowed the space for the other passengers so much that there was no room to place the ladder to the hole that led to their quarters, and they had to climb over our things to get on deck. It is atrocious the way people are treated, but nothing else is possible with the hold packed full of merchandise and sealed so that water from overhead cannot enter and damage it, and with the ladies' salon likewise filled with ballast. This certainly cannot be customary. The water casks are stored on the deck, as is the wood for cooking, and wine casks also are lashed fast there. In fact, the entire deck is covered almost completely with objects of all kinds, so that only forward at the captain's station is there a little clear space. One can get to the galley only by climbing over wood piles and water casks.

SATURDAY, JUNE 4

Splendid weather. Light wind in the morning, better in the afternoon. Still in the channel, with the French coast on the left and the English on the right. Cold weather. Several ships passed near us, most of them in the direction of England. A beautiful English frigate with two decks and forty-eight cannon came so close that our captain had to adjust the mid-sail to reduce speed in order to avoid collision. We were greeted with fine music. The wind strengthened at noon but drove us NNW so that all of a sudden we could see the English coast so clearly that we could distinguish not only elevations but wooded areas. This was a magnificent sight in the twilight. The sails had to be adjusted to keep us from running ashore, and we held a SSW course. More persons began to feel the effects of seasickness, which some had experienced as early as the first night out.

Our ship's personnel of 24 is headed by Captain Funk, who speaks only English. Then there are 2 helmsmen, 1 of whom speaks some German; 11

sailors of various tongues and nationalities; 5 cabin boys, mostly relatives of the captain; 2 stewards; a cook; a cook's helper; and a woman mulatto.

The 10 cabin passengers include a young American doctor fresh from his university studies; an Italian from near Rome who loves to travel; a Frenchman with a young daughter and a boy whose father lives in New York State; 2 French boys six to eight years old en route to their parents in America; and 3 Frenchmen thirty to forty years old on their way to settle in northern New York above Utica.

The 156 between-deck passengers include, besides our 24-person association, 3 in a small enclosure adjoining ours. So we have a total of 190 passengers aboard. Later I will also describe the ship itself as well as I can.

SUNDAY, JUNE 5

Beautiful weather, but a strong west wind, forcing us to tack to the north. Increasing wind in the evening. Many ships and the coast of Ireland in sight. In two leagues we would have reached land, but with an adjustment of sail we flew southward. The tacking and the rolling of the ship caused the most vomiting.

Of our fellow passengers, we came first to know Mr. Weinmueller, a brewer from Munich who occupied the small enclosure adjoining ours. This good man with his two comrades paid 750 francs for this poor bit of space which Mr. Barbe had described as a small cabin in the agreement. On embarking, Mr. Weinmueller had had to make do with it. We understand that this man had rented out his brewery because he was alone except for an only son whom he had left in a boarding school. He lives comfortably on the rent from his brewery and is going to America to see if he can find something better. No longer young, with sparse gray hair on a balding head, he has a cheerful demeanor, and originally we took him for a merry Tyrolean because of his accent.

The two men sharing the tiny enclosure with him are from the Black Forest, good, honest craftsmen, the one a watchmaker and the other a painter. They are on their way to Lancaster in Pennsylvania.

Of the between-deck passengers in the forepart of the ship, I must tell first of the old high bailiff Faehnrich from Laufenburg in the canton of Aargau. We pass many pleasant hours with this loquacious man. He and his elderly, infirm wife and a pretty daughter are going to Philadelphia, where his son is employed as a merchant's clerk. Two years ago the son sent them a fine travel diary, which we find most informative and interesting. A second son working in Paris as a lithographer, an able one according to samples of his work shown us, plans to emigrate in another year.

Another person deserving of mention is a young Frenchman, a pattern maker, who with his young wife hopes to make a living in American printing establishments. He too had been cheated out of four hundred francs by Barbe. After having been promised a closed-off space for his wife and himself, they had to content themselves with a bunk among 129 other persons, with no semblance of privacy.

In speaking of the people around us it occurs to me that I have told little more about Mr. Hitz than his name and the size of his group. He was well regarded in his homeland, where he had served ably as grand bailiff (analogous to district bailiff), and he had lived most recently in Klosters [in the canton of Graubuenden] where he operated a tin mine. Previously he had been merely the manager of this business as well as of another establishment and a silver mine, which belonged to a joint stock company. Recently he had taken over the tin mine himself. Enormous operating costs and apparently too little experience in smelting, combined with a big drop in metal prices, reduced his profits to nothing and drove him to find a better life in America.

His married son, a former schoolteacher and a thoroughly good man who had acquired a family, attended the institution of higher learning in Freiberg[6] to perfect himself in metallurgy, and he had been serving for some time now as overseer of the tin mine. But they were working on a new method of producing zinc which was diametrically opposed to current theory, namely to reduce zinc from sulphate of zinc. Up to now it had been obtained only from calamine. Only recently had they made discoveries that a year earlier would have saved them.

They found that hitherto they had thrown away as useless slack as much metal as they had produced, so the loss had been tremendous. The man's misfortune was that he had only one buyer for his product, who constantly lowered the price he was willing to pay. It would not have been necessary for him to do this, because the zinc plates that his buyer rolled from his product depreciated in value very little.

Swedish calamine with zinc is much cheaper because it is easier to reduce, but it is said to be much softer, not so durable on roofs, and almost

6. Suppiger must be referring to Freiburg im Breisgau, at that time in the grand duchy of Baden.

impossible to roll unless mixed with zinc from Graubuenden. According to Mr. Hitz the rolling mills in Chur would regret his departure as soon as his zinc was processed. This plight is similar to our own. Year after year we had to lower our prices to compete with poorer English [textile] products, and necessity forced us to make discoveries that a year earlier would have helped us in every instance.

MONDAY, JUNE 6

Since yesterday, favorable WNW wind enabling full sail all of last night. Cold but clear weather. More seasickness. Still many ships in sight, so we must still be fairly close to land.

TUESDAY, JUNE 7

Favorable wind all last night but violent movement of the ship. This morning we were passing Ireland. At noon today our position was 10° longitude (reckoned from Greenwich) and 49° latitude. Steady wind all day and in the evening WNW under full sail. We met two ships this day. Ships at times pass so close to one another that they can easily be seen by the naked eye or can be called to with speaking trumpets. These two ships hoisted their flags to show their nationality. Generally ships passing one another ask each other where they are from and compare their positions, that is, each tells the other its ship's reckoning. The last of the ships seen today, an English schooner (two-master), was questioned by our captain but seemingly had an unfriendly captain, for it gave no answer. Tonight we are again under full sail. Continued cold but clear weather. Less seasickness.

It is not my plan to give daily reports about those who are seasick. It would be too monotonous. Later I will tell how it affected this or that member of our company. G. Duden gave detailed descriptions of birds and fish,[7] but in this account—as much as possible—they will be mentioned only in passing.

7. See the discussion of Duden's account in the Prologue and its listing in the Bibliography (Gottfried Duden, *Report on a Journey to the Western States of North America . . .*, ed. and trans. George H. Kellner and others [State Historical Society of Missouri and Univ. of Missouri Press, 1980]).

WEDNESDAY, JUNE 8

Strong WNW wind. The sea began to run so high that it seemed as though we were passing through mountains of water. Alternating rain and sunshine. Wild tossing of the ship causing much discomfort. Most appetites disappear. All night the same high waves.

THURSDAY, JUNE 9

Beautifully clear morning but still plowing through mountains of water at seven miles an hour. In the afternoon sudden variations between sunshine and showers. Toward evening all sails had to be furled. Stormy all night. Continued seasickness.

Still the same high waves. Only four shortened sails in use. Cold wind. All day alternating showers and sunshine. Large fish sighted (called marsouins or porpoises). Improvement in weather toward evening and lessening of seasickness (but today I experienced the most violent vomiting and could hold no food or drink). Night a bit calmer, easing the sickness. (WNW) A storm in these parts usually lasts forty-eight hours. Hurricanes are said to rage most furiously at the Azores, which is entirely natural, that being the high point of the waters between the two continents. The greater the mass of water and the longer the time the wind can work on it, the more force it has to stir up the waves, and the longer it takes for them to become calm again. If at times there are islands nearby on which ships can founder, the danger is increased. But the duration of a storm lessens as one approaches America, for the closer to land, the smaller the force.

I do not propound this theory as universally applicable, for local conditions can play too great a part, for example the Gulf Stream and the like. This time in any case, it held true. From Wednesday morning to Friday morning the commotion lasted, and I do not doubt that if we had been farther west, we would have been bounced about by even worse waves.

SATURDAY, JUNE 11

Moderate but still wet weather. Sighted a two-master at a great distance. Wind unfavorable. The sails could be put to use again, but all day we had to sail back toward the southeast. Not until 5:00 P.M. could we get on a

NW course. The wind strengthened, held all night, and became even stronger in the morning. Boring as this account of the wind and weather may seem, it could well be of interest to those who wish to know how conditions really are on the ocean, for it is easy to harbor misconceptions.

SUNDAY, JUNE 12

In the morning NNW with strong wind. (When the ship's direction is given, it must not be assumed that the wind is blowing from directly behind us. This would make it impossible, given the same wind, for two ships to pass each other in opposite directions. To be sure, one could not proceed in the direction of one's goal with a completely contrary wind. For example, if we should be heading northwest, the direction from which the wind was blowing, our sails could not catch the wind except by going toward the north or south in a somewhat more easterly direction. But if the wind then came from the west more northerly or southerly, we could again be carried nearer our destination by tacking, that is by going alternately almost northerly or southerly in zigzags. A good wind is one that blows from the north or south, for with it one can head directly west, but the sails must always stand oblique, which makes the ship slant, so that one side is out of the water. The more the wind turns from north or south toward the east, so much more evenly can the sails be set. It is therefore possible to sail toward one's destination with any wind except an absolutely contrary one. In the case of such a wind the sails must be set so that the ship does not backtrack, or at least not to a significant degree. An unfavorable wind, however, is better than a dead calm, which, although comfortable for travelers, could cause the available provisions to be consumed before the end of a voyage.)

I now resume my interrupted account of our voyage. Because it was Sunday we used the time to read aloud and also played a hilarious game called "tossing around." Picture the size of a ship about 40 feet longer than our factory building, or 120 feet; from keel to foredeck 18 to 20 feet; and to the highest mast approximately 70 feet. Such a ship can spread more than twenty sails. So that the force of the wind when it must be taken obliquely does not cause the ship to capsize, it is so loaded in the bottom with stones or other things that it always acts as a counterweight to the wind. This is the function of the ballast, as this weight is called. A properly ballasted ship may be compared to the charming little wooden mandrakes that always hold themselves upright through the weight of nails driven into them from below, no matter how hard one tries to push them over. When a ship has proper ballast, all the other freight has little effect, especially when it is only merchandise of a lighter kind. It is not difficult to understand that a structure of this kind, solidly built and watertight as it must be, can carry such a tremendous load only because it floats on the water. Thus if there are side winds, the ship must head against the waves. The result of this is that the ship's bow and then its stern is lifted upward so that one, depending on the size of the waves, believes that the bow is going down into the depths, and then that it is going heavenward. This movement, however, is not bad, and when it is the only motion and is not too strong, it is actually beneficial to one's health. But when the ship rolls on waves running sideways, it is swung over to the opposite side, from which the wind from that direction drives it back. Because the ship is narrower than it is long, the movement is faster, so that it is repeated very quickly. This ever-changing motion causes one discomfort at sea and provokes the vomiting which Mr. Duden describes so well. In a strong crosswind the ship is alternately low on one side and high on the other, so that the deck and, of course, the masts are sloping. This, of course, can easily cause passengers to run around without being able to stop, and it also makes it necessary that all objects and effects be lashed to the deck if there is not to be a lot of damage. (It had seemed odd to us when on the first day the sailors came to make fast all of our trunks, chests, and things.)

Today we had a strong south, or cross, wind. We were gathered in a small circle on the deck, some of us on chairs, near the mainmast. I was reading aloud Mr. Faehnrich's travel description, and all were listening intently, when suddenly without warning a very large wave struck us, drenching most of us thoroughly. My brother, Mr. Luethy, and I were sheltered by the high ship's rail, but our doctor, his daughter, and old Mr. Hitz, who were sitting facing us on chairs, as well most of the others, received the full force of the water. This was the first wave we had seen strike so hard, and for a moment we were all astonished. After the water had run off, we all had to laugh heartily, and everything was remedied with a change of clothes.

In the evening the sea became rougher, so that only four sails could be carried. The weather continued to be violent until almost 5:00 A.M. For us sleep was out of the question.

MONDAY, JUNE 13

Fine morning but unfavorable wind, toward NNW. By 9:00 absolute calm. We did not move forward a league all day. Not until almost 11:00 P.M. was there any wind. During the night we must have made substantial progress. Rain in the evening. Calm sea, aiding recovery from seasickness.

Now something about our cooking, which is not well regulated on our ship. A principal cause for complaint is the policing of the galley. There is a well-equipped galley available for the cabin passengers, cared for by a Negro. The one galley available to the other passengers is so inadequate that it must have been intended that as little cooking as possible would be done in it so as to save wood, which is so expensive in France. The hearth resembles a sentry box constructed of boards, the inner part of which is walled up two feet high with bricks. On this is a kind of trough over which iron rods are laid. Under this the fire is built, and on it the cooking utensils are placed. The smoke is suffocating, as is easy to imagine, especially in a strong wind, when it is scarcely to be endured. Added to this is the fiendish rolling of the ship, which throws many a pound of butter into the fire and overturns many a soup. All of these troubles could be combatted, however, if only a specific time were allotted to each family to cook. But the first person to arrive on the spot takes possession of the hearth, and from then on the strongest and most unconscionable ones prevail. It is not unusual for the women to get into arguments, and it sometimes happens that a number of passengers get nothing warm to eat for half a day. We complained to the captain, and he gave us permission to cook in the cabin passengers' galley from nine to twelve and from three to four, the Hitz and Koepfli families taking turns. Unfortunately this galley is often unavailable to us.

It must be said that our cooks are becoming ingenious, for only meals that can be cooked easily and quickly are practicable here, and our stomachs are not adjusted to the ship's regulations as laid down in Havre. They would leave practically nothing for us to enjoy. For example, one regulation requires that no captain may sail unless there are one hundred pounds of *zwieback*[8] and one hundred pounds of salt meat for each person. This is really a beneficial regulation, because inexperienced travel-

8. Literally "twice-baked." The earliest recorded usage of *zwieback* as an American word is 1894 (*A Dictionary of Americanisms on Historical Principles* [Chicago: Univ. of Chicago Press, 1951], p. 1911). Suppiger refers to *zwieback* again in

ers would take hardly any provisions, believing that they could predict the length of the voyage. The pressure of hunger eventually causes one to feel fortunate to have biscuits and salt meat. But at the start when one is seasick and at the end when one has recovered and still has other provisions, the prescribed biscuit and salt meat do not taste very good. In Havre we had resolved to provide ourselves with plenty of wine to kill the monotony of the trip. We had also provided ourselves with spirits, but unfortunately, if there is not more drinking than has been the case so far, the casks will still be full when we reach New York.

What tastes best to us are cereals, dried fruits, and eggs. We enjoy our potatoes, but we have only a small supply. Good, fresh roast of beef such as they carry past our noses into the cabins would also suit us, but unfortunately we have to eat bacon and dry salt fish. The cabin foods are served American style. May they not run out of geese and chickens! But the sailors can put up with *zwieback,* salt meat, and fish, and sparing amounts of cognac.

TUESDAY, JUNE 14

Early in the morning all sails up and filled with the most favorable wind since we set sail. Continued rain. In the afternoon freshening wind required several sails to be taken in. Fairly severe rocking of the ship throughout the night, with heavy rain. We are said to be approximately 250 miles from the Azores.

WEDNESDAY, JUNE 15

In the morning strong but not unfavorable wind. Dreary weather all day. Great speed toward midnight. Beautiful shining sea.

One often fails to appreciate what is constantly at hand. For example, the right we had been accorded in advance, as against the other between-deck passengers, to use the main deck along with the cabin passengers. We are treated with a certain respect, and it seems as though the captain is a little apprehensive about us because we have complained a good bit, and

---

his advice to travelers at the end of part 2, and Dr. Koepfli gives advice about it to travelers in part 5.

he probably knows about our dealings with Mr. Barbe. Moreover, on boarding, Mr. Weinmueller spoke so loudly and abusively against Barbe that Mr. Funk may well regard us as people who will not submit to being treated like dogs. Furthermore, we conduct ourselves circumspectly, so that he has more respect for us than for the rough and dirty occupants of the forward quarters. The large mast on the foredeck is the point beyond which the other emigrants may not go, while we may go anywhere, even into the upper salon for cabin passengers when the weather is bad. Only their lower salon is off limits to us. The exit through the cabin stairs therefore is of great value to us, as is the nearness of the pantry, from which many a plate of food and many a cup of tea or coffee comes to those of us who are seasick, albeit not free of charge. However, it is off limits to the other between-deck passengers. Except for the food and our less comfortable quarters, we are treated as well as the cabin passengers, who seem glad to talk with us.

THURSDAY, JUNE 16

Toward 8:00 A.M. a strong hurricane began to rage. The sky became completely overcast, and the rain poured down. Toward 9:00 A.M. half of the horizon cleared, the sea began to reflect the sun's rays brightly, and the wind blew ever more intensely. All of the sails except the lower ones on the mainmast were lowered. The seas had never been rougher, and the storm continued all day. Having experienced the earlier storm, we watched with indifference the mountains of water looming before us, assured that they could not harm us. Finally the last sail had to come down, and the so-called lug sail was put to use on the mainmast.

Toward 6:00 P.M. we glimpsed a ship that seemed bent on sailing right beside us in the same direction. Quickly our captain changed the set of the sail. A tremendous effort was made to keep a safe distance between the two ships, for in such rough water they easily could have been dashed to pieces against each other. We succeeded in placing three valleys (as I must call the tremendous troughs) between us and the other ship. It was in the main like ours, presumably a Liverpool packet. The sailors estimated that the waves must have been seventy feet high, for the other ship disappeared from our view every time a wave rose between us.

The cold winds whistled over the hills of water and seemed to impart new energy to them. The foam of the shattered water rolled over the waves like streams of lava, and the storm continued all night.

The captain and the sailors had begun the day before to rearrange the deck passengers' effects, placing them closer together to make more room. Furthermore, the deck was scrubbed with vinegar. The captain spoke of coming next into our quarters, where, however, he would be able to clear little space because all of the space under our bunks is filled with trunks.

FRIDAY, JUNE 17

The storm continued with unabated force. The ship we had evaded the evening before remained in sight all day long. It seemed to be following the same course. In the afternoon we were running with three sails and the lug sail. Occasional sunshine which, although its warmth could not be felt because of the cold wind, seemed to hold out some promise of better weather for the night. But with the coming of night our worries increased again. All sails except the lug sail had to be furled once more. All of the captain's preparations caused us to believe that he too was worried about the ship's being tossed about like a ball. Then the deck began to leak down upon our heads. Trying to stem the leaks helped very little. What with the cold, cutting draft it was disagreeable to lie in completely soaked bunks. Most of us contrived to lie outside the bunks while the storm raged on. We lay beside one another fearing the worst, while the wind whistled through all the cracks, and the objects that were hanging up made ominous sounds. The ship tilted alarmingly to one side or the other, and sleep was not to be contemplated. Everyone had to hold on to something to keep from being thrown around. Now we understood the precautions that had been taken to lash everything to the deck. We spoke very little, waiting hopefully for the storm to abate.

Shortly after midnight the ship suddenly was thrown upon its left side with tremendous force, and there was a sound three times as terrifying as thunder on the deck. We thought the ship was sinking as we heard the rush of water above us. Dead silence followed, terror paralyzing our tongues.

Even the lantern was extinguished, and we believed our last moment had come. But before long we began to realize that the ship was still intact and our lives had been spared. The tossing continued, and the entire ship began to come alive again. Anxiously we awaited the break of day. It was a long night.

SATURDAY, JUNE 18

As soon as day began to break we examined the destruction on deck. During the night we had heard the captain's authoritative commands, trying to bring about order, but everything still lay piled in confusion. In our closed quarters below deck the cause of that fearful noise had been a mystery. Now we learned that a towering, thirty-foot wave had hurled its full fury onto the deck, causing great destruction amidship. A boat serving as a pen for livestock, which had been lashed to the deck with strong ropes and surrounded with water casks, had torn loose, as had the water and wine casks, which had rolled down the deck and caused much damage. One of them and several meat casks had gone overboard, firewood was floating about, and much of it had been lost. Chaos was everywhere. The ship's rail was damaged in many places. Fortunately no one had been hurt except that in the morning a young sailor's finger was crushed when the water casks had to be put back into place. The lug sail had three large rents.

Now Mr. Faehnrich reported about our neighbors enclosed forward, from whom we had heard nothing but wails and prayers. When the huge wave struck the ship the night before, those on the right side of the ship had been tossed very roughly out of their bunks. Many of the upper bunks had collapsed and fallen on the ones below. The hatch had been loosened by the force of the water, and a large volume of water had poured in, causing women and children to scream and men to pray. Then they had spent the rest of the night cowering in their gloomy hole, where more than a foot of water was swirling around under the bunks.

The sailors now had much to do, but by evening everything was back in order, with water casks lashed to the deck again. Except for the fact that the loss of firewood and several casks had made for more open space, one would not have realized that there had been any damage other than that to the ship's rail. However, the broken places in the ship's rail gave the dashing waves more room to play.

The sea continued to tumult until late evening, so we feared that the night might bring a repetition of the uproar we had experienced the night before. But thank God the night passed quite calmly, and the weary passengers enjoyed uninterrupted sleep, not to mention surcease from seasickness.

SUNDAY, JUNE 19

The sea must have been in a terrible upheaval because it continued to be rough, with fog persisting all day. Around midnight the stormy north wind quickly turned into an equally unfriendly south wind, which permitted the use of only five shortened sails, and we made no progress.

MONDAY, JUNE 20

Strong wind from the north again last night. Today cold, unfriendly weather. A two-master flew by with full sails in the direction of Europe. Odd that they would venture out on the high seas in such a small vessel.

TUESDAY, JUNE 21

At times, such a strong wind that we could carry hardly any sail for fear of capsizing, and at other times no wind at all, so that with all twenty-two sails we could make no progress. Although the sea has calmed, the surface is not yet smooth. The masses of water still rock to and fro, causing a constant tossing of the ship, because the wind is too weak for us to move ahead. If we were moving along, this rolling would not be noticeable.

The captain keeps the sailors occupied constantly. Even when it rains they have to clear the deck, scrub it and dry it, making it difficult for us to move about. Too much is too much! I too love cleanliness, but this excessive dousing seems nonsensical. In America it is almost as bad, where houses have to be scrubbed from top to bottom once a week, quite unlike the filthy French.

When they are not swabbing the deck the sailors repair torn sails, splice pieces together and make new ones of them (or at least ones that cannot easily be distinguished from new ones except for their darker color). Then with the old ropes they make such things as mats to place before doors for cleaning the shoes.

We almost lost the passageway to the cabins. In the night of the storm a beam was thrown against the door, and it broke the lower hinge. Since there had been always stronger and colder wind since then, the doctor wanted the door closed, which normally is nailed back to keep it open. The captain believed the door would be broken by repeated opening and closing, so he had it nailed back.

WEDNESDAY, JUNE 22

A good wind that came up last evening held until 8:00 A.M. and was followed by calm, foggy weather. Then another favorable wind came up to carry us along at seven miles an hour.

THURSDAY, JUNE 23

Beautiful weather but calm again until 9:00 A.M., when the wind began to come up a little. We saw a ship on the southern horizon, and we enjoyed watching ducks, fish, and birds. In the afternoon we saw another brig.

FRIDAY, JUNE 24

Thick fog all day but fairly good wind, permitting us to move forward. We deduce from the weather that we are fairly far north, but according to the ship's reckoning we are below 45° NL, and we have reached 33° WL.

SATURDAY, JUNE 25

Fog, but favorable wind, that is, for us, for we are making about six miles per hour. (Normally a favorable wind means twelve to fourteen miles an hour.) Today we saw two brigs and a three-master within the space of three hours, passing by on the horizon.

SUNDAY, JUNE 26

Favorable but not strong wind. Sky overcast and noticeable drizzle. The antics of the many flying fish amused us as they sailed three or four feet above the water. According to Mr. Barbe's estimate, we should have arrived in New York today, but we are still far from it! However, we submit to the will of the wind and its divine guider, and in doing so, recall the words of our companion Weinmueller, who says to everything: "If it doesn't come right away, I'll wait a little while." Calm evening but more favorable wind at night.

MONDAY, JUNE 27

A small storm began before daybreak and continued all day, preventing our making any headway. These rough seas supposedly originate from the Gulf Stream, and they are quite usual in the region of Newfoundland Banks, so our crew, also taking into consideration the continuous foggy weather, reasoned that we were near the large Banks. That would mean that most of the distance would now have been covered and most of the dangers overcome. The fact that we never sighted the Azores is the best proof for me that we passed near the ice masses of the north, which would account for the disagreeably cold wind. In the evening calmer and somewhat more favorable wind.

TUESDAY, JUNE 28

With the break of day the sea became calm again. This appears to be the finest day that we have experienced on the ocean. To be sure, we had no wind until 8:00 A.M., but this also could be considered a pleasant factor. We are said to be nearing the Banks. The beautiful day also ended happily. A sailor gave a good performance on the violin, a German passenger played the clarinet, and dancing began as women made themselves available as partners. The sailors made merry, waltzing and square-dancing as well as if they were on a stable floor, which really required skill. We still had trouble walking, but less than at first.

WEDNESDAY, JUNE 29

Beautiful, cold weather, but no wind until noon. Several whales amused us with their spouting of water which resembles little fountains. We met a French fishing brig.

THURSDAY, JUNE 30

Strong wind from the southwest drove us in a northerly direction. Cold weather. Afternoon west wind, by which we proceeded in a southerly direction. The sounding lead found bottom at sixty *toises* (about 250 feet), so we have arrived at the Banks. Even yesterday the water had begun to lose its dark blue color, and today it was getting quite green.

FRIDAY, JULY 1

Wild weather and continued unfavorable wind from the west, forcing us to tack south. It is depressing to be forced to proceed continually at an angle toward the north or south instead of toward our goal in a direct line.

SATURDAY, JULY 2

Rainy weather and continued unfavorable wind. We have seen so many fish of all kinds and have spotted so many porpoises that I am no longer tempted to go the ship's rail to look at them.

SUNDAY, JULY 3

Favorable wind almost half the night, followed by calm, so twenty-two sails unfurled today, the first time we have had so many. Toward noon the sky clouded over. Today we met four ships. Plumbing showed no bottom. We are below 43° NL. We were not told the longitude.

Early in the morning we saw a ship behind us following the same course. The captain took it for the three-master *New Orleans*, which had left the harbor of Havre at the same time as the *Henriette*. All day it followed us at a distance of five miles. Our captain seemed determined to maintain the advantage, unfurling as much sail as possible.

In the evening we met an English brig heading directly toward us. Then we noticed an already departing sloop with four sailors and a coxswain. Our captain struck sail. We were surprised to see the cold-blooded meeting that took place when the coxswain came aboard. There was no handshaking or any other kind of greeting. The coxswain seemed entirely confused, but we gathered that they had come from a West Indian island and had suffered damage in a storm. He asked us for tar and cordage, which they badly needed. But our captain declined, saying that we had no oversupply. He suggested that a French ship following us might be in a position to help him, and he took leave of him just as coldly as he had received him. Then he ordered the sails set again, and we proceeded on our way. It seemed unnecessarily rude, cold-blooded, English behavior. Surely Germans would have behaved in a much more friendly manner.

Incidentally, we had another very pleasurable evening. The sailors made merry with music and dance, and we and the cabin passengers with jumping games. When occasionally someone fell, there was happy laughter, and the person who had fallen got up, joined in the laughter, and continued to take part in the game. The captain joined in the fun.

MONDAY, JULY 4

Bad, wet weather and strong wind forced us to tack in too much of a northerly direction, an unwanted excursion.

I have quite forgotten until now to report that we have been acquiring more room on the main deck every day, for every time a water cask becomes empty, it is broken up, the hoops thrown overboard, the staves marked and bound together and laid aside with the ends.

Two casks last three days, two gallons of water a day being issued to each person at 4:00 P.M., generally by the second mate. He has a list of the families, calls them one after the other, and no one receives an extra drop. With care one could make do with this, but there is no possibility of washing the dishes with fresh water, so they have to be done with sea water. Also the wood is being used up each day, so that gradually one can get to the galley without climbing over it. This pleases our women who do the cooking.

TUESDAY, JULY 5

Again on the foggy Newfoundland Banks. We wanted to break the monotony by fishing for cod, but if we had been forced to rely on them for sustenance, we would have despaired, for all of our efforts were like those of the holy Simon Peter as he cried to the Lord that he had worked the entire night and caught nothing. The sailors thought our fishing lines were too short, but I think our ship moved so fast that the cod did not take the hooks baited with bacon. In the afternoon we actually met a codfish vessel, an American schooner. Course WSW. Splendid sunset following a bit of calm. Some wind at night.

WEDNESDAY, JULY 6

Beautiful daybreak but calm with a fairly good wind coming up after seven. According to today's ship's reckoning we have reached 44 ° north latitude and 55 ° longitude (from Greenwich).

THURSDAY, JULY 7

Fog. Good passage until evening. Today a number of *schwarzfische* (as they are called), or porpoises, came quite close. Our powerful coxswain threw a harpoon at them and hit one, but it was able to free itself. I would have enjoyed seeing it brought aboard, although the meat is not good to eat. The brain, however, has a kind of oil that is said to help wounds heal. The blubber is put to the same use as that of the whale. In the evening the wind worsened again.

FRIDAY, JULY 8

Unfavorable wind and course. Foggy and unpleasant. If the wind does not become favorable we will be under way a good part of this month, for the north and south tacking is of little help.

SATURDAY, JULY 9

Smooth sailing all last night. Pleasant morning but calm. Weak but favorable wind in the afternoon. We are beginning to wash and clean up more. Our crew appears to think land is near. Stronger wind toward evening. Three full days of such wind, we are told, would bring us to our destination.

SUNDAY, JULY 10

Another warm day at last, warm enough, I should say, so that we are not freezing as we have been. We must still be quite far north. Only a south wind today but we made some headway. We are supposedly in the vicinity of the "sand islands," and we are being assured that with favorable winds we should see the coast of New Jersey by Tuesday evening.

MONDAY, JULY 11

Hard rain nearly all last night and all this day, but fairly favorable wind. We saw a large three-master sailing toward Europe from New York, and we called greetings to be extended to our loved ones at home. It may well have been one of the packets that usually leave around the beginning of the month. We must hurry if our ship is to leave again from New York on July 15.

TUESDAY, JULY 12

Wonderful weather. All last night the ship made better time than ever, but all through today only a very light wind. Our water on the deck has been used up, so the hold has been opened and a large quantity of merchandise taken out in order to bring up the reserve casks of water lying in ballast. We saw a man-of-war, called frigate by the French. The little craft with its bright colors gleamed in the sun. Weather unchanged. Surface smooth.

WEDNESDAY, JULY 13

Beautiful weather all day but no appreciable wind until early afternoon. Many large and small fish of all kinds amused us with their antics.

THURSDAY, JULY 14

Last night the wind strengthened in our favor, and we sped along. Rain threatened in the morning, but the temperature was entirely different from that of Newfoundland Banks. Notwithstanding all this, we really felt some warmth from the sun. We enjoyed watching large numbers of flying fish making their long but low flights. Approximately a half yard in length, they seemed disturbed by the course of the ship, for all of the ones we saw flew away from the foaming furrows produced by the ship's passage.

The wind remained favorable until evening, and if it continues this way all night we shall have the pleasure of seeing land in the morning. The nearer we come to our goal, the more our anticipation increases.

FRIDAY, JULY 15

Yesterday's favorable wind held only until 2:00 A.M., when it strengthened so much that all secondary sails had to be furled one by one. This did not decrease the speed of the ship, but the rolling was somewhat checked. The sea grew rougher, and at 5:00 A.M. the ship had to tack northward. The wind blew so hard that the spinnaker boom broke in two with a great crash. At the point of the break it was seven inches in diameter. The jibsail could not be pulled in quickly enough. At five the wind changed enough so that the course could be set southwest again. The sea continued to rage. Around ten we saw a brig heading south. Toward noon the wind increased and became more unfavorable, but it improved by evening, and a northwest course was maintained.

Today I saw a fine whale again, as well as a good number of terns that we enticed to our ship for several hours with bits of bacon we tossed overboard. We also used a good fishing line with several small hooks baited with similar bits of bacon. Every bit that was thrown free was snapped up, but the bacon on the hooks remained untouched, and we caught nothing. The fish cavorted gaily as they competed for the booty, and they often pursued one another for quite a long distance before hurrying back to the ship for another handout.

SATURDAY, JULY 16

Little progress throughout last night. This morning calm. It seemed that the dear Lord wanted to have us experience all possible happenings on the sea so that we would be able to recount them. The roll of thunder awakened us early. Black clouds all about except in the east, where the sky was a bit lighter. Blinding flashes of lightning, and thunder rolling on all sides. But the loud echo to which we are accustomed in the high mountains was lacking, and it was easy to distinguish rumbles on the open sea from those coming from the direction of the nearby continent.

We are said to be a mere 170 miles from New York, a short distance, but with unfavorable winds still a journey of many days. On our left a schooner was sailing eastward. Gusts of rain drove us below deck. Later there was a repetition of the thunder concert, with occasional showers. In the interval we had some favorable wind, but later it merely let us tack north or south. Twice the sounding lead was used, showing bottom at four hundred feet both times. Splendid clearing in evening, but the wind remained unfavorable.

SUNDAY, JULY 17

Another Sunday, the eighth since we last saw land. God grant that it may be the last. Promise of a beautiful day, but unfavorable wind. Sailed in a northerly direction all morning but quite steadily northwest in the afternoon. We should see land in two hours. At 7:15 P.M. (while you were probably fast asleep in Sursee) we were happy to see the coast of North America to the north. It was the western shore of Long Island. The hills became ever clearer, bathed in the golden light of the setting sun, and from the distance they looked like mountains. We all wished we were there, and in a half hour's time we could have reached the shore, but it would not have been at the right place. With the sinking sun the sails had to be changed, which meant a complete turnaround to the right, and our ship sped south in order to be able to sail into the bay, still more than a hundred miles distant, for we could expect only west wind.

MONDAY, JULY 18

Not until daybreak were we able to head northeastward again toward land. Six ships were in sight on the horizon. The day began with wonderful weather, but toward eight a thick fog enveloped us, doing away with all visibility, almost as if we were not to be permitted to observe our approach to land. By two the sun broke through the cover of fog for a few minutes, but heavy showers followed.

The sailors had been so busy all day clearing and washing that there was not a dry stitch on them. But for the first time everything was being doused with fresh water, since there were still ten or twelve casks full of water. Even the masts were washed down and the heavy hawsers freshly treated. The ship's rail, which had been repaired during the past few days, was painted jet black on the outside. The coverings used to protect the hawsers controlling the yards were removed.

In the evening the horizon cleared a little. Several vessels showed toward the north, but no land. According to the sailors, we were on the best possible course, and within an hour we should have sighted lighthouses. Later some good eyes saw them twinkle, but around 9:00 P.M. our captain headed southeast to the open sea again.

The sounding lead, used repeatedly, showed the depth gradually diminishing from thirty to fifteen fathoms, so we must be nearing land. Soon it was being said on the ship that the captain did not trust himself to sail in at night. But I really believe his reason was that the between-deck could not yet be cleaned, a procedure that is said to be standard practice on incoming ships.

TUESDAY, JULY 19

Not until 5:00 A.M. were the sails changed again, but the wind turned against us and let us head only to the northwest. Many clouds at daybreak. At seven we saw the coast of Long Island again, and we were able to distinguish houses and clusters of trees. At eight the sails had to be changed again, and we headed southwest.

At nine a two-master appeared with the speed of an arrow, turned in an arc around us, and came up in our rear. A small boat brought a well-dressed man aboard who brought us the latest New York newspapers, collected the European ones, and returned at once to the two-master, a so-called press boat belonging to newspaper publishers, which meets incoming ships to get the latest news from abroad. This kind of boat is so well built and the handling of its sails is so cleverly arranged that they [sic] utilize the wind from all directions advantageously. It is amazing to see them cruise about apparently at will and without regard for the direction of the wind. And they are quite large, at least sixty to eighty feet long.

Through the telegraph the time of our arrival in New York must be known by now, for our expected arrival had been announced in today's paper brought to us by the boat. Our approach must have been noted on Long Island the evening we first sighted it, the fifteen to twenty-foot-high black letters on the topsail of the foremast having identified us. In any case, ships are expected according to a schedule of departures determined a year in advance.

A little later a second press boat came, collected other newspapers and letters, and disappeared as quickly as the other had. Captain Fritz with his *Henriette* was already in New York, and in a news item in today's paper he was quoted as saying that on June 24, at 40° north and 43° west, he had spoken with a ship departing from here. The date of his arrival was not given in the news item, so he must have arrived some time before.

Toward noon it became calm, and for the first time we felt the heat. The entrance to the bay lay before us, but we did not move forward. At 3:00 P.M. they raised the middle flag with the letter *U* displayed (which means Union, or United States). Very slowly the ship began to move as in a solemn parade. Two three-masters passed on either side of us toward the open sea.

Today the between-deck was straightened up. All of the middle bunks were completely torn out and the lumber cleared away, the lower bunks along the side walls taken out, and the partition of our enclosure torn away. All of our trunks and chests were carried forward, the space cleared as for a wedding, and everything was scrubbed.

Now prospective passengers visiting the ship, especially if they examined things superficially, would believe that the incoming passengers were splendidly lodged. They would not realize that very different conditions obtain on the open sea. Mr. Funk's apprehension that we might bring complaints was not unfounded, because we had made no secret of our dissatisfaction.

The sailors who in today's cleaning had received too much wine and brandy from the passengers, something that was forbidden at other times, turned rowdy this evening. During the voyage they had appeared to be busy and polite, but now they began brawling, and the first mate, trying to interfere, was hurt in the hand. They were on the whole somewhat vexed and repeatedly let it be known that they had never had to work so hard on any other ship. Normally twenty sailors would be required on such a ship, but here there are only eleven, and the cabin boys (as relatives of the captain), instead of performing hard jobs as on other ships, have done what they liked, even giving order to the sailors.

They are actually young men who want to become shipmasters, but in

America everyone has to start at the bottom. As a matter of fact, the cabin boys on our ship, one of whom especially is said to be quite rich, have no better quarters than in the forecastle and no better fare than the regular sailors. But when the sailors are not watching, they beg from the steward.

The sailors receive thirteen dollars a month, the head steward twenty dollars, his wife ten, and a relative of his, the galley boy, five. The second steward, who serves both as waiter and servant, receives seventeen dollars, and the cook twenty. The life of a sailor is really hard. Double pay could not attract me to it, and I marvel that it is possible to continue to find men to serve at this wage, for life in America is said to be so easy. Their dissipation enters into it; hardly is a voyage over and they have collected their pay than they squander every bit of it. As long as a sailor still has a cent in his pocket, he will not go near a ship. Not until he is again a poor devil does he look for a job. This prodigal way of life results from a feeling that the next trip might be the last, and he had better enjoy himself while he may.

With approaching night the ship began to make better time. After sunset we saw the beam of the first lighthouse on Sandy Hook in the far distance to the left. On the bow of the ship a lighted lantern was hung as a signal to the pilot who appeared at eleven as swiftly as had the two ships in the morning. In line with practice everywhere, these pilots guide ships in and out of the harbor, because ships at the end of their voyage often run aground. As soon as the pilot is aboard, he takes over the command and with it the responsibility for the ship's safety. These men are familiar with every foot of space in the harbor. It seemed odd no longer to be hearing the irascible voice of our own captain. We had come to believe that the ship's command could not be handled otherwise. But now that we heard the pilot, who seemed to be a good man give his commands without stridency, we changed our opinion.

WEDNESDAY, JULY 20

It was too exciting to think of going to sleep. Everyone gazed out into the starlit night. We could see nothing but the glimmering of the lighthouses' beams. We passed the first lighthouse on Sandy Hook at exactly midnight. Immediately after that we saw three others at different points on Staten Island. We were all sorry that it was night. Now that we were so near the end of the voyage, we were not impatient to see the end of this last night. At

2:00 A.M. we passed between Fort Lafayette and Fort Richmond. The bay here is not particularly wide, and we could distinguish buildings on both sides. During the entire passage a sounding lead was regularly operated by a sailor who sang out the determined depth. At certain places we saw piles in the water on which the depth was marked, as signals for the ships. Soon thereafter we reached the quarantine station, which is on Staten Island; the anchor was cast, and the ship stopped moving. For some time we had noted in the distance a faint redness which gradually became stronger as we moved westward, but it seemed to be north of us. Word spread that it was the glow of a conflagration in New York. Thus during our first night we witnessed from afar an instance of the extremely frequent fires in the city of New York of which we had read in Mr. Faehnrich's travel description. Several houses must have burned down, for although we were almost five miles from New York, the fire appeared to be fairly widespread.

Wearied, everyone went to bed after 3:00 A.M., but soon after daylight everyone was up and dressed festively for the inspection. Everyone aboard was well except a Wuerttemberg boy who had not yet entirely recovered from a bilious fever he had contracted through carelessness on the part of his parents. A wonderful day. We want to see everything, but we don't know what to look at first. Everything is equally new to us and of equal interest. Round about us are small hills. The entire shore is dotted with buildings of every size, comparable in charm to the splendid shores of Lake Geneva and Lake Zurich. We lie at anchor almost in the center of this animated basin. Toward the southeast towers the entrance of the immense Fort Lafayette, seemingly out of the sea. On the opposite side Fort Richmond lies concealed behind hills, only the buildings of the town in front of it gracing the waterside. Toward the northeast lies the green coast of Long Island with its tall trees, a veritable paradise, and to the west the neat palaces of the quarantine station. Twenty-five ships of various sizes lie at anchor awaiting inspection. To the north the New York battery at William Castle and to the left little Bedlow Island.[9] At 6:30 A.M. two steamers sped by along the the west shore between the "Kills"[10] and Staten Island Sound on their way to Philadelphia, and later several others in various directions. One of them stopped at our ship. In it were Captain Fritz and his cox-

9. Bedloe's, or Bedloes, Island later became the site of the Statue of Liberty and was renamed Liberty Island.
10. Kill Van Kull, about 4 miles long and ½ mile wide, connects Newark Bay and Upper New York Bay between Staten Island, N.Y., and Bayonne, N.J.

swain, who were on the way to the city and had recognized us. He told us that he had entered the harbor the previous Saturday but had not sailed to New York with the big ship because he had learned that another French captain had already been waiting several weeks for sailors who had deserted. To avoid this he had decided not to land but to have the passengers and their effects taken to New York in small boats. We were very happy to see Captain Fritz again. We had recognized the *Henriette* some time before among the ships lying at quarantine and thought it might have been detained because of disease aboard, the possibility of which had caused our Captain Funk to smirk maliciously.

About 8:30 A.M. a large, corpulent, elderly looking health officer boarded our ship. He was very friendly and extremely courteous. He first visited the lowermost quarters and had the captain give him a list of the passengers. Then he lined up the ship's complement, counted them, and required each one to show his tongue. After this was over he placed himself behind the big cabin lantern, and all passengers had to gather on one side of the ship and march past him to the other side. In the process of looking us over sharply and counting us as we walked past him, he spotted the convalescent, although we were moving quite fast. He placed him to one side, asked some questions about his condition, and with that the visit ended. He took leave of us in the same friendly manner.

Now we weighed anchor, which took until noon. While still at a distance from the city we could see the towers of the many churches of all different kinds. What caught my eye were the city's red brick structures, new to us, which seemed to be encircled by a forest of ship masts. Wherever one looked, ships were moving up and down the bay. We had not imagined such activity.

The heat was oppressive, and we were perishing for a glass of cider or beer, so our first order of business upon landing in the city shortly after noon was to hurry to a saloon and gulp down some glasses of cider.

We were plagued with persons wanting to direct us to lodgings. Even before we had left the ship, small boats bearing landlords and boarding-house operators had come out to invite us to lodge with them. Mr. Hitz and I had shared food on board, and now we decided to stay at Tensier & Frère, who operated a French pension at 75 Fulton Street. Dr. Koepfli and his family found lodgings nearby at 7 Gold Street with an Alsatian. We had to pay three dollars a week per person. Except in miserable noxious holes no cheaper lodging is to be had in New York.

Thanking God for having let us arrive here well and happy, we decided to spend some days in New York to recover from the sea voyage. Soon our fellow countrymen appeared. Sebastian Keller had arranged for the carriage to go by steamer to Albany, which is on the route we were planning to take. He was in good health, as were his traveling companions, and they had nothing but praise for the captain of their ship. There had been various incidents on their ship involving Picoli, some of them including quarrels with his friends.

Advice to Sea Travelers

1. Departures from Europe should be made earlier in the year than ours, in April at the latest. At the time we left, mostly westerly winds prevailed, as we learned only too well. For the return journey mid-June and July would be advisable. If the entire distance we traveled were laid out in a straight line, it would be equal to at least three times the distance from Havre to New York. One reckons twelve hundred leagues or thirty six hundred English miles as the actual distance. As a rule the trip from America to Europe is never so long as from Europe to America, usually taking twenty to thirty days. On the other hand, starting from Havre, a voyage of thirty to thirty-eight days is considered fast, while one of forty to fifty days is considered good, according to other immigrants here with whom we have talked, and their information is more reliable than that of a man like Barbe.

2. There is little possibility of danger on a good, solidly built ship, especially if one has a good captain. Ships are so constructed that on the open sea they cannot sink, no matter how severe the storm. This can be a comforting thought when waves are wildly tossing one's ship about (unless one is given to excessive worrying). Without some actual catastrophe, which is just as likely to occur on dry land, one need have as little fear of a sea voyage as of a journey by land. Shipwrecks, strikes by lightning, water spouts, lack of water and food, and sickness have their counterparts on terra firma. When fate wills it, one can be killed on land in an avalanche or other mountain mishap as easily as in a shipwreck. Floods on land are perhaps more dangerous than the waterspouts on the sea, from which one can safely flee. Exceptionally severe waterspouts, like floods, can be dangerous, but rarely does either prove fatal. Lightning is more to be feared on land. There are few known examples of a ship's being set on fire by lightning. Guarding against a shortage of food and water can be easier

on a ship by proper provisioning than on land. As for illness, this depends largely on the traveler's physical condition. Seasickness kills nobody, and if one takes reasonable care, one will not be ill at sea any more than at home.

3. Therefore one must provide oneself with good clothes. Even if a voyage might miraculously prove to be storm-free, one cannot assume that the entire trip will be free of cold, rain, or penetrating fog. Even on a good ship one has to contend with penetrating moisture, which is not the least trifling nuisance of sea travel, for it can have unfortunate consequences on one's health just as it can ruin one's personal effects.

4. Sea air has a destructive effect on one's digestion as well as on the colors and durability of one's clothes. It is necessary to select in advance enough heavy clothing for the voyage, laying out plenty of changes of linen and keeping all other effects carefully packed in good chests. One cannot wash clothes in sea water, for the soap does not dissolve, and the garment so washed is soon ruined. Also, careful though one may be, one must count on occasionally being soaked by spray. And these baptisms usually do not take place during a storm (for most people go below when it is rough), but mostly during good weather when one must sail with a crosswind. Also, the waves do not strike from the side of the ship which lies lowest in the water, but from the high side from which the wind blows. Since sea water works such damage on clothes and especially on colors, and everything is affected by the sea's spray, one can readily imagine that clothes worn at sea will no longer be fit to wear later except as work clothes, and then only after they are properly aired or when one is out in bad weather.

5. Seasickness is not, as I can attest, hazardous to life, and there is no reliable remedy for it, although Duden gives good advice about the malady. Some are more susceptible to it than others. Since it is not a universal evil like cowpox, for example, no universal remedy for it can be prescribed. We did not have a particularly calm voyage, for even seasoned seafarers like the first mate were seasick. On the other hand, Dr. Koepfli was never seasick, always had a good appetite, and was healthier than at home where he never would have tolerated such foods. His health and appetite persisted, and he withstood hardships that surprised us. It was the same with his daughter Rosa, who had only a slight headache occasionally but was cheerful throughout the voyage. Mrs. Koepfli stood up until the day of the storm when fright, more than the tossing of the ship, may have made her ill, for she recovered very quickly. Bernard and Salomon Koepfli, as well as our brother Anton, were never really sick. Salomon and Anton had to vomit only once, and Bernard never. For a long time nothing happened to Joseph Koepfli and Vonarx, and they had begun to regard themselves as safe when they finally fell victim to it, long after the storm. After some three or four days they were free of it again. It affected me most severely, the vomiting beginning quite early in the voyage. I was not seriously ill, but I did not feel like doing anything, not even reading. It was good that I often had the pleasure of hearing others read, or I would have been quite bored. To mention several other cases: Mr. Hitz, more than sixty years old, didn't feel unwell a single day of the entire trip, and the same was true of his two grandsons, four and five years old.

6. A principal effect of seasickness seems to be that one loses one's appetite for many foods and especially wine and spirits. It affects some one way and others in seemingly the opposite way. Some feel best in the fresh air on deck, and others feel better on their bunks. I felt best when I alternated between the two. One's eating habits, in my opinion, definitely affect the rate of one's recovery. I finally had to accustom my stomach to hard zwieback and raw salt meat. However, I am convinced from my experience and that of the cabin passengers that the more one can keep to one's customary regimen the less one will suffer on a sea voyage. I want to devote a number of pages to this important subject, but will interject here some comments about the preparing of the food.

7. Please believe that I am not exaggerating when I insist that the between-deck passengers also must have a good, efficient cookstove in order to come through tolerably well. We were cheated of that in two respects. First of all, one hearth for 156 passengers does not permit each family the necessary time to prepare its food properly. If the food had been prepared for all 156 passengers in large pots, we would have had galley space for a group three times as large as ours. But since the captain issued no regulations or time schedules, there was irregular access to the hearth, and a family had to consider itself lucky if it got to use it once a day to cook enough to last for three successive meals. The more shameless and aggressive one was, the better one fared. But this often resulted in scuffling and brawling. If we had not been able to prepare our food now and then in the cabin passengers' galley we would, simply to keep peace, often have had to go hungry or content ourselves with uncooked food.

The other bad feature of our hearth was its construction. It was truly an infernal torture machine. Our cooks were half smothered, red-eyed, and sweat-covered by the time they brought us our food. Occasionally they were drenched by waves which would splash into the place where the galley was built. Saving wood in the process of preparing the food was considered secondary to escaping the galley as quickly as possible. Although the cabin passengers' galley was provided with an iron range and other conveniences, even here those doing the cooking suffered a good bit from smoke, but hardly a twentieth as much as those in the other galley, the construction and location of which had been poorly planned.

8. A simple cast iron range like the one we recently got at home from Dole[11] (Jura Department), with a stovepipe leading through the galley ceiling would remedy all troubles and concomitantly, through the conservation of wood, serve the interest of the ship's charterers. And if there were two such stoves for 150 people, and if definite times for their use were allotted, it would be far more satisfactory than using the present infernal contrivance.

A mere 5-franc charge per person would provide a total of 750 francs, which would be enough to ship two such stoves to Havre with all appurtenances. Finally, if the passengers coming from the same general neighborhood could agree to having their food prepared in common, they would fare better and save much time. In fact, it would even provide time to prepare special dishes to tempt the appetites of those who were seasick.

9. I return to the matter of provisions, a subject that seems all the more important to me because of the fact that one can get only the most inadequate information from the tradespeople in Havre about the kind and amount of provisions to take. These insensitive dealers consider all between-deck passengers to be no better than common sailors and consequently offer them inferior provisions. So every emigrant must have enough judgment to be able to select provisions that he will be able to enjoy. Cabin passengers, of course, need do no special purchasing, because the meat for them is brought along on the hoof, as is a cow to provide them daily with fresh milk and butter, and there is a bake oven to provide them with fresh bread.

We were not able to make a proper judgment as to the most suitable provisions to purchase, what with everyone clamoring for zwieback and salt meat. We could tell in advance that such fare was not for us, and we provided ourselves with many items that did prove satisfactory. At the

---

11. La Doele is a high peak in the Jura mountains. The stove in question probably was cast in Choindez, at the foot of 600- to 800-meter mountains, the site of one of the largest ironworks in Switzerland (*Georgraphisches Lexikon der Schweiz,* 6 vols. [Neuenburg: Geographische Gesellschaft, 1902–10], 1:495–96).

same time I also noticed what edibles are to be had in Havre that are good and cheap and what one would do better to bring from home.

Here are our findings on this subject:
1. Of the large supply of real zwieback we purchased, we did not eat a single pound, and none of the other passengers particularly enjoyed it, although for lack of other provisions, some had to eat it. Others, who had not brought enough flour, used crumbled zwieback as a substitute.
2. Ordinary fresh bread keeps very well for nearly two full weeks before it begins to mold, so a fourteen-day supply can be taken. It keeps better hung up in the open than packed in chests.
3. Another kind of zwieback, really a twice-baked bread that recently has become available, comes packed in small casks. Stored in a dry place it keeps well. There are two kinds of this bread, round and rectangular. The first kind is torn apart after baking and looks like ordinary bread. The second kind, long pieces of which have been cut apart, appears to be better. Both keep well, but the latter kind absorbs odors, and I prefer the round kind, since it seems to go better with the other foods on board.
4. With the right kind of oven one could bake fresh bread daily, as is done in the cabin passengers' galley. This probably would be the greatest boon of all. In America fresh bread is prepared daily and is considered part of the preparation for a meal. It is important to take enough flour along. Packed in barrels it keeps very well. Without it our meals would have suffered. More emphasis should be placed on it in the recipes for meals to be prepared aboard ship. I need mention only some of the many things requiring flour, such as soups, pastry, and bread, with which one can make do in the absence of meat.
5. Canned butter keeps very well. I would prefer it in properly soldered tin containers because crockery breaks so easily and wooden casks give it an aftertaste. One can readily get these tins in Havre, and the butter there is better than ours. After it is boiled down it should be cooled before it is put into cans so that it may congeal better. In order always to have sweet butter I would wash it very thoroughly with fresh water mixed with a little pulverized sugar, pack it carefully into small tin containers holding one to two pounds, and as a precaution have the cans either hermetically sealed, or soldered by a tinsmith. I would prefer the packages to be small, so that when opened the butter soon would be used up. If as an additional precaution some cans of it were mixed with some salt and these saved for later use, I am sure they would keep well.

6. Eggs keep quite fresh packed in flour, salt, and sand. Our packing them in lime water was not successful. One must be sure to take along enough of these little gifts of God. When we were seasick they were the only food for which we did not feel an aversion after having vomited. One should also keep in mind the dishes made from flour that are tasteless without eggs, as we learned toward the end of the trip.

7. If one cannot take along meat on the hoof as did the captain (who had a pig or sheep slaughtered almost every three or four days, and was well supplied with chickens and geese), one must make do with dried or salted meat. We also brought fresh beef, but in the first days of seasickness almost no one had a desire for meat, and later it turned bad and had to be thrown to the fish.

8. Dried and smoked meat, including dried tongue, bacon, and sausage, all of which keep well, should be brought from home, because in Havre only very heavily salted meat is to be had. In foreign countries the cooking is done to please indigenous palates, and we prefer cooking to which we are accustomed. Meat for the voyage must have all fat cut away and then cut into thin slices so that it can be thoroughly dried.

9. Rice, macaroni, grits, and vermicelli keep well and taste good as alternate dishes. One should not expect to get along with just one of these dishes with the thought of saving money or simplifying one's work. What is left over can always be used, and it is good to have some variation in the meals on board ship.

10. Potatoes keep quite well, although those obtainable in Havre are not so good as ours. It certainly would be well worth the trouble to dry a supply of potatoes to take. This year potatoes in France were very dear and poor.

11. Dried fruits such as apple slices, raisins, figs, and prunes had to be brought from home because the only dried fruits available in Havre (mostly apples) could not be eaten with relish, and one must keep in mind that on the ship no fresh water is allotted for washing, and salt water imparts a very offensive taste to food.

12. Lemons and oranges keep well in salt and sand, and wrapped in paper they can be carried overseas in baskets. These truly wonderful fruits require no special care, are cheap in Havre, and are effective in relieving seasickness.

13. Coffee keeps well. Not everyone enjoys it black, but enough do to make it well worth while taking. I would advise having it roasted on the Continent for reasons easily imagined.

14. Spices of every kind should be taken, as well as dried almonds and chestnuts. All of these can be had very inexpensively.

15. An especially large amount of white sugar should be used prodigally on the ship to sweeten lemonade, wine, water, and tea, for a steady diet of fresh water for four to seven weeks is not particularly pleasant.

16. Milk boiled with sugar can be counted on to keep eight to ten days. In hermetically sealed containers with some sugar added it would be sure to last the entire trip. Milk in Havre is much better than in Paris. Mr. Faehnrich in his travel diary says that a measure of cream boiled with five pounds of sugar keeps and is so strong that one teaspoonful is enough to sweeten a cup of coffee. Conducting such experiments at home might well prove advantageous. Here again I would use small tin cans and seal them hermetically, or even better, have them soldered. One could began testing these at home by setting them aside for two months and then determining which kind has kept best.

Our captain, because of too much baggage, had to leave his cow behind, which we learned about later, so he brought some prepared milk in small square cans of thin tin, closed and soldered tight. It is said to be expensive. Prepared milk is most readily available at J. Colin, rue de la Salorée à Nantes, manufacturer of sweet milk. I would still prefer some of my own making because I would then know what I had and would not have to rely on a stranger's products, which are said to be made according to a secret formula which yields substantial profits.

17. Chocolate without cream or milk is tiresome, and it is not very good just cooked with water. Some may like it raw. With milk or cream it is not bad.

18. Cheese keeps well, and those who like it even moderately well will not feel their stomachs rejecting it in the stimulating sea air. Holland cheeses are available in Havre, but it would be cheaper to bring Swiss cheese.

19. Gelatine tablets for soup should not be forgotten because little suitable broth can be cooked from dried and salted meats. The tablets (simply evaporated meat extract) can be found in Paris if one does not wish to prepare them oneself.

20. Lentils, beans, and peas provide variety and keep well.

Beverages

21. Wine vinegar is prescribed by ship's order and cannot be omitted. Four liters are required for each person.

22. Various kinds of tea such as English, linden blossom, elder blossom, etc., are recommended as medicine as well as beverage.

23. Wine keeps well in casks, but would be better in bottles. We used little.

A good rule is to bring a moderate amount of it but to choose a good variety. Ours was used mostly for wine soup and mixed with water and sugar. We had red Bordeaux (*vin de Montagne,* according to the wine merchant), which we found astringent. In France one must watch carefully where and from whom one buys wine for it is probably more adulterated than natural. In the area of Paris and Havre, at least, one seldom finds pure wine.

24. Cider (apple or pear) and beer, of which on the advice of the French we took none, keeps very well as we found by sampling some from the cabin passengers' galley which had been brought from America to Havre sealed in bottles. Cider probably would taste better to more people than wine and quench the thirst better. One finds excellent cider in Havre at low prices.

25. A limited quantity of liqueurs and whiskey also should not be overlooked. Syrup in jugs would not be superfluous (raspberry syrup as well as ordinary syrup), because it is scarce in Havre, as is cherry brandy. I will not repeat here what is said in Gottfried Duden's work about medicine for seasickness. His advice is not only good but correct, and one should pay it heed.

In order to be able to regulate the purchase of these things and in order to judge what can best be brought from home, in addition to that already noted, I am adding a price list showing this year's (1831) cost of provisions. Many items are very cheap and better than ours, especially the butter, which is well worth more than five times its cost. Sugar, coffee, and rice should be bought in large quantities, in common. In this way they are much cheaper than at home.

For the packing of provisions it undoubtedly would save much expense in Havre to have boxes with partitions made at home for the small things. On the other hand, flour, bread potatoes, and also dried fruit can very well be packed in small casks or tins.

26. Current Prices (in francs and centimes), May 1831.

Beverages

1 French liter is about ⅔ quart.

	Francs	Centimes
Bordeaux or de Montagne in casks of 114 liters (about 150 bottles)	45	
White wine in a similar cask	60	

	Francs	Centimes
Best cognac per liter	1	10
2d quality cognac		90
Cider (in small quantity), per liter		20
Liqueur per bottle	4	
Champagne	5	
Vinegar, extra quality, per cask (74 liters)	32	50

Victuals

100 Kilograms (K) = 189 pounds

		Francs	Centimes
Bread (ordinary white per ½ K)			30
Zwieback (1st quality per 50 K)		28	
Zwieback (2d quality per 50 K)		24	
Twice-baked bread with cask about 45 lbs.		15	
Beef, good	(per lb.)		55
Bacon	”		75
Sausages	”	1	20
Sugar (in large quantity)	”		70
Salt ”	”		90
Coffee ”	”		60
Chocolate ”	”	1	50
Rice ”	”		25
Lard	”		75
Wheat flour	”		50
Macaroni and Vermicelli	”		45
Shelled almonds	”	1	60
Grapes	”	1	50
Holland cheese	”		75
Holland tea	”	5	
Bees' honey	”	1	20
Ham, heavily salted	”		75
Lemons and oranges	”		10
F. oil[a]	”	1	22
Roasted coffee	”		90

		Francs	Centimes
Rock sugar	,,	1	90
Raisins	,,		80
Saltpeter	,,	1	50
Tallow candles	,,		75
Dried prunes	,,		55
Barley	,,		60
Potatoes, c. 25 lbs.		3	
American flour per cask;			
about 180 lbs., extra good		42	50
Peas per gallon measure			80
Milk ,, (about 2 liters)			20
Eggs, per 13			55
Ground cloves, per ½ oz.			10
Cinnamon, ,,			10
Ground pepper, ,,			7½
Nutmeg, ,,			50

[a]The translator was unable to determine the meaning of "F."

Wood in Havre is very expensive, but that is of no concern to us on the ship because it will be provided. However, it is interesting to know that one small bundle of beech wood, some five or six logs, costs twenty-five centimes and a bundle of pine wood twenty centimes.

New Way to Smoke Meat

27. Instead of going to the trouble of smoking meat one could simply dissolve chimney soot in water and let it stand some time to penetrate, so that it takes on the flavor of smoke. One can increase the amount of this ingredient, depending on how smoky one wants the meat to taste. After this brew has been filtered, the meat—cut in thin slices—is suspended in it. It is left for some time to absorb this fluid (depending on how smoky one wants it to taste) and after that hung up to dry. An experiment could do no harm.

28. One usually should provide provisions for a sixty-day voyage from Havre to New York. Some voyages, in rare instances, are said to have taken longer. It might be of interest to know what a particular group such as ours used. As accurately as possible I have compiled a list of provisions that were used by fourteen persons in fifty days:

Fresh bread	18 lbs.	Cheese (no more	
Twice-baked bread		was available)	5½ "
(3 casks)	135 "	Macaroni	9 "
Fresh meat (that spoiled)	60 "	Vermicelli	9 "
Meat, pre-roasted	8 "	Barley (became moldy)	12 "
Sausages	17¾ "	Potatoes (25 lbs.	
Bacon and ham	16½ "	not enough)	24 "
Lard	4¾ "	Eggs (not enough)	22 doz.
Melted butter		Bitter oranges (too few)	½ "
(not enough)	100 "	Lemons (too few)	3⅓ "
Prunes (not enough)	20 "	Peas and beans	3 gal. mea-
Rice	25 "		sure

Coffee, unimportant
because of lack of milk

Beverages [bottled]

Sugar, white	46 "	Vinegar	38 liters
Saltpeter for salting		Wine, red	228 "
down meat	½ "	Wine, white	20 "
Various spices totaling	1½ "	Juniper brandy	
Sweet butter	2 "	(not enough)	3 "
Tea	1 "	Cognac	4 "
American flour	225 "	Brandy	14 "
Wheat flour	2 "	Liqueur	1½ "
Salt	12 "		

It is well to understand that much of this, especially the drinks, necessarily went to the stewards, cooks, and sailors to maintain a good relationship.

This ends the story of the sea voyage. Part 3 will describe our journey from New York to St. Louis in the state of Missouri.

PART THREE

River Journey from New York to St. Louis on the Mississippi

THURSDAY, JULY 21

One of my first concerns was to acquire a map of the City of New York in order to be able to find my way around in this fairly large city. Although there is little difference in size, it is not so confusing to get about in New York as in Paris, what with the French city's confusion of streets. However, because of the very uniformity of the streets, with almost all the houses of red brick, it is not so easy to identify landmarks for the purpose of instantly recognizing a street. To be sure, the names of the streets are posted on the corner houses, which really helps locate them on the map, but it is difficult at first to keep in mind how many streets one must pass on the left and on the right in order to find the one being sought. To walk the entire length of the longest street, Broadway, takes an hour and a half.

Today everything was unloaded from the ship, and I was surprised at how well things went. Not a single trunk of the immigrants was opened, everyone being permitted to take his effects ashore duty-free. Except for a roll of carpet we had bought in Paris, they questioned nothing, not even our many new clothes, shoes, and boots.

FRIDAY, JULY 22 TO TUESDAY, JULY 26

During these four days I have been extremely busy doing nothing, walking the streets, visiting the shops, and writing letters. When I reviewed my work at each day's end it seemed I had accomplished nothing.

After such a cold sea voyage we find the climate in New York unbearably hot. Someone coming from the interior, where he might well become somewhat acclimated, would undoubtedly have endured it more easily. Everywhere there is talk of this year's mild and wet weather. But in order not to be overcome by the heat we had to put aside our wool clothes and purchase the kind of linen garments worn here. I found the prices reasonable and quite satisfactory.

Fires here are literally a daily occurrence because most houses are heavily insured and no one would rather see it burn than the owner himself, because he generally comes out ahead with the insurance and then builds a house more beautiful and substantial to replace it. When finally the frame houses, of which there are still some here and there in the old streets, are all burned down and replaced by brick palaces, fires will occur less frequently. During our stay the many fires often involved several houses. The fire on the night we entered the bay reduced twenty buildings to ashes. The fire stations are splendid, and men who have served as fire fighters for five years are excused from military service. The fire engines, though, are said to be more elegant than efficient. Suction pumps utilize the water mains leading to every street.

Everything here is expensive. There is no incompetence. Everyone manages to make some profit. Only when an article is overproduced does the price drop. Last year the manufacture of knives, previously very profitable, was adversely affected by overproduction. Several factories could not stop producing, and foreign imports of this product caused a price drop, but not below what you pay in Switzerland. Although watches of many kinds are offered for sale at almost every shop, the price is uniformly high.

Beaver hats, of which none are produced in Europe, are of superior beauty and inexpensive here in America. Compared with them, straw hats, of which many are imported although some are manufactured here, are much more expensive. They are being replaced by a kind of *Holzhuete*[1] that are good looking, strong, and cheap.

Also there is no lack of copper engravings and stone lithographs, and many of the works displayed would rival the best European ones. But it would be incorrect to assume that these are made only by Americans, for there are of course just as many Europeans here as Americans. There are especially good maps here that are far more accurate than one would be able to imagine in Europe. This is the result of exact surveying. What country of Europe could reliably show how much arable land it contains, and where and how it lies?

What surprises me, however, is that the environs are not utilized to raise garden produce, which surely would be profitable. To be sure, the soil is of inferior quality and it is sandy, especially on the west side, but with a little labor one still could make considerable money. I can explain this neglect in no other way than that the land has long been in the hands of speculators who hold it for sale at high prices, and in addition to this the tracts are too large for any one person to work. In America fallow land is also a good investment.

When one becomes accustomed to the red brick houses of this country, the architecture is not bad. Especially the new buildings are in good taste and are admirably suited for the climate. All are built of durable brick and

---

1. Wooden hats? The Suppigers in Switzerland, questioned in 1983, had never heard of *Holzhuete,* and the word occurs in no dictionary, English or German.

so expeditiously that at home it would be considered fabulous. A five- or six-story house that is not only erected but completed in six weeks! Each has its own side walls so that it can burn without injuring the neighboring house. The floors, made of very narrow boards, are durable and very quickly laid. There is only one kind of window: machine-made. One can dispense with window frames if one has a glazier. The casing is constructed during the erection of the building. Hinges and clasps are not needed. The two halves of the windows can be moved only up or down. The doors are *galant*[2] and hang just on hinges. The rooms are papered. They are heated by French fireplaces, and the kitchen contains an ingenious cast iron stove. The roof is light weight and its shingles usually are painted red.

WEDNESDAY, JULY 27 TO FRIDAY, JULY 29

The shops here rival in splendor those in Paris. I would not have expected to find shops filled with such fine wares. It appears that the different classes of merchants have developed specialized kinds of merchandising. There are streets where only wholesale business is carried on and others where retail business is conducted with the wholesale, and again shops that are only retail, etc.

It is much more agreeable to walk through the straight, regularly laid-out streets here than in Paris. Although, comparatively speaking, it is just as lively here, there is not the danger of being run down by vehicles because all of the streets are wide and there are somewhat raised sidewalks on both sides for the pedestrians. Most of these are overhung with awnings from the buildings, which makes for pleasant, shaded walks during the heat of the day.

The horses here are generally of a better grade than ours, comparable to our most powerful ones. I have seen no huge draft horses like those in France that cost from one thousand to two thousand francs, but there are carriage horses here that compare most favorably with ours in speed and beauty.

The horned livestock here surpass my expectations. Cows and oxen are

2. The Swiss in Lucerne (in 1983) could only suggest "elegant." But Suppiger uses the German *elegant* in instances where he wishes to describe something as "elegant" in the American sense of the word.

definitely as good as ours. I have seen cows without horns too, a contrast to those with huge spreading forks, but I have seen few goats, probably because feed for the cattle costs nothing, running free as they do summer and winter. In the city even pigs roam freely.

I must comment on the pleasant farm houses I saw on an excursion last Sunday. I really was astounded at their style and neatness, especially after learning how inexpensively and quickly they can be constructed. It is true that they are not planned for hard winters or for permanence. Nearly the entire frame of the house consists of studding roughly five centimeters thick, set three feet apart. Windows are set in every so often between two studdings. The outside of the house is covered with six-inch-wide siding, each strip of siding overlapping the one below it one inch like roof shingles. The whole is painted (usually a light pearl color). Inside, it is lathed and plastered, all smooth like a plaster ceiling, and papered. It is not difficult to understand that a house of this type can be built quickly. But it is surprising to see the varied patterns of these wooden structures and the ornamentation and numerous pleasing details that are added to make these elegant dwellings. Still, such a small two-story house, in which there are not much more than some four rooms and a stone floor, costs two to three hundred dollars.

Mr. Iselin, Swiss consul[3] and reputedly one of the largest landowners in the State of New York, offered to have us deposit with him any of our money at 5 percent until we needed it, at which time we could draw on him at any bank, wherever it might be. We accepted this courtesy with thanks, since we believed our money could be in no safer hands. Thus at this time we drew only what we thought necessary, and for the balance we were given a letter of credit on the house of Messrs. DeRham, Iselin, and Moore, who from then on served as our bankers. For ready cash we were given a draft on a bank that immediately paid us in bank notes. From this New York bank we went to the United States Bank to change our various bills of exchange into those issued by the United States Bank. It is amazing the way millions of transactions can take place in these banks so quietly without a raised voice to be heard. It is carefully arranged that the banks open at a certain hour and close at a specified time. Specific tellers cash one's checks, others convert one's bank notes into currency, still others interchange

3. Henry Casimir DeRham was named New York City's first Swiss consul in 1832, according to the *National Cyclopedia of American Biography,* 57 vols. (New York: James T. White, 1892–1977), 54:197. The Mr. Iselin referred to by Suppiger was Isaac Iselin.

bank notes, etc. One has only to stand in the proper place in order to transact business, and without further ado one gets what he wants, that is, if it is not contrary to the rules and regulations.

Banks are organized as follows: They are not managed by the state but are simply business enterprises. If the state enters into it, it is only as a depositor. There are numerous banks in North America whose principal business consists in putting into circulation as legal tender bank notes bearing their name and then working with the acquired cash. It can be risky, therefore, to have one's wealth in bank notes since such enterprises, through unsound speculation, might become bankrupt and no longer able to redeem their own bank notes.

But now there are laws regulating the opening of banks. If such a paper money factory wishes to organize, it must first specify the amount of paper money, for example fifty or one hundred thousand dollars, which it intends to put into circulation. The institution must then give security for this amount and have available an equal amount in cash. It is understandable that bank notes are so printed that they cannot easily be forged, and counterfeit bank notes rarely get into circulation.

Thus one can exchange his cash for such paper money anywhere, and every bank must upon demand cash its bank notes within ten minutes' time (that is, its own notes, not those of another bank). Therefore it is wise to acquire bank notes that are accepted at the places one plans to go.

Nearly every state has several banks, and the bank notes of those in adjacent states are always exchangeable. The Bank of the United States, however, is the safest, with branches in all important cities of every state. Within the state of New York, for instance, the notes of its banks would be readily exchangeable, but one could travel anywhere in the United States with notes of the United States Bank and have no trouble.

You may ask what help it is to me to be able to cash my money for paper rather than to keep my silver and be safe. The American feels quite different about this and regards these enterprises as beneficent institutions, which in fact they really are. I still do not know all the merits involved, but I will explain what I know. Concerning the United States Bank, it pays the state some millions of dollars annually in taxes, lightening the tax burden of the inhabitants. Government deposits or withdrawals all go through the bank without a cent of loss or handling costs, the money of the government is available in any part of the country it is needed, and much saving is effected through avoidance of unnecessary expenses.

Now let us consider convenience as well as political economy. How convenient it is for the citizens of the United States, especially merchants who must make payments to places as much as a hundred or thousand miles distant, to pay debts without paying for exchange. If they want to transfer funds by mail they will have only the expense of postage for the letter. Payments of sums of money which with us would cost heavy service or exchange charges can be made here very easily and for nothing. One can provide oneself with a letter of credit for the entire sum or take bank notes. When one arrives at one's destination, one gets his gold or silver without any charges.

Anyone who has money for which he has no immediate use can take it to the bank. He can have it back whenever he wishes with 3 percent interest, or if he leaves it for a specified period it earns 4 percent. If one wants to borrow money, he goes to the bank, shows his identification and gets what he needs. For example, to finance the purchase of land one generally can borrow up to half of the purchase price. If someone buys a building lot in town, he can borrow the value of the place at 6 percent interest as soon as the first story of the house is built, before it is even under roof.

The legal rate of interest here is 6 percent, actually ½ percent per month. In the state of Missouri there is no bank other than the United States Bank. I understand that another bank started there once, but that it did not last long.

SATURDAY, JULY 30

Although we had not yet finished with our affairs, we went early this morning to make our reservations on the steamboat scheduled to leave for Albany at 6:00 P.M. We were very happy to leave New York, for we found the heat so unendurable that we feared we might all become ill. Furthermore, New York has no good water. It is bath water that probably is impregnated with some salt (for New York is on a peninsula). It is quite laxative for the foreign immigrant at first, and drinking too much is unhealthful in any case. We hurried to make our purchases, which now consisted primarily of iron utensils and tools that we had begun to choose at a wholesaler before. We believe we got good value for our money because buying as a group we made our purchases at a wholesale house and not only received 5 percent discount for cash but benefited by saving the retailer's profit, which in America is considerable.

We hurried to get everything packed this afternoon and taken to the boat. Our effects now had increased quite a bit. Dr. Koepfli still had an unopened cask of wine he had brought from Europe, which was to go with us into the interior where it is said to be quite expensive.

Our family coach was shipped to Albany last Saturday because in New York no one had been willing to pay a fair price for it. Having been for so long in the ship's hold, where things rust and deteriorate, it had come to look shabby, and we had neither the time nor the desire to do anything about it. Such carriages are said to be expensive in the interior of the country.

We almost left New York without hearing a word of our Hitz, who, although grey headed, continued to enjoy life as much as he had in Europe, seemingly as little affected by the passing years as he was in Graubuenden. After the first few days in New York he and his family had rented a house in order to stay there for a time. He had changed his mind about going to Missouri at this time for good reasons, holding that with such a large family it would not be economically feasible. He regretted not being able to accompany us, just as I regretted having to take leave of this good man. To be sure, he promised faithfully to come later, but if one once settles down somewhere it is harder to set out again.

Because he wanted a less noisy neighborhood and also because his family wanted more open space, he immediately looked around for something more comfortable in the environs, and just last week he moved into a little country house, the Wilhelm Tell Inn above Hoboken. At first he contemplated renting the little inn itself which was being offered for two hundred dollars per year, but now he seems inclined to resume his former occupation. God grant him good fortune. I believe for his declining years a cottage on the Missouri and a few acres of good land would have served him better and been a more fitting compensation for his active life.

Mr. Weinmueller also has remained in New York for a while and often visits us. He and Mr. Gutmann, a young German whom we met here, want to accompany us to Albany. A bookbinder by profession, Gutmann is as good a soul as his younger brother, for whom he was able to find a place in the custom house. These honest, upright men are exceptions to the other Germans, who try to cheat one while professing friendship. "Good man" is their name, and they do not dishonor it. Without any desire for remuneration these people, with their knowledge of the language, most generously made things easier for us and even offered to serve as *correspondenten* [correspondents ?] for us on the distant Missouri as far as it lay in their power. Mr. Weinmueller will take one of the brothers with him for a short trip into the interior. Both are still single, have no family, are able to earn a good living, and the bookbinder can afford to absent himself for a time.

Incidentally, we experienced no cheating at all in New York, and we live confident in the hope that from now on we will experience no more of the exploitation we endured in France.

SUNDAY, JULY 31

As we were loading our effects on the launch at 6:00 P.M. yesterday, we were still awaiting the arrival of the steamboat that was to carry us up the river. Mr. Iselin came to bid us farewell.

What an entirely different impression our new quarters made on us! Only someone who had been confined with us during our fifty days at sea could understand our pleasure at having plenty of room, clean beds, wonderful food, safe and fast passage, and honest people. In short the only similarity was the fact that we were aboard a vessel.

One can travel very inexpensively on these steamboats that leave daily and often twice daily. The trip to Albany where the canal starts, a distance of 145 English miles (about 50 leagues) costs two dollars for cabin and meals and one dollar without meals. A steamboat makes the trip in one day, a towboat in one and a half days.

Hardly had it begun to dawn when everyone came on deck to see as much as possible of the picturesque region. During the night we had made considerable time, for we were just passing the national military academy at West Point. In the background toward the south rise the peaks of Bear Mountain and Anthony's Nose. On the right and left the river banks are crowned with hills. Some places here rival those on the Lake of Lucerne, except that here the banks are much more heavily settled and even the highest elevations are covered with forests. Flourishing communities are to be seen alternately on both sides of the river. Further north the banks become less steep. In the far distance to the left, blue mountains, probably spurs of the Alleghenies, provide a lovely background. It was as if we were again in the fatherland. Primeval forests with the most varied kinds of trees alternated with farms. What seemed incredible to us was to see oak, maple, nut, and fruit trees growing wild in colorful profusion among acacia [locust], savin [red cedar], and plane [sycamore] trees. Wild grape vines covered some trees so completely that they looked like one immense tree.

Toward noon our ship had to make a stop because the engine had overheated. We obtained permission to go ashore. The captain, a friendly, obliging man, came with us. Anchor was cast directly before a farm. It may have been near Livingston, more than a hundred miles upstream from New York. Though we were eager to get to Albany, it was pleasant to be able to inspect the productivity of the land in the settlements along the Hudson. The path, which at first rose steeply from the river bank, led us past an attractive farmhouse shaded by hundred-year-old acacias, a number of them with trunks more than four feet in diameter. In the garden, which we were permitted to inspect, there were fruit trees growing beside the wild flora of the region. The winding footpaths, bordered by fruit-laden trees, might have been laid out by a landscape designer except that it was obvious that all of this previously had been virgin forest. Beyond this was a garden plot carefully protected from the animals, and adjoining it were wooden cattle stalls erected more for shelter in bad weather than for feeding. The horses were better provided for than were the cattle. Next to this was a fine orchard, mostly apple trees of different varieties. The fruit had a good flavor although it was not entirely ripe. Here one saw the abundance of this country, for under every tree lay a quantity of fallen fruit that would not be gathered, but left to rot or be eaten by the hogs. Although the soil would not be regarded as the best, it would be considered excellent at home. The mowed orchard showed that farming is not carried on here as profitably as it could be. There seems to be no effort to take advantage of nature's bounty, much less to increase production.

After about two hours the bell called us back on board, and the boat proceeded rapidly upstream. The current is not at all swift. In some places the river widens out over a mile, with many small islands; in others it is quite narrow. The current is so insignificant in comparison with that of our European rivers and the surface in calm wind so mirror-smooth that one seems to be traveling on a lake.

The city of Hudson seems to be quite an important place, but Athens, facing it across the river, is growing, and with its more favorable location could in time probably become even more important. There are a hundred small communities on this beautiful river that may perhaps become large cities after some years. We had lost time, since the steamboats usually reach Albany at noon, but yesterday's delay and today's stop cost us a half day.

The day began to fade, and the approaching night robbed us of the view. Those who believe there is only wilderness in America would find it difficult to believe how heavy river traffic is here. Steamboats and other vessels proceed up and down the river constantly. There was not an hour in the entire day when we could not see several ships going in both directions. There is not this much activity on any waterway of the old world.

We finally arrived in Albany at 8:00 P.M., having covered the 145 miles in about twenty hours. The steamboat that had left New York at 7:00 A.M. landed a few minutes before we did. It had many passengers, including Mr. Iselin, who called to us while we were still aboard. We could see nothing of Albany except the lights. Our captain permitted us to sleep on board, saving us a good bit of money. There were twenty-four beds in the men's cabin, and twenty in the women's.

MONDAY, AUGUST I

At sunrise we went ashore to see the city, which already boasts a population of more than twenty thousand. So many steamboats, barges, canalboats, sailboats and the like made the landing place look more like a lively seaport than a city in the wilderness of America. In a short time Albany will attain a size which no Swiss city can rival. The city is rapidly being expanded, with streets being laid out everywhere in a regular pattern. The developers cut into elevations that we would call hills, using the material to fill depressions that we would call valleys. Here again the ingenuity of the Americans becomes evident. The clay obtained through this digging is used on the spot to make bricks, which are needed in enormous quantities here, for they are used in all new construction.

In Albany the new statehouse under construction is being built entirely of hard granite blocks with a gilded cupola which brings light into the interior. The style of the building resembles that of the Bourse in Paris except that the one here is much larger and is several stories high. That is all I will say about Albany, and as we proceed I will describe only the most noteworthy things we encounter in the places we visit.

Toward 10:00 A.M. our effects were unloaded from the steamboat's launch directly into a canalboat, for in New York we had made arrangements to go to Buffalo, which would save us some time. All of our things were weighed as they were loaded, and no time was lost. An efficient weighing scale was suspended on a pulley block, and stones of different weights were used to balance the various loads, saving labor as well as time. No attempt was made to charge us for every ounce, small items going through free.

We finally left at 6:00 P.M. But instead of going directly into the canal here, the captain enlisted the help of a steamboat to take us up to Troy so that we could enter the canal through a branch. Not long after our canalboat was tied behind the steamboat, seven other irregularly-shaped vessels, some behind and some beside each other, were being towed by one steamboat. One could hardly help laughing at the spectacle. Our procession looked like a squadron of warships ready for battle. On our arrival at Troy they cast loose, one after another. It was too dark a night for us to see anything of Troy, and the steamboats had lights fore and aft on poles in order to avoid damaging each other.

Just beyond Troy two locks led up to the canal. A great many boats already lay before the entrance, and they moved quite slowly from their places, for above the second lock was the weigh house where the boats together with their loads are weighed. This arrangement is found at all entrances and points on the canal between which the boats go. It is simply a large steelyard with a weight lever[4] from which the pan is suspended in a sluice which permits the water to be drawn off. After the water has run out, the whole boat with its load hangs free on the scale. Such a scale must have tremendous power for often the loads are more than forty tons. A ton is two thousand pounds or one thousand kilograms in weight, or forty French cubic feet. These boats usually charge by the weight of the loads they carry, while ocean ships charge by the space taken up by the loads.

We did not move up into the canal until midnight. The canal is the private undertaking of a company of stockholders. It has its own bank notes, which are current in this region. To cover expenses a toll is imposed. Anyone who wishes may travel on the canal. A captain is charged seventy-five cents for every person he is carrying and fifty to seventy-five cents per hundredweight for the freight, and he has to determine his charges accordingly. This sounds expensive, but if one takes into consideration the distance of 362 miles, it really is not so exhorbitant, because overland transport would cost ten times as much, not to mention the loss of time. It

---

4. *Hebel* = lever; *Gewicht* = weight (*Hebelgewicht* is not in standard dictionaries). *Schale* is a pan or scale; *Schleuse* is sluice.

is necessary to know all of the factors involved before one can make a judgment.

As night set in we began to make our sleeping arrangements. The berths are very simple and are removed from sight in the daytime. The uppers are suspended frames, on which the mattresses and sheets are spread. The seats open out double width to provide lowers. Everything is arranged so as to utilize all of the space. The curtains that hang at the windows by day provide bed curtains at night, and everything looks very neat. A cabin has just two berths on each side, providing space for four people. In the women's room, where the extra bedding is placed during the day, the suspended bed frames always remain in place. It is remarkable how well one sleeps in these berths and how comfortable one can be on these vessels.

TUESDAY, AUGUST 2

When we awoke, two stout horses were trotting ahead of our boat along the canal. We must have made good progress during the night, for we had passed a number of locks. We found ourselves in the valley of the Mohawk River, with the scenery changing constantly. Especially remarkable is the design of the canal where it passes over the river, the first time near Midletowe and then at Alexander's Bridge.[5] The shallow river is quite wide. At the first-named place we counted fourteen, and at the second sixteen, supports over which the canal is carried. Toward noon we came to a nice little town by the name of Schenectady, twenty-nine miles from Albany.

Here there are said to be many mechanics who have made themselves famous through inventions. Fine buildings resembling palaces have been built on a pleasant hill beyond the city, as we understand, for a university of the state of New York.

The weather this morning forced us to remain on the boat. A soft-spoken English lady who had come up from New York on the same steamboat with us remained our only companion. She too was happy to

5. The name "Midletowe," not identified, apparently was a reference to the starting point of an aqueduct over the Mohawk River, 1,188 feet long, resting on 26 piers, the longest aqueduct on the canal (Robert E. Shaw, *Erie Water West: A History of the Erie Canal, 1792–1854* [Lexington: Univ. of Kentucky Press, 1966], p. 135). Alexander's Bridge was probably near Alexander's Mill, later Rexford. The aqueduct here was 748 feet long and was supported by 16 piers.

have seen the last of the coarse, dirty Irish. At this point the valley is quite monotonous except for occasional country seats that are worth coming here to see. The soil on the average is much better than ours, as is evidenced by the splendid green forests with their various kinds of trees. The canal generally follows alongside the unnavigable river, which would be deeper if it were narrower, but the land is too flat and the current too weak to dig a deeper channel.

On the average, one must describe the distinctive architecture of the country houses as tasteful. Nearly everywhere they are built of wood, with pleasant arbors, and painted a pearl color. Large shingles, also usually painted, comprise the roofing everywhere. We saw many log houses built by the first settlers, as well as old fences which looked more like woodpiles than enclosures.

Not only the valleys are largely cleared, but many hills in the area are also under cultivation. And no one who found himself transplanted here like *Blondin von Namur*[6] would believe he was in a new uninhabited world. I am sure that no Swiss farmer would want a better tract of land. But since nearly everything is privately owned, the price of land is already very high. Land along the canal costs fifteen to twenty-five dollars per acre. Food prices are also high, making it possible for the farmer to sell his produce at good prices. Horses cost from fifty to one hundred dollars, and cows ten to fourteen dollars.

We approached the lock at Amsterdam at dusk. Thus since yesterday we have progressed only forty-five miles, which at home would be considered quite a distance. The name Amsterdam should not suggest anything European to you. Usually at these places with high-sounding names there are only two or three miserable huts. In this instance it is a small village which must grow, if only because of its location on the canal.

WEDNESDAY, AUGUST 3

We were awakened by a bell that is rung each morning as well as at mealtime. We had already reached Lock 23, which means that at Utica we

---

6. This improbable tale by Johann Heinrich Daniel Zschokke (1771–1848) can be found in Zschokke's *Werke*, 12 vols., ed. Hans Bodmer (Berlin: Bong, n.d.), 4:173–221. *Blondin* is a blond; *Namur* a Belgian city on the Maas.

had that number of locks ahead of us and thirty-one behind us because the fifty-fourth is at Albany.

The pleasant little village of Canajoharie was the first place we saw today, and we also saw many medicinal plants growing wild which in Switzerland grow only in the garden. Toward 4:00 P.M. we reached Little Falls where four successive locks raise the canal more than thirty feet. Here, where the waterway winds through a rocky canyon which has counterparts only in the Swiss mountains, we saw the first bare rock in America. The canal at this point is a daring new adventure. The rain of the day before had swollen the river, and the foaming waves swelled over the jagged rocks. A large mass of rock just below the village separates the river into two channels, and next to the canal the two branches are divided again by a rocky ledge. Further along, all three channels are again united. Cut from the rock on one side and protected from the river with walls, the canal appears here to have been wrested from nature.

Upon emerging from the canyon we came unexpectedly upon a flourishing town on the opposite bank. A fine bridge built of granite blocks connects the canal with the town. It has two arches, and the walks for pedestrians along each side of it have iron balustrades. The bare rock on which the town is built has not even enough earth for a small garden. It rises gently from the river, with steep, wooded hills to the left and right. Beyond the town is a small valley with beautiful estates. I would expect this town to grow rapidly. The magnificent bridge attests to the inhabitants' sound financial status.

After another lock above the town the canal passes through a landscape which can be described as a pleasant contrast to the cliffs below the lock. Here the river has resumed its smooth, quiet flow. I had pictured the rivers in America as wilder. The Mohawk, like the Hudson, has little flow, but at several places, like the Hudson above Bemis Heights, it has falls that must be bypassed by canals in order to make it navigable.

The activity on this canal must be seen to be believed. Not the busiest waterway in Switzerland or any other country can be compared with it. There are said to be thirteen hundred canalboats operating on it. This estimate cannot be an exaggerated one, for on the average we saw a boat in transit every quarter hour. Today we counted sixty-five vessels. Just as many, or perhaps even more, probably are following us, because nothing has overtaken us but mail boats that carried no goods and were drawn by three horses that had to run steadily at full gallop. On these boats passage cost three cents per mile including food, half that amount without food. They make eighty to one hundred miles per day.

Today we counted 101 bridges that cross the canal. When a boat passes underneath these, its passengers have to lie down; most of them allow barely one and a half feet head room. When two boats are about to pass each other it is done without unharnessing the horses and without delay. The horses are so accustomed to the procedure that it is done without the slightest trouble. As with carriages on the street, each one knows which is to pass on the right or on the left. The pilot steers the boat. One set of horses stands almost still so that the long rope by which the boat is pulled can lie slack. The other driver passes over it with his pulling equipment and continues on his way. Since the boats continue to move forward for some time through their own momentum when the horses stop pulling, this procedure causes no delay. In the meantime the boat has passed over the rope lying in the water, and as soon as this has happened, this driver, too, continues on his way. So each proceeds without a word having been spoken. At night the lanterns furnish enough light so that the journey need not be delayed.

THURSDAY, AUGUST 4

Last night we passed Herkimer and Utica. We would have enjoyed seeing the latter place. Toward 8:00 A.M. we reached Rome, which lies in a broad, fertile plain. If stone and good water are not lacking here, it really could become a large, important place. At present it is little more than a large village with several churches. There are said to be many Swabian immigrants here. Only the fact that Utica is so near can be a disadvantage.

Today the canal took us through a monotonous region that still has its virgin forest. The occasional smaller settlements we passed might possibly, after fifty to a hundred years, become more pleasant as they develop.

In order to give an accurate conception of the canal I find it necessary to explain at some length and at the same time to add a small diagram which for lack of space must be divided into three parts. Imagine that the lines at Utica and Clyde fit together to make a whole. The canal begins in the Hudson River and ends in Lake Erie.

The first part on the diagram, from Albany to Utica, ascends approximately 390 feet through fifty-four locks over a distance of 119 miles. The

middle section has the fewest locks. To be sure, the canal descends and
ascends twice in this section, but then from Utica it continues for 60 miles
at the same level, then descends three times, ascends twice, and descends
again by way of four locks, and then ascends once more at Clyde, so that
there it lies 20 feet closer to sea level than Utica. This section is 112 miles
long. The western section then ascends toward Buffalo through twenty
locks. This part has two fairly long, level stretches, of which the first
measures 70 miles, but the canal ascends steeply at Rochester and Lockport. Buffalo lies 550–555 feet higher above sea level than the Hudson at
Albany. The last section is 150 miles long. The length of the entire canal is
360 miles.

This canal is a gigantic undertaking, particularly when one considers the
cost of the locks, which are all built of hewn stone. The boats are mostly of
such size that they fill the space in the locks so completely as barely to leave
room for the gates to be opened and closed.

The locks are only 80 feet long and 15 feet wide, inside measurement
(and our boat is almost 76 feet long and 13 feet wide). Although very

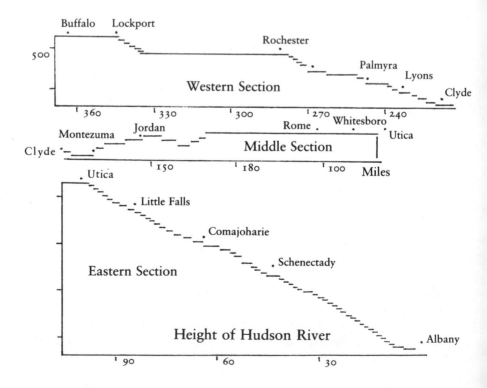

simple they are much more serviceably contrived than the wide, more expensive gates on the Monsieur Canal in France.

Toward evening the monotony of today's trip changed. Earlier there had been clearings at intervals along the banks of the canal, but we had seen no hills in the background. Now some pleasant ones came into sight, and there was more evidence of habitation on the hillsides. At this point a pleasant little place called Canastota came into view, a young village with thirty or forty attractive houses. We had not seen any settlements until now with such attractive and tastefully situated dwellings.

Here there are houses on both sides of the canal. Two fine bridges connect the two halves of the town. Between the bridges the canal is double in width to provide room for boats to tie up. It could become one of the most important points on the canal, for there are indications that the soil at this settlement on the gently rising slopes of the hills is of exceptional quality.

FRIDAY, AUGUST 5

We went to bed late and regretted that it had been almost dark when we came to this attractive region. The view of the lake at Syracuse would have been especially interesting to see. We felt nothing but the jolt of the boat as it entered a lock, for travel is so gentle on the canal boats that the passenger really is pampered. No other kind of travel is so pleasant, quiet, and completely free of bumps and rattles. One is protected from heat, cold, and wet, and a well-appointed table is provided without the slightest effort on our part. The tossing that plagues one on a seagoing ship and the roaring and rattling of the steamboat are lacking. Gently and efficiently the boat glides over the ever-smooth surface, without the constant getting in and out of a vehicle, the unsatisfactory meals, and the overnight stops of land travel. Also without the monotony of sea voyages, where one sees only sky and water. On the canal one travels constantly past changing scenery.

Today Canton, very much like Canastota, was the first little town that greeted our eyes, still half-drunk with sleep. Not long thereafter we came to Jordan with its two attractive wooden churches, which attest to American taste. The first was especially attractive because of its little tower decorated with three galleries. The stone foundations of both structures enclosed space used for school rooms. Jordan is situated on fertile, gently rising hillsides. Unfortunately levees had to be constructed to carry the canal through here, creating conditions for the possible formation of a marsh. If the deep lock at this point could have been located a short distance away and the river flowing under the canal protected against flooding by engineering devices, it would have been a more satisfactory solution. However, these places are increasing in wealth rapidly, and soon there will be adequate levees along the canal.

Today we passed two more settlements with pleasant homes, and then came Montezuma, another attractive little town with a fine, large, three-story mill, part of which was still under construction. It was of hard stone, which is scarce in this region and very expensive. Each wing was 50 to 60 feet long. Near it, part of the same enterprise, was a one-story building at least 150 feet long, likewise of hard stone, housing a workshop for coopers who make nothing but flour barrels. All flour made here is shipped in small casks holding two hundred pounds. The size of such a workshop may give an idea of what such a mill produces. Clyde (at the end of the second section in the diagram) also has a pleasant location and attractive buildings.

SATURDAY, AUGUST 6

We were asleep when we passed Lyons and Palmyra. We saw no important places this forenoon, but there were many fine settlements. Before Pittsford the canal is an imposing piece of engineering. Here the canal crosses a valley, and an eighty-four-foot-high levee has been constructed to carry it for a distance of more than a mile. A tremendous mass of earth must be piled up here. Pittsford itself is still small.

Toward 4:00 P.M. we reached Rochester, a forty-year-old city that already has sixteen thousand inhabitants. It is located in a fantastic, heavenly setting, with the Genesee River in its rocky channel carrying its clear water to the city and supplying countless factories with water. The river is 110 paces wide and the stone channel in which the canal crosses it is 270 paces long, protected on both sides with iron railings. Beside the main river are ingenious conduits that carry the water to the most varied enterprises. This is what made necessary such a long basin to carry the canal across the river. At the edge of town the river drops precipitously a hundred feet over bare rock, creating a marvelous waterfall 150 to 175 paces wide. The water basin is walled in on both sides, above which the upper level slopes gently in the far distance toward the outlet. It seems like a good place to install waterwheels, several of which are already in operation on the left side.

The city has spread for quite a distance on both sides of the river, but there is still room for a thousand dwellings. Several saw mills, flour mills, tanneries, spinning and woolen weaving mills, as well as nail factories are in operation. Two large bridges cross the river within the city. There are so many buildings on both sides of the bridge that it looks like a regular city street. The principal business is carried on along the canal, where the streets resemble those of a European city. On the average the streets, including sidewalks, are sixty feet wide. Farther from the canal the residences are set back from the street about twenty feet behind attractive gardens, giving the place a rustic appearance. In many places trees have been planted between the street and the brick sidewalks. All streets are laid out in regular squares. The environs, although flat, are not swampy but healthful.

There are virtually no Germans here except for a few laborers. Most of the inhabitants are rich English. The place is only nine miles from Lake Ontario. Day wages are high, from 50¢ to $1.50 per day plus board, depending on the time of year and the supply of workers. Land around the city is already $200 to $500 per acre, and only at a distance of four miles can one still buy for $14 to $25. In my opinion this town has all of the advantages it needs to become a city. Rural and urban life unite here. If there were more German culture, I should like to live here.

SUNDAY, AUGUST 7

Early in the day we set out to look for Germans in order to become acquainted with this place, but all we could find was a tailor from Baden who has been in this country only eight months. He said that he was the only German in the town and still not fluent in English, but happy with what he was earning. We did not leave until quite some time later, for our boat had had to make a long stop, not only because it had freight to unload, but because repairs twenty miles ahead on the canal would necessitate a delay.

The most important place we saw today was Brockport, which has three churches of different denominations, with classrooms below each one, as seems to be the custom in this part of the country. From here we went on as far as a canal inn (a saloon), where a dozen canal boats had already found it necessary to stop. A small culvert underneath the canal, serving as a drain, had sprung a leak and broken through, and it had to be rebuilt. Because we had an agreement for passage and food to Buffalo the captain had to bear the cost of the delay.

The trip from New York, together with subsistence, costs $8 a person. Passengers' effects cost 75¢, and merchandise one dollar per hundredweight, the operator paying the canal toll. Thus besides being fast and pleasant this trip is cheaper than it would be in Europe. In Europe one could not travel 170 leagues (507 miles) in this most comfortable style and with the best board for thirty Swiss francs, and this in the so-called wilderness of America! It seems hard to believe!

The repairs were made so quickly and so easily that we were amazed. The canal had been dammed immediately on both sides of the break for a distance of six to eight hundred paces so that no more water could run out. A large beam was placed diagonally across the break in the floor of the canal, planks were placed side by side on this and covered with dirt to calk the seams. Supports were put under the planks as braces, and the dam was finished. It not only served its purpose for the moment but could be removed quickly, and it caused only a minor tieup of traffic on the canal. It should be explained that the water in the canal at this point is not flowing, so it is fairly simple to dam it.

MONDAY, AUGUST 8

We are still in the same spot. There are only a few residences here, and as far as I can make out this place has no name, but it must be near Clarkson. On an excursion today, in the wilderness of America, we found a threshing machine for wheat of such a simple construction that it would serve as a model in our populous and civilized Europe. It is only unfortunate that in this flat part of the country there is no waterfall that could be harnessed to run it. It has to be operated with cattle, and this would be less expensive than a waterwheel except that it requires a man to drive the cattle. Keeping cattle here is simple, for they are not kept in barns, and they must forage for their own feed winter and summer.

TUESDAY, AUGUST 9

The repair of the culvert was ingenious. As soon as a foot's width of the top of the culvert had been repaired, it was cleared of stone and covered, first with cement, and then immediately with clay-like dirt. Then the entire bottom and wall were treated in this manner. Water was added continually and it was worked into a mixture as if a plate were to be molded of it. At home such a mixture would not have been considered capable of holding together, but upon reflection it will become clear that it must become more effective as a sealer through this treatment and that it would soon set and be watertight.

Finally about seven o'clock we were able to proceed again. More than fifty boats had gathered before and behind us, and there would have been several more if the news of the canal break had not spread quickly, making it possible for boat operators to stop at places of their own choosing along the way. If we had been forced to delay much longer it would have become necessary to bring our provisions from some distance. Our captain had no more fresh meat, and the supply in the next town had run out, which was not surprising in view of the large number of people from so many boats gathered at the same time in such a small place.

The west end of the canal is eighty-eight miles from here. Albion, Medina (where several threshing machines were displayed for sale), and Lockport were the most important places we passed today. When one nears the high ground of Lockport the region acquires a charm which makes it stand out from the plains through which we have been passing. From afar a gently rising hill dotted with attractive houses meets the eye. On the left side fairly long rows of brick houses begin to appear, giving the impression that one is entering the city of Lockport. On the hillside stands a six-story-high mill, beside which a wooden fifty-to-sixty-foot-high bridge leads to the right side. It looks as if the end of the canal has been reached, when suddenly a large gap opens up. On both sides are high, steep slopes. Further on, the ampitheater of the quintuple double lock comes into view. At first the traveler is so confused that he does not trust his eyes. He appears to be seeing a series of terraces and galleries which look from a distance like the approach to a magnificent park. Then as the boat approaches, he can see the black double gates. On one side the boats ascend, on the other they descend, so there is no delay. Everything is expertly constructed of hewn stone. Over each lock is an attractive little pearl-colored bridge, over which the operators of the locks pass back and forth. At first sight it seems impossible that boats can be raised or lowered more than fifty feet within the short distance of four to five hundred feet. The locks had to be blasted out of rock. The cost of construction and maintenance must be tremendous.

Not until one arrives at the top of the lock does the city, with its two-hundred-odd buildings come into view. It is not much older than the canal. When the high ground is reached, the sight that unfolds staggers the imagination. For a three-mile stretch the canal bed has been largely blasted out of rock, in some places to a depth of more than twenty-four feet, although the average depth is fifteen to twenty feet, and the width, including the towpath, is thirty-six feet. Immense masses of stone and earth are piled up fifteen to twenty feet high on both sides, and when one considers the fact that every laborer involved in this impressive engineering feat received at least a dollar per day, one wonders whether the old world can produce a counterpart.

Wherever there is a possibility that a public work can be built in America that will produce a fair percentage of return on an outlay of many millions, the money is soon forthcoming, for this is not the only canal in the free states nor the only one in the state of New York. There are two others in this state alone, namely the seventy-two-mile-long Champlain Canal that joins the lake of the same name with the Hudson River, and the fifty-mile-long Hudson Canal that leads from the Hudson to the Delaware River.

WEDNESDAY, AUGUST 10

We woke up in Buffalo, our destination. We breakfasted on board and compensated the captain for the enforced stop, for we had cause to be satisfied. The freight charge for our effects, which altogether came to more than seventy American hundredweight, was fifty dollars, every passenger being permitted a hundred pounds free.

Our plan to make an excursion to Niagara Falls was canceled because during the morning bad weather had set in which would have spoiled our view of this awesomely beautiful, natural wonder, and the considerable expense of the trip for our entire party could well have been wasted. It would have cost one dollar per person to go the twenty-four miles each way on the vehicles that are always standing ready. The steamboats going there have to stop three miles above the big island, and from there one must walk.

A letter of introduction we had brought from Albany for Messrs. Joy and Herbster almost cost us an outlay of some dollars for storage. Our half-German Captain Strohmann wanted to unload our effects immediately into a warehouse. When we told him of our decision not to go to the falls, but to continue West without delay, he helped us book passage on a steamboat. The cabin price from Buffalo to Cleveland is $6 per person, but because there were so many of us, we were able to get a group rate for $60, including our effects, which ordinarily would cost 75¢ per ton. Each passenger was allowed a hundred pounds free. Without food and bed it would have cost only $2.50 each. Our effects were transferred as quickly as possible, for after 9:00 A.M., the scheduled time of departure, nothing more could be loaded. All of the steamboats here hold to this deadline. One leaves every day and makes the trip to Cleveland. The schedule is so arranged that one always arrives before the other departs. The departing boat must leave the dock at the stroke of nine, which was the case with our boat, but we only went to the other side of the harbor, because the lake was so rough that it was not safe to venture out.

With the short stop in Buffalo we hardly had time to take a short walk through the rapidly growing town. Although it is said even now to compare in size with Rochester, and as a harbor on Lake Erie may well become more important, it impressed me less. Possibly the cold, stormy wind made it seem more unpleasant.

Toward evening the wind diminished somewhat, so that after 7:00 P.M. the steamer set out on the 170-mile trip to Cleveland. The water was still so rough that most of the passengers became seasick. Here we were able to determine clearly that the cause of this affliction is not the ocean and not the sharp air, because we had breathed this same air while the ship still lay on the other side of the harbor, and all of us had enjoyed the midday meal there, but out on the rough lake most of us skipped the evening meal. Seasickness is caused by the movement of the ship stirring the gall. The ones who did come to the evening meal took only tea for the most part.

To the north we could see the low coast of Canada, which lies under England's dominion, and to the south the higher-lying coast of the state of New York. The beautiful view of a plain rising gently toward a low range of hills reminded me of Rolle and Geneva on Lake Leman, with the difference that here there are still stands of primeval forest to give the hills a greener look than the vineyard-covered ones at home. Everywhere appeared settlements that had penetrated the immense forest cover.

THURSDAY, AUGUST 11

A good sleep had refreshed all those suffering from seasickness, and the ensuing calm had cured the malady. Almost everyone appeared for breakfast. Although more than thirty places had been set, there had to be a second seating. No ship upon which we had traveled had had so many passengers: fifty cabin passengers in addition to the travelers on the deck. Europeans who have not been here cannot imagine the pleasure of traveling through the vigorous young country of America. The food on the canalboats and steamboats is not only better than that enjoyed by our upper classes, but it even exceeds in quality the food of the larger restaurants. However, the wine is lacking, and this has to be made up for with distilled liquor, tea, and coffee. And the farmers here are said to fare the best of all?!

What Mr. Duden says about the hurried attitude at table, where everyone looks after himself, is just as true as their eating of meat for breakfast, but our stomachs became accustomed to this from the first day. One customarily eats only three times a day: mornings between seven and eight, afternoons after one, and evenings after seven. On some boats something is served between these times. Meals are taken at these times in all households throughout America.

Our ship was scheduled to stop at two places during the night to let passengers debark or embark, but I slept soundly through it all. Just after breakfast we reached Erie. The ship stopped only at the outer pier, so we could see the city only from a distance. A spacious harbor constructed by nature, with some help from man, lies at the foot of the steep rise on which the city is built. It seems large, and because of the important factory business of Pittsburgh, will always be an important warehouse center, although it suffered through the construction of the Ohio Canal.[7] As soon

7. Upon its completion in 1832, the canal was known as the Ohio and Erie Canal and ran from Cleveland to Portsmouth on the Ohio. As the reader will discover, our travelers in 1831 were to traverse the northern portion only.

as some passengers had debarked and new ones embarked, we moved on. Horses and wagons also were loaded here and in Buffalo. The freight charge for a horse from Buffalo to Michigan is seven dollars.

On our trip from New York we met many natives from Zug [in Switzerland] who were going to Michigan to settle there. On our steamer were many persons from the states of New York and Pennsylvania who praised Michigan enthusiastically. If immigration to it continues at this pace, the state of Michigan will develop quickly. There is still much United States land to be had for $1.25 per acre. The price of land already under cultivation, depending on its location, is like that in the state of New York. A well-located site can be worth three hundred dollars after three or four years.

Our view of the coast toward the north has disappeared, and toward the east and west too there is only an endless expanse of water to be seen. The route of the steamer follows the southern coast at a distance of one and a half miles, and we continue to see gentle hills still largely covered with virgin forest except for occasional settlements.

At 2:00 P.M. we stopped for a few minutes at Salem, at 5:00 P.M. at Ashtabula, Ohio, and at 7:00 P.M. at Painesville, Ohio, on the Grand River. From what we could see of these places from the lake, they did not look very important. The towns proper probably lie somewhat farther inland, for only a few warehouses were to be seen on the shore.

The night wore on. We had been scheduled to arrive in Cleveland at noon, but the steamer had not been able to start from Buffalo immediately after loading. When night came we lay down on our beds in our clothes. Toward midnight the ship's bell signaled the arrival. The steamer stopped only an hour, long enough for loading and unloading.

FRIDAY, AUGUST 12

Some members of our party saw to our effects, while Joseph Koepfli and I went to make arrangements for a canalboat. At three lines there were already people assembled. (A company that has several boats is called a canalboat line, and it will have boats arriving and departing almost every day. All such boats are identified with large letters, although each still has its own name. For example, the steamboat on the Hudson was called *Henry Eckford* and belonged to the Albany and New York Line. The canalboat to Buffalo belonging to the Pilot Line was called the *New Philadelphia*. The large steamer on Lake Erie that we had just left was called *Enterprise*.)

The prices on this canal are higher than on the New York canal. The fare is one and a half to two cents per mile, meals fifty cents per day, and charges for the effects fifty cents per hundredweight. This canal is not yet finished, only some 168 miles having been completed to date.

There is so little competition here that we could find only one line willing to give us favorable terms, namely $50 for freight, passage, and food for eleven persons for the 151 miles to Dresden, where we would have to veer off toward Zanesville.

At 3:00 A.M. all our possessions were loaded and we lay down to sleep in our new quarters. Our canalboat, the *Citizen*, belonged to the Farmers Line, and our captain was Timothy Capen.

Our present steward speaks only English, and it is an effort to communicate with him. Awake at daybreak, we now were able to see this place, which has a steep street in a gully leading up to it. On the shore there are a few warehouses, and on the heights is the city with its magnificent view over the lake. Only the fairly wide main street has brick houses on both sides. The adjoining streets, already laid out, contain only a few buildings. Cleveland has a population of one thousand, and so far there are only sixty canalboats operating, but after completion of the Ohio Canal business will boom.

When we came back to the boat our goods had to be unloaded and weighed, for there were as yet no scales on the canalboats. At first everything was carefully brought to the scales, but as soon as the inspector turned away, much was shoved back in the hold and the captain had to pay toll on only about 40 percent of the goods.

We left during breakfast. No attendants have yet been assigned to the locks, and the boat crews have to operate the gates. All day we traveled through a wooded region with only a log cabin to be seen now and then. The heavy growth of the trees showed good soil. It may have looked just this desolate a scant four or five years ago along the New York canal. Commerce will also come to these regions with the development of the canal. The lowest lock at Cleveland is Number 44, while Number 1 is on the hilltop at Akron thirty-one miles away. The cost of constructing the locks here is probably not so high as it was for the New York canal, for the use of sandstone here must have made the construction less costly.

SATURDAY, AUGUST 13

We must have been ascending all night. Jolts often caused us to wake up as the boat rose in the swirling waters of the locks. When we got up in the morning we were at the thirteenth lock. The canal led upward through a rugged valley with fairly high locks at intervals of 100 to 150 paces. If the valley were shorter I would like to call it *Tobel*.[8] Constructing a canal here required very little work beyond removing the *Tobel* and making a towpath. Were it not for the cost of the locks it would be much cheaper than a road.

The pleasant little town of Akron lies on a hill. Just above the uppermost lock the canal leads into a small lake that furnishes the water for the lock, doubtless the reason for the canal's having been constructed here. The region appears to be very fertile. A fellow passenger, a German laborer from a tannery in Canton (Ohio), told us that the tannery, operated like a German tannery by a German foreman, did well. The raw hides are bought from farmers at four cents a pound, and the sole leather then sold at twenty-five cents. A cord of oak bark costs two dollars, but it is not very effective, because the farmers take it only from the old tree trunks without bothering to peel the branches. Oak bark costs six dollars in Philadelphia, but it is more effective. Every tanner has his own mill of cast iron, which can be purchased inexpensively anywhere. A horse powers the entire simple arrangement which closely resembles a large coffee mill. Although the American leather tanned in six weeks may be cheaper, the superiority of that tanned the European way is recognized and commands a better price.

Late in the evening we reached Massillon, where we stopped for an hour to unload gypsum stone and barrels of salt. This place was started as recently as 1826 and may become important because a railroad already under construction from Pittsburgh is scheduled to come through here.

8. According to the Grimms' *Deutsches Woerterbuch,* (16 vols. [Leipzig: S. Hirzel, 1885], 11:528) *Tobel* was a Zurich word for *Tal* (valley), found in the Zurich *Bible* of 1530, p. 336, where it says: "Let all *Tobel* be built up and all hills cut down."

SUNDAY, AUGUST 14

Since leaving Buffalo we have had hot weather constantly. Although there were no places of importance or interest along the canal before, the country we passed through today had some attractive settlements. The reddish soil (four to eight feet deep) does not seem very rich. Underneath it is coarse sand, and it lies mostly on a limestone stratum, but it supports a sturdy growth of trees and a good stand of corn and wheat, etc. In the morning we passed Bolivar and in the afternoon, to the right side of the canal, Zoar. There are said to be many Germans and Swiss here—a good many of them from Suhr in the canton of Aargau—as well as vineyards from which wine is sold at forty cents a bottle. Here, for the first time in America, we saw roofing tiles of the type familiar to us.

MONDAY, AUGUST 15

In the morning when we got up we were greeted by a brief rainstorm. As we approached Dresden we left the main canal through a two-mile branch that led to the Muskingum River.⁹ Here the descending locks are still under construction. The little city of Dresden is fourteen or fifteen years old and already fairly large, about the size of Muenster in the canton of Lucerne.

It is strange that we could not get exact information anywhere about the waterways of the interior. Everything is new and under development and changes every year. We could only learn a little as we proceeded from one place to another. One should buy good, new maps on which one can depend. Our first business in Dresden therefore was to find someone who could give us the most nearly reliable information. Good luck led us straight to a man whose name deserves mention, John Jacobson, the town's top official. We were told later that he was the town's founder. He advised us to travel by water, since we were undecided whether or not to go overland to Dayton in order to get to the canal leading from there to Cincinnati. He assured us that with so much baggage, 160 miles of land travel would cost us much more and be much more uncomfortable. He

9. The Ohio and Erie Canal, when completed, ran southwest from above Dresden over the Licking Summit, eventually running south from below Columbus to Portsmouth on the Ohio (Harry N. Scheiber, *Ohio Canal Era* [Athens: Ohio Univ. Press, 1969]).

said that with this year's high water level the boats could go all the way, and he did not doubt that in Zanesville [on the Muskingum] we could find transport to Marietta and from there steamboats to Cincinnati. He was even kind enough to present us to a man called Wilson, a local transporter who had not quite completed a warehouse where we could unload our effects.

The keelboat had left for Zanesville just before our arrival, but in the afternoon the steamboat which had been put into service only two weeks before between Dresden and these places was expected. The distance of eighteen miles is covered in about three hours. The fare is twenty-five cents a person and the freight ten cents per hundredweight. The little steamboat did arrive, but was not scheduled to leave until morning. However, it seemed that our effects would make enough of a load, so we agreed to pay eight dollars with the understanding that it would leave this day. Since the locks were not yet finished, we had to have our things transported to the steamboat. I mention this because only in the new world is such a conveyance possible. The bank of the canal, still without stone paving, was soft and full of deep ruts from the rain, but still the carter, driving four horses, brought our possessions safely aboard in three trips, all for the low price of one dollar! Who in Switzerland would take four horses over such a route as that? We did not have to pay anything for the warehouse, and the accomodating German gentleman, Mr. Jacobson, gave us letters of introduction to take with us to Zanesville to his friends Messrs. Brak and Smith.

At 5:30 P.M. the loading was finished, and we reached Zanesville toward nine. Our effects remained on the steamboat with a watchman while we went to look for Mr. Brak, who arranged accomodations for us in the National Hotel, where we lived like princes, but inexpensively.

TUESDAY, AUGUST 16

We were amazed last evening when we disembarked to see Messrs. Kappeler and Geisshuesler. They had waited in vain for a keelboat for four days. However, we learned that they had met their old ship's company again. Helfenstein had remained behind in Albany where he got a job with a farmer. The news about the keelboat hit us hard. Two or three days' delay here would cost us more than the trip to Marietta.

Tied up at this place lay a kind of fishing boat of the type in which American families usually travel down the Ohio. It would cost thirty-five dollars, but since we did not yet feel experienced enough to be helmsmen in this new world, we did not want to have anything to do with the undertaking unless someone would take us down. For the sixty miles from Zanesville to Marietta on the Ohio they demanded one dollar per person and twenty-five cents per hundredweight for the freight. We would have to furnish our own food. When Mr. Smith assured us that the boat would be exclusively at our disposal, we contracted for fifty dollars to have it get us to Marietta by the eighteenth, with the understanding that the passengers would be limited to the members of our group. Otherwise an Irish family would have accompanied us.

The city of Zanesville, some twenty-five to twenty-eight years old, has become important because of its many industries, including foundries, nail-making machines, glassworks, weaving mills, and saw and flour mills, etc. The great National Highway from Pittsburgh and Wheeling serves the city. Also, traffic on the Muskingum River (which presently is possible only in the spring during high water) is expected to increase, for the state is having locks installed which will make the river navigable throughout the year.[10]

At 2:00 P.M. our goods were under cover again, virtually filling the floating palace, which measured scarcely eight by twenty feet. Because the most dangerous place was right at this point, the two oarsmen and the helmsman cast off by themselves laboriously but safely, after which we all came aboard. Like many American rivers the Muskingum is too shallow, and the water spreads out too much at low water level. Wherever rocks appear which the quiet flow cannot move, the river creates an even wider channel (because the earthen banks are more eaily washed away), and then the volume of water is not enough to cover the rocks sufficiently to enable a boat to proceed without passing around them. Still we moved along nicely except that the boat leaked. We stopped in the evening because the boat operators did not feel it was safe to travel at night. The water level had begun to drop rapidly several days before, so that in a number of places we had trouble getting through.

---

10. While a canal following the Muskingum was eventually completed, its design was faulty below Zanesville, from which point the river could best be described as improved (See Scheiber, *Ohio Canal Era*).

WEDNESDAY, AUGUST 17

I slept better last night in our moving boat than the night before on the overly soft mattress of the National Hotel. In such hot weather soft beds are no pleasure. A rural inn on the river bank served as lodging for the other members of our party. Bread had to be baked when we arrived, and in an hour's time there was a fine supper on the table, with many kinds of food. At home this would be considered impossible!

At 6:00 A.M. we set out again. The region so far much the same, with hills rising to the left and right of the narrow valley, both sides of which had been cut away alternately by the river, so that the tree-covered slopes come down close to the water, now on the one bank, now on the other. The land seems fertile. The banks are lined for the most part with sturdy trees, behind which attractive settlements often can be glimpsed. At various places on both sides of the river we could see salt works steaming. The facilities looked cheap and temporary, somewhat like our saltpeter works. The springs are mostly close to the river banks, where they are dammed with earth. A horse on a treadmill pumped up the brine, which from a distance seemed to run through a conduit directly into the kettle. Judging by the length of the oven there must have been several kettles in a row, the brine flowing from one to the other until the last held dry salt.

We passed no communities of significance. Here and there stood a new frame building near an old log cabin. We saw corn ten to fifteen feet high, and in the garden of our last lodging we had seen a single sunflower plant with fifty-six flowers and a stalk as thick as an arm.

Toward noon we met a real keelboat coming up from Marietta. These boats are much like the canalboats except that they are half again as narrow and have a board walkway along the sides on which the boatmen can move to push the boat with poles, since rudders would not be practical when going upstream. The interiors of these boats, designed to carry freight, must be depressing, for there are no windows, the only openings being those for loading. It was having trouble getting upstream, and it was doubtful whether it would reach Zanesville on this day. There is supposed to be a McConnelsville at about this point, but we didn't know whether to look for the town on the left or the right bank. However, a skiff was maintaining an active water taxi service, which indicated that there were settlements nearby. The Muskingum here was wider than the Aare [in Switzerland] but we often scraped bottom with our flatboat, which even with the heavy load required only one foot of water. The water seemed to foam a lot.

Today I have time to describe the steamboats between Dresden and Zanesville. It may surprise some of you that it was possible for a steamboat to operate on the river above Zanesville, when farther downstream on the same river it was difficult for flat bottom boats to operate. To be sure the Muskingum River is narrower above Zanesville, but yesterday the water was less than two and a half feet deep almost everywhere. The little steamboat was about fifty feet long and twelve feet wide. Just above the water line it had a boardwalk about three feet wide all around it, which gave it the shape of a large ship. This served as a passageway around the boat, and narrow stairs led from it to the deck, where benches were provided for the passengers, who were protected from the rain and the heat of the sun by canvas shades. On the steamboat's floor, which with a full load was approximately one and a half feet in the water, there stood forward in the open an iron firebox with two steam boilers. A pipe led the steam to the rear of the boat where the machinery and condenser were. Right and left outside the structure itself lay the steam cylinders (like small cannons). Out of these came the pistons to which the levers were attached that turned the crank of the paddle wheel at the boat's stern. Eccentric wheels on the axle of the paddle regulate the gears for the valves, and one lever drives the water pump in the manner of a balance. The length of the cylinder and lever are housed in the space customarily used for the cabin, and the space between the firebox and the condenser are used for storing the firewood and the freight. The rudder hangs out over the wheel on a curved wooden beam. With such a small vessel one could very easily navigate the Suhr at Sursee. The canal is nowhere more than four feet deep, and yet it can accomodate ships carrying tremendous loads, depending on the style of the boat and the depth of its hull.

THURSDAY, AUGUST 18

Whenever possible, the largest cities excepted, it is better in America to put up at the first regular inn available, unless one has grounds for avoiding particular places. The price is the same in all of them, and lower class establishments would charge essentially the same but would be unsatisfactory. I believe that no more than twenty-five cents is ever asked for a fine meal, and lodging in the inns is usually half this amount, certainly never more than twenty cents. In large cities like New York and Baltimore, and even in smaller cities like Cincinnati and St. Louis, one can always find boarding houses where living is still cheaper and just as good.

The country offered very little variation as we proceeded. Perhaps the fertility of the soil improved somewhat toward the south. It certainly seemed favorable for growing fruit. Along the New York canal it had been sandier. Until now we have not found anywhere the surface soil rich in humus of which Duden tells of having found along the Missouri River. This surprises me very much, for I would expect the eternal rotting of plants to result eventually in such soil. But this does not seem to be true, different kinds of soil being peculiar to different regions and subject to change only through cultivation.

At 6:00 P.M. we arrived in Marietta after a monotonous trip. Marietta is situated on the left bank of the Muskingum where it flows into the Ohio. The Muskingum had become so wide at this point that our first sight of the Ohio led us to believe it was the smaller of the two. Transportation between Marietta and a town on the right bank was provided by a boat that operated by means of a simple arrangement. From the one high bank to the other a strong rope was kept taut by means of a windlass. Across the rope moved two pulleys, from which ropes reached down to the boat. The current of the river drove the boat, which was attached of course to the pulleys, diagonally across the river, and in this manner provided transportation for persons on both sides of the river.

FRIDAY, AUGUST 19

The steamboat we were expecting did not come until 10:00 A.M. The fare for the 325 miles from here to Cincinnati is $8 per person cabin class; without meals and on the deck $2.50. The deck passengers can prepare their own meals on a stove which is provided or buy them from the captain at 25¢ a meal. Every traveler has sixty pounds free, but this is not strictly adhered to. Excess weight costs 20¢ per hundred pounds.

The fare for a large group is very advantageous here. For all of our baggage and eleven persons[11] cabin class we had to pay only $25. By 11:00

11. Ten of the eleven are easily accounted for: six Koepflis, Catherine Huger (the maid), two Suppigers, and Joseph Vonarx. The most likely candidate for the eleventh person is Sebastian Keller, who was with the settlers from their early days in New Switzerland.

A.M. all of our things were loaded, and the journey began. Now in the middle of the Ohio we saw that we had been much mistaken the day before concerning the size of the two rivers. The Ohio here is almost twice as wide as the Rhine below Zurzach [in the canton of Aargau], but flows very gently. The surface is smooth as a mirror. At high water it may be different. At a few places there is a slight fall, and there are frequently large islands. In many places the river is more than twenty to forty feet deep, while in others it is hardly four, but the channel used by the boats is seven to eight feet deep. If high water did not rip trees and stumps from the wooded banks, creating a hazard, travel on this river could be most pleasant. Boats have been wrecked here and there on the river, but in no instance with loss of life.

SATURDAY, AUGUST 20

Our steamboat makes good progress. Yesterday at 10:30 P.M. we already had reached Point Pleasant opposite Gallipolis. I had expected the settlements on the Ohio to be better developed. With the exception of important communities there were small, recently established general stores. Nearly everywhere the shores and the low hills still are covered with virgin forest, with space enough for centuries to come for thousands of settlers.

So far the country along the Ohio offers little variation. The banks are twenty to thirty feet high on the average, very rarely more than fifty feet, and yet seem to be subject to flooding, although this cannot be estimated properly in passing by. Almost everywhere is evidence of the constant erosion of the soft earthen banks. The region seems to be especially fertile and easy to cultivate. Yesterday we saw corn twelve to sixteen feet tall, grown on rich land that had been plowed twice before planting and cultivated only once after the corn came up.

The quiet, gentle flow of the North American rivers is an indication that the United States is fairly flat and only attains variety from the many, but not particularly tall, ranges of hills. Deciduous trees comprise the virgin forests, as described by G. Duden. Coniferous trees are not seen here. On the New York canal we found white pines and firs among the scrub, but none of either among the large trees. Everything here is more luxuriant than in Switzerland even during the spring. Places that are subject to seasonal floods, especially the low-lying islands, can be recognized by the yellowish green of the trees.

The construction of the steamboats here is entirely different from those on Lake Erie and the Atlantic coast, but it is perfectly adapted to the depth of the waters on which they operate. Here on the Upper Ohio, where at low water stages there are often places that have only a depth of five or six feet, the vessels that can keep running the longest are built for a depth of only four feet. And since the engines as well as the passenger salons must be kept above the water line, it requires two decks in order to have space for all. The hold, or what is below water line, is now generally used for freight. On the lower deck just above the water line is the boiler, toward the bow, and just behind it is the engine with cylinder, pistons, condenser, and pump. The working beam extends to the cranks of the paddle wheels, which are approximately in the center of the boat. In all of these vessels the flywheel is on the axle of the paddle wheels.

On both sides, next to the engine, the space is used for the galley, toilets, sailors' bunks, etc., and the stern for the deck passengers, with an iron stove. The upper deck has a place forward for the pilot as well as the office and sleeping quarters of the captain, and, inside, the cabins for the men and women. On many steamboats the captain is situated below, behind the engine, and the deck passengers occupy the upper deck. Our boat, the *Emigrant,* commanded by Captain Thomas Baylett, runs between Pittsburgh and Louisville and has sleeping accommodations for twenty males and eight females. The occupants of the men's cabin eat at one table.

Most of the steamboats are neatly painted and the interiors most beautifully decorated and carpeted. Each berth has its own small window that can be opened or closed according to the weather, and this is fitted with jalousies. The berths can be curtained off for privacy. The steamers on Lake Erie are just as pleasant and possibly even less expensive. However, because of the deep, stormy waters of the lake, a high ship would capsize easily, so it must have space below the water line for cabins, engines, and cargo, dispensing with the need for an upper deck. In the stern are usually the women's cabin, the galley, and washrooms, and forward there is space for wood storage, horses, etc.

At 6:00 P.M. today we passed Maysville in the state of Kentucky. This place must have developed recently, for it already has a good deal of masonry along the river, partly to facilitate the landing of boats at every level and partly to prevent the washing away of the earthen banks. Our boat had a substantial load of freight for this place from the factories of Pittsburgh. We did not proceed again until midnight, and at 6:00 P.M. we arrived at Cincinnati.

SUNDAY, AUGUST 21

We were not sure whether we would be continuing to Louisville on the same boat or whether we would be staying awhile and then taking another boat from here. The captain wanted to stop here for only two hours. We went immediately to look for a young Frenchman by the name of Paul Lacroix, who was supposed to be established here with Mr. M. Reilly. We had got his address in New York from Mr. X. Blanc, a friend of Mr. Wanner's in Havre. Our inquiries were in vain. Returning to the steamboat we read on the bulletin board that it would not leave until 9:00 A.M. the next day (probably because additional freight was going to be taken on). This pleased us because it gave us time to look around Cincinnati and escape from the endless loading and unloading taking place on our boat, which we had come to find wearisome. There seemed no point in looking for a steamboat that would take us from here to St. Louis, because the river was too low for such a vessel to make it over the rapids of Louisville, and we would have to change to another boat there in any case.

Sunday is strictly observed in the United States. No games and no business—much less hand labor—may be carried on. Also, the steamboats stand idle except with special permission. There even had been efforts to stop the stagecoaches and other means of transportation, but for good reasons they had failed. Thus we could not transact any business on this day. In Cincinnati all of the stores were closed, and this gave us opportunity to go sightseeing in the city.

G. Duden describes the docks built at such huge cost below the city. But how astonished Duden would be now. In the year he wrote, the place probably was less than half as large, for most of the buildings, including the finest ones, date from the years 1828–1831, after his time. Last year alone fifteen hundred new buildings are said to have been erected, and this year even more would have been built except for a shortage of workers. The growth has been incredible. The [Miami] Canal from Dayton will lead into the heart of the city. It is still under construction inside the city and will lead down into the Ohio.

Hills are being leveled and gullies filled. Above the *Ansteigen* [terrace?] everything is being leveled all the way to the hill in the background, along which the valley of the Miami opens. It is a magnificent location and must be very healthful. There are a good many Germans here, even some from the canton of Lucerne, which was quite a surprise to us. Of course we sought them out. They had come here in the years 1816 and 1817. On the way they had suffered terribly and been robbed almost blind. This gave rise to the bad reports that had discouraged travel to America. One can rightly say that these people had fallen into the hands of pirates at that time. One of the victims was Sebastian Toes of Fischbach, who had come by way of Basel and Amsterdam to Philadelphia and was on the water twenty-six weeks. His present wife, who had started from Wuerttemberg, was on a ship that sailed around from April 26, 1817, until New Year, 1818, until no one on the ship had a bit of money left. Such examples were bound to discourage and retard emigration!?

Now Toes makes cigars. The others are Franz Weibel of Gross-Dietwyl, Johann Mueller of Willisau, who is thinking of moving to Missouri, and N. Gruenenwald of Weggis. Although these men [all from the canton of Lucerne] have acquired no wealth, they nevertheless do not wish that they were back in the homeland. We had not spent much time with them before we learned why they had not done so well as their contemporaries. In addition to the fact that they were unskilled, their religious fanaticism might be a principal reason. Individuals who need to make their way in America cannot insist on settling in a place where they can attend mass on a daily basis from the very first, and the Catholic Church had been very weak in this place when they first settled here. Now it is easier to find places where there are several priests. Cincinnati and St. Louis have become the seats of bishops.

Because it was the first good liquor we had tasted since leaving Europe I think it is noteworthy that we enjoyed genuine American Vevay wine here.[12] It cost all of twenty-five cents a bottle, but this Swiss gift is worth it. It must be that Duden did not get to taste the genuine product, or he would have accorded it higher praise.

The attitude here toward the states to the west is extremely bad, and because there is a shortage of laborers here the region along the Missouri is denigrated in every possible way. Every kind of fever and disease is said to be endemic there, etc. Because of the labor shortage, craftsmen and day laborers are in demand and are paid so handsomely that it is possible for them to accumulate savings. The usual wage is two dollars per day without board, and a man can live well for two to three dollars a week. Farm workers get ten to fifteen dollars a month with subsistence.

---

12. French-speaking Swiss from Vevey, canton of Vaud, settled Vevay, Indiana, on the Ohio, early in the 19th century and established there one of the first wineries in the United States.

But those who come here now to settle must bring money with them, for building lots and plots of land are quite expensive. A building lot in the city costs three to four hundred dollars, and it would take many a day's wages before one would be able to have his own window to look out of. There is little land for sale around the city except to those who really have money, and even three to four miles from the city it already is fifteen to twenty dollars and even more per acre.

Cincinnati could well become the second largest city in the United States after New York. It already has won the advantage of becoming the largest in the interior. Many steamboats are being built here, and there are numerous other industries. A good number of steamboats arrived today and many departed, all to different places. The steamboats on the canal are more elegant than any we have seen up to now. Each seeks advantage through commendations from its patrons.

MONDAY, AUGUST 22

At 9:00 A.M. we left for Louisville, 150 miles distant. The country continued to look the same. Duden's reports about it should suffice. We passed Vevay at night and regretted not being able to see the vineyard plantings there which are said to be well advanced.

TUESDAY, AUGUST 23

At 5:00 A.M. we were in Louisville. The $37 charge for transporting our freight from Cincinnati to this place was only half as much as from Marietta to Cincinnati. As for steamboats to St. Louis, it was just as we had been told, for we had not been here long before a captain asked us if we would not like to travel with him. He told us then that his boat definitely would have to stop at Shippingport.[13] On arriving there we found several steamboats larger than any we had seen before.

There was another steamboat scheduled to leave for St. Louis in addition to the *Cumberland,* about which the captain had told us earlier in the day in Louisville. The *Cumberland* was just being reconditioned, which

---

13. Shippingport is located at the lower end of the falls and of the canal around them. Later it became a part of Louisville.

would require at least three days. Since the other steamboat, the *Talisman*, was due to leave this very afternoon, we made arrangements for passage on it, and the competition unquestionably helped us to get a better rate.

At Louisville we were still six hundred miles from St. Louis. For this distance the cabin fare is usually $12 per person plus 50¢ for freight charges. The captain of the *Cumberland* had wanted to take us with all of our freight for $120. On the far superior *Talisman*, however, we had to pay only $100, with the captain standing the cost of carting our things over to Shippingport, two miles below Louisville. These two captains were so competitive that the captain of the *Cumberland*, who spoke German, now offered to take us for $20 less.

They formerly had operated a ship as a joint venture but had taken separate paths a few weeks before, hence their enmity. Especially in the spring the steamboats earn a tremendous amount of money. A company that procured a new ship this year for nine thousand dollars is said to have earned thirty-six thousand dollars in the past eight months. This is the absolute truth! However, it is said to be one of the largest and most beautiful of vessels. On its maiden voyage from New Orleans it had more than 300 deck passengers and 150 in cabins, not all at one time, but on its entire trip to Louisville.

A canal has been built from Louisville to Shippingport on which steamboats will be able to operate at all times, with no worry about water level. It has been blasted entirely through rock, the cause of the rapids here, and the work is still going on. The cost is said to run into many millions of dollars, and its success is being questioned because of the possibility that at low water level there still will not be enough at its beginning at Louisville. However, the canal is not yet finished at that very point, and I cannot believe that such a gigantic and costly work would have been undertaken without the sponsors' having considered all contingencies. It is laid out in a straight line, and at Shippingport four locks lead back down into the Ohio.

Its dimensions can be calculated from the following: The steamboat *Washington*, which was just there, equals at the very least an oceangoing ship in size. It lies almost as deep as a three-master and can therefore operate only at high water. It is 150 to 170 feet long and 44 feet wide at the top deck. It has three decks and will be driven by a double steam engine, each of which has three boilers. Just next to it lay the *Enclyde*, nearly as large, with two decks and powered with only one steam engine but with four boilers. The cylinder was open, and the piston measured 2½ French feet in diameter.

Although we brought our things aboard hurriedly at 5:00 P.M. yesterday and the boilers were already being fired, we are still here today. Apparently our captain was expecting more freight or passengers, for this afternoon quite a few more passengers came aboard. The delay had given us time to look at the saw and flour mills built at the falls. They are water-powered, but because the fall is so insignificant the power must be generated by wide wheels.

We left at 3:00 P.M. As soon as one has arranged for passage on a ship, one is eligible for board and lodging on it. For some miles below the falls the current of the Ohio was somewhat brisker, but then it gradually resumed its gentle flow, moving along a rocky channel that must be considered potentially dangerous for vessels, for the depth was being measured constantly. It looks much like the Aare region at home except that the hills are low and covered with splendid woods. Naked rock was visible in only one place near the falls.

A clattering noise of the left paddle wheel gave us cause for disturbance last night. It had torn something loose in the paddle wheel box which broke several paddles and crossbars. Today it was quickly repaired. It appears that such accidents are not rare, for a good supply of crossbars is kept in readiness. These are shaped to fit in the cast iron sockets of the paddle wheel frame and merely need to be screwed on.

The country below Henderson, which we reached at noon, continued to look the same. After this the hills receded a bit more, but the view had an ever-changing charm. The trees were luxuriantly green everywhere, although on the average the river banks below Louisville were less heavily wooded than on the Upper Ohio. The communities have not as yet become so important as they will with the passage of time.

We continue to enjoy the ever-changing spectacle as we proceed. The soil seems to be getting somewhat darker. The trees are not so gigantic as along the New York canal. There, almost all of the trees had straight trunks eighty to one hundred feet high up to where the crowns began, and this is all the more impressive when one considers that they were deciduous trees.

Toward 5:00 P.M. we reached the Mississippi. Before this the Ohio had spread out in some places like a large lake, but here at the confluence of these two great rivers the width was even more impressive. Quietly and gently they merged, much as if the arms of the Ohio—separated by islands—had united again. Our progress now changed in that we were traveling upstream and through far murkier water. Just as beautiful to my mind had been the mingling of waters at the junction of the Cumberland and Tennessee rivers with the Ohio, where the clear waters of the tributaries delayed mingling with the murky waters of the main stream. For almost six miles the muddy water of the Ohio had been visible suspended in the clearer waters of the tributaries.

SATURDAY, AUGUST 27

At 8:00 A.M. we passed Cape Girardeau, as yet an unimportant place. Above this point the west bank begins to grow higher. The woods in this area are very dense, but the tree trunks are smaller, so they cannot be old. The soil is still like that along the Ohio.

SUNDAY, AUGUST 28

Last night we strayed from the channel twice. On the Mississippi, as on other rivers, it is always necessary to know exactly where the channel is in order to be sure of deep water. It flows just as gently and smoothly as the Ohio and the Hudson. At one place this morning where our boat had to back up for some distance in order to find another channel, the river formed a lake-like basin more than two leagues wide. For Swiss eyes today's journey offered much charming scenery. The west bank is bordered by fifty- to one-hundred-foot-high cliffs whose rock formations are not unlike old stone walls, fortifications, and knights' castles, with niches, windows, and doors. Herculaneum has a pleasant location just above these rock formations. There are several foundries and ammunition factories here but it is an unimportant place.

From this point the hills along the river begin to spread out more, and only small thickets cover the ground. A beautiful spot on the river above Herculaneum, but probably not the most fertile, has been chosen for the military school of the state of Missouri. It is equipped with fine buildings.[14] Here, as in every other state of the Union, are regular troops that have enlisted voluntarily. The soldiers receive six dollars per month in addition to food and clothing. The military exercises take the smallest part of their time, the greatest part of which they must spend working the land belonging to the military school. Incidentally, in the United States too [as in Switzerland] every citizen from his twenty-first to his fiftieth year is subject to militia service, with the difference that in the spring and the fall he is called to an inspection that sometimes lasts two days. In Missouri they are called for review only once a year. The younger the state, the less exacting it is in this respect, as well as in the observance of many laws that in Switzerland are regarded so literally that if it were forbidden to play with three or nine ninepins, ten would be used.

Carondolet, six miles below St. Louis, seems to be a pleasant place. It is a settlement of French who planned to lay out a large city here. The streets are actually laid out and if St. Louis had not won the lead, the project would have been successful. Nevertheless in time it may become an important place, for the location is wonderful.

At 3:00 P.M. we finally glimpsed the long-awaited St. Louis. I cannot describe the impression this place first made on me. We expected a small town something like Sursee, but it exceeded Lucerne in every respect.[15] "Here," my heart spoke, "must I remain. Here it is good to live; let us build here." No, it is not prejudice. The really beautiful and healthful location on a magnificent, gentle slope leading to a great, beautiful plain, the charming greetings in French and German, the activity—in short, everything was so pleasant that we could not have wished for anything more except to have all of our dear ones here with us. After our long journey through many American cities we find that we are not in the least disappointed, but happy and contented that we have come this far. This is saying a great deal! But it is really true that our expectations have been exceeded.

14. Suppiger is evidently referring here to Jefferson Barracks, which had been established a few years earlier as a training site for federal soldiers recruited for service in the West.
15. The population of St. Louis in 1830 was nearly 5,000. Beginning in the middle 1830s, with the coming of large numbers of Germans and Irish, the city expanded very rapidly.

It would be hasty and presumptious if I should now try to advance my judgment of this country and the state of Missouri in particular. These notes are intended to serve as nothing more than a mere account of our journey. If anyone should decide from this account that this land is the place for him, I wish him luck, for in my heart I firmly believe it. But it is not my intention to be urging immigration at this early stage. What I have seen has been good and beautiful, but I saw it only in passing. I have seen the flower and the bud, but I have not yet had occasion to feel the thorn, so I will live in the land for awhile and see how things work out. I must confess that all my investigations and everything I have seen with my own eyes agree with Duden's reports, except that in the short time since his writing many things have progressed substantially, but that is nothing against him and only confirms his account.

Everywhere when we asked an immigrant how he was getting along and whether he would not like to go home, we got as an answer: "I am satisfied now that I am doing well. The first two years after coming here were sometimes hard for me, but after having become accustomed to the country, its customs, and its language, I have long forgotten my old homeland." This is the kind of talk one customarily hears, and it is no wonder, for the most ordinary man lives well here! I have seen no beggars in America.

MONDAY, AUGUST 29

We rented a house on the hillside and moved into it. This will give us time to look around and make proper assessments.[16]

16. The first days spent by the Swiss in St. Louis are described in Salomon Koepfli's *Geschichte der Ansiedlung von Highland*. He relates that before renting a house of their own in St. Louis, the group members stayed in the City Hotel, where they met a man from Bern called Peter Rindisbacher, who encouraged them to buy land in the area. An Irishman named John Mullanphy wanted to sell them a two-hundred-acre tract in the general area for seven dollars an acre. They also went to a place at Dutzow on Lake Creek in Missouri, approximately fifty miles west of the confluence of the Mississippi and Missouri rivers, where Gottfried Duden had lived. But the dense woods, which hindered cultivation, as well as the practice of slavery, made them decide against establishing a Swiss colony in Missouri.

From this point on, excerpts from Salomon Koepfli's 1859 *Geschichte* are used to supplement the material in the *Reisebericht*.

With this I end my diary except to add some information about money, weight, and measures in order to show how they compare with those at home.[17]

Units of Currency, Measure, and Weight

Currency

Exchange. The United States has its own standard of coinage, based on the decimal system. There is the silver dollar (a very scarce coin) worth 100 cents. The cents are copper coins. There are also 20 cent,[18] 10 cent, and 5 cent coins. Gold coins include the so-called eagle, the equivalent of 5 dollars. The real value of a United States dollar according to the Swiss standard—where the Brabant taler is valued at 36 batzen and 6½ rappen, and the French 5-franc taler at 33 batzen and 6 rappen—is 36 batzen and 4 rappen. With this information everything can be calculated.

A good deal of Spanish and French money also circulates here. The Spanish dollar is equal to the U.S. dollar, the ¼ dollar is 25 cents, the ⅛ dollar [real] is 12½ cents, the ¹⁄₁₆ dollar is 6 cents. The Spanish dollar is actually worth only 36 batzen and ½ rappen. The Mexican dollar is equal to the United States dollar. Also found here occasionally is a Brabant taler, which is not accepted for more than a dollar. The same is true of the French 5-franc taler except that it is accepted at 94 cents, or more often, at 93½ cents, which, with ¹⁄₁₆ Spanish dollar added to it makes 1 dollar. Small French silver coins are heavily discounted. The names of the small silver coins are different in nearly every state. But it probably is of little interest to you that in New York ⅛ Spanish dollar [real] is called "shilling," in Ohio "eleventens," and in Missouri "pitt."[19]

Measure and Weight

The foot here is exactly equal to that in England, and the English yard also is used here. According to the French measure, the foot here is 11¼ inches, and the yard three such feet, or 33¾ French inches (or circa ¾ *aune de france*).

17. See Appendix for complete listing of units of currency, measurement, and weight used in this work.
18. Suppiger may mean 25¢. 20¢ coins were minted 1875–78, four decades after publication of the *Reisebericht*.
19. Probably a Swiss hearing of "bit" (12½¢).

When measuring large areas one would estimate 34 French inches to the United States yard. Long distances usually are expressed in English miles, of which there are three in what we term a *Stunde* [league]. Land holdings are expressed in acres, a unit of measurement that is defined in Duden [as "160 square rods" in his fourteenth letter]. The only unit of measure for fruit that I know is the so-called bushel, which is more than 6.5 French inches in height and 13.3 French inches in width. It is cylindrical like our ordinary half-*viertel*.

Liquids are measured by the gallon, which I have not yet had occasion to use. It contains four quarts and comes close to our Lucerne unit of measure for milk. I will look into this more carefully.

The English terms are used for weight. We have compared the units of weight here with the apothecary weights brought from home, but we have not been able to work out an exact equivalence. The American pound is roughly equivalent to 29 *loth*.[20] Wood is calculated by the cord, which is longer than our *klaster* but not so high, being eight feet long and four feet high.

---

20. The Grimms' *Deutsches Woerterbuch,* (16 vols. [Leipzig: S. Hirzel, 1885], 6:1205) gives the equivalence as 32 *loth*, which makes a *loth* equal to ½ ounce.

PART FOUR

Letters from New Switzerland

Map of Illinois from the 1833 *Reisebericht*

Courtesy of New York Public Library

The Koepfli family in New Switzerland to that [of Kaspar Mauris Koepfli] in Sursee [by Salomon Koepfli].

NEW SWITZERLAND, DECEMBER 11, 1831

Dear Brother!

We have heard nothing from you since we left Havre, but when I look back on the route we took, I am not surprised at the delay. We have received no German newspapers up to now, but the *Schweizerbote*[1] probably will be forwarded to us in the future from New York through Mr. Iselin. He wrote us quite briefly in his last letter: "In your fatherland things really are happening." His words cause us worry, for we do not know how they are meant, although they obviously do not indicate that things are going well. We hate to think of unsettled conditions in Switzerland, which is still so dear to us. Would to God that you and yours and your friends and ours were here. All of you would find far greater opportunities here, and New Switzerland would soon become a colony that definitely would be a credit to the homeland.

But you still do not know what a heavenly area we have found in which to settle. Some time before I sent you my last letter from St. Louis,[2] a young man from the state of Illinois [Ross Houck] offered to sell us his 450-acre farm twenty-seven miles east of St. Louis, consisting mostly of woods. Later we learned that this young man, who had made a good business as a bookseller, had been planning to marry. He had bought a beautifully situated farm to please his prospective bride [a daughter of a farmer near Edwardsville], but unfortunately he had been turned down most emphatically by his intended. Not wishing to settle on the land by himself and knowing that he could put capital to good use in his book business, he offered to sell us the land for the exceedingly low price of nineteen hundred dollars cash.

Not wishing to act impulsively, we decided to look at a number of tracts before making a decision. Father, Suppiger, and Bernard accepted the invitation of a native Hanoverian who happened to be in St. Louis, to look

1. This weekly newspaper published in Aarau reprinted this letter in its May 19, 1835, issue (after it had appeared serially in the *Nordamerikaner* May 25 and June 15, 1833).
2. No known record of the content of this letter exists.

at some land near Vandalia. Some ten years before, he had come to Vandalia, capital of the state of Illinois, with three hundred florins and through small investments had accumulated a fortune of at least sixty thousand dollars.

He showed them some apparently acceptable places to settle, but they learned later that the area was quite unhealthful and that the soil was not particularly good. So they went to look at the land they originally had planned to examine and found it to be located in a surprisingly pleasant region. The man who had the land for sale was not there, but he had just put it in charge of a German near Edwardsville named Barnsback,[3] who had been a university student in Germany (at Sand's time),[4] had settled near Edwardsville and had been named a justice of the peace some years before. He turned out to be most helpful and spent a good deal of time on our behalf.

When Father Koepfli, accompanied by Joseph Suppiger and Bernard Koepfli, returned to St. Louis he spoke to our assembled group as follows:

"At last, my dear ones, we believe we have found what we were looking for, namely, a new home, an answer to our needs. Thirty miles from here lies a lovely district, richly endowed by nature, where a domain awaits you. You will find it has good, fertile soil in which most products can be raised at a profit. There is prairie as far as one can see, with sufficient grazing for herds of a thousand cattle, and no doubt enough will remain to support large herds for the next century. Also, there is enough wood in the forests for building a large number of farms.

"The region has good water, with springs in the woods. The woods also contain limestone and there are indications of coal deposits which we will leave for future generations to develop. Furthermore, it is near enough to the Mississippi so that produce can be hauled to St. Louis without great expense.

"So you see, the region we have selected has all the qualities that are necessary for a new settlement. Yet, I do not wish that any one of you should have illusions regarding your future life.

3. Julius L. Barnsback of Osterrode, WSW of Schleswig in northern Germany, accompanied his uncle George to America in 1802.
4. The reference to "Sand" remains unexplained.

What awaits you is not much better than a wilderness now, and your life will be full of privation and hard work. With this choice we will be separated from the rest of the world for many years, and we will be entirely dependent on ourselves for entertainment.

"What will provide peace of mind and cheerfulness for us is the satisfaction we will find in our own accomplishments, and we must rejoice in the fruits of our labors. Not only your fortune depends on your resolve but that of many other families who undoubtedly will follow us.

"Now once more consider everything. If you think you are not equal to it, stay away. Look instead for an easier life for yourself and a more certain living close to an already established city. For after the land is bought from Mr. Houck you cannot change your mind. When the work is started, it must be continued in a firm and vigorous way. If your strength and endurance, of which I have no doubt, permit it, you will be successful. God almighty, who has led us safely here, will also in the future not withdraw His hand from us, for what we are striving to do is in harmony with His law of creation."

The transaction was completed on October 5. The seller agreed to leave us all of his harvest, comprising four hundred bushels of corn, sixty bushels of wheat, and some oats. (A bushel is approximately the size of a Sursee *viertel*.)

An even more important consideration, for us, led to our decision to purchase this acreage. The great National Highway[5] the government is having constructed from Baltimore, one of the nation's principal cities, west through the entire country, has been laid out as far as Vandalia and will be extended to St. Louis, and this vital highway is to pass within a mile or two of the acreage in question.

On the same day we went to the land office at Edwardsville (fifteen miles distant) to purchase three [additional] well-situated tracts through which the highway also is scheduled to pass. We had to pay the federal price of

---

5. Also known as the Cumberland Road, this highway was planned to pass through Pocahontas and continue through what later came to be called Grantfork, thence through Marine Settlement, and southwest from Troy and Collinsville to St. Louis.

$1.25 per acre for the 240 acres, which adjoin our property. (We estimate an acre to be somewhat larger than a *juchharte*.)

The week following the purchase we prepared to make the move to our beloved New Switzerland (as we have named our new homeland). Up to now it had been known as McAlilly's Settlement, inhabited by Samuel McAlilly, an Irishman who came here from Tennessee; his son John and his large family; and Joseph Howard, his son-in-law.

All of us were looking forward to living in such a surprisingly pleasant little fatherland, all the more attractive because we had been homeless for such a long time. On the acreage are twelve American [log] buildings, two wells with excellent water, approximately 150 beautiful fruit trees, more than eighty acres of cultivated land enclosed by fences, and the rest of it in good woods through which flows Silver Creek with several little tributaries.

There are some springs and, comparatively rare in this area, a limestone formation adjacent to bituminous coal strata. The many trees include varieties of nut and oak, acacia, sassafras, ash, linden, mulberry, maple (not sugar maple), red and white elm, wild apple, plum, cherry, and grape, in addition to a good number of others with which I am not familiar.

After making necessary preparations of all kinds we left St. Louis with four heavily laden rented wagons and a horse we had bought. We crossed the Mississippi River on a ferry set in motion by skinny, blind horses, and at an ill-kept place called Illinois Town we separated from the two oxen-drawn wagons with which our workmen were traveling. In two horse-drawn wagons we took the Edwardsville road to Mr. Barnsback's farm where we settled for the night.

We bought two cows with calves which were led alongside our wagons. After making our way through woods and across creeks to Marine Settlement we felt we had left civilization. We crossed another stream, and at the edge of a prairie we were pleasantly surprised to come upon German-speaking men building a log cabin. We learned that it was for a man called Deck[6] and his two sons who recently had come from Virginia.

We pushed on through dense young woods to Silver Creek

6. Michael Deck (1759–1843). The area had come to be known as Deck's Prairie by the time the Swiss settlers arrived.

where we had to get off the wagons during a difficult crossing. Leaving Silver Creek we came eventually to the farm of James Reynolds, who lived just north of the land we had bought from Houck. We met his family and, with Barnsback serving as interpreter, learned that the members of this household made their own clothes, either of home-tanned deerskin or of wool from their sheep which they had dyed, spun, and woven. We were served a fine meal which included, among other things, wild turkey, venison, homemade hominy with milk, and honey from wild bees.

Leaving the hospitable Reynolds, we reached the crest of a long shoulder separating Silver and Sugar Creek valleys,[7] and here the lack of woods permitted us a bird's-eye view of the area in which we were to live.

I can state unequivocally that in our entire travels we have come across no other place to which we could more aptly apply the biblical words, "Here let us build."

All around for a distance of several miles beautiful, gentle hills rise from the luxuriant prairie, and all of this is a part of Looking Glass Prairie, stretching more than forty miles westward and southward, and it in turn is part of a three hundred-mile-long stretch of prairie enlivened here and there by a hill, stream, or patch of woods.

What Duden says on pages 48 and 49 about the Illinois prairies is correct on the whole, but not in all respects. We have not yet found the [acrid] drinking water he claims to have come across.[8] On the other hand, the advantages of prairie land to a farmer can be appreciated only by one who knows the difference between readying prairie, as against woodland, for farming.

7. Silver Creek, some 50 miles long, rises in Madison Co. and flows south. Sugar Creek rises in Twp. 4N, R5W, and runs south through the eastern border of Madison Co. Both creeks flow south into St. Clair Co. and enter the Kaskaskia River.
8. He wrote: "These large meadow areas did not make a pleasant impression on me. Also, for miles between Vincennes and St. Louis the water tasted of iron vitriol and repelled me because of its sulfurous odor. This is due to a stratum of earth, which is said to be very extensive. However, the water is not considered unhealthful and the farmers have become accustomed to it" (Gottfried Duden, *Report on a Journey to the Western States* [Columbia: The State Historical Society of Missouri and Univ. of Missouri Press, 1980], p. 50).

We came down from the watershed and walked through the
prairie to McAlilly Settlement, only to discover that the old man
had not vacated his cabin. We set out angrily for the place his son
John had been occupying, and found it after passing a small
planting of cotton and a luxuriant corn field.

We paid our drivers, climbed over a rail fence, and entered the
larger of two log structures. It was 16 x 18 feet, with no windows, but it had two doors constructed of large oak slats fastened
together with wooden pegs. The chimney was made of wood plastered with clay, the roof was of clapboards held down by long,
heavy poles, and the flooring was of heavy boards hewn from tree
trunks. It was obvious that from floor to roof neither saw nor
plane had been used, and there was not an iron nail to be seen in
the entire structure.

There was not even a chair to sit on, for the wagons carrying
our furniture had not arrived. We made a seat from some pieces
of wood lying about, collected some maize leaves for bedding,
and started a fire in the open hearth. A messenger sent to old man
McAlilly to try to buy provisions was unable to make himself
understood and was set upon by his dogs. We had left the calves
with the cows, so we were able to get only a little milk from
them. We gave it to the women to drink before they and Father
lay down on the improvised bedding to sleep, using their coats as
blankets. The rest of us sat around the fire talking and roasting
corn until long after midnight.

The next morning saw the arrival of the other two wagons,
each drawn by three yoke of oxen. The trunks they brought were
taken into the smaller log structure, completely filling it, and we
stacked as many of the other things as possible in the larger building, but much had to be left in the yard.

Soon we had a table and chairs set up, and food was being prepared in the fireplace. But the fire base fell in, milk and water
poured over it, and an explosion sent a rain of ashes over everything. Twenty minutes later, however, we were all sitting around
the table in the open air, eating bread we had brought from St.
Louis.

Suppiger opened a trunk containing tools, and he and Sebastian
Keller constructed bedsteads, one above the other to save floor

space. Kitchen cupboards were made from large bedding boxes, and at the end of this weary day everyone enjoyed a refreshing rest in his own bed, the workmen on the trunks.

Directly after breakfast we set about mowing 16-inch-high prairie grass with a scythe. We loaded the hay on a sled borrowed from Reynolds (his wagon could not be spared), using a fork we had brought and several two-pronged ones hewn from wood and saw to its stacking for winter feed. Meanwhile Suppiger changed the north door of the larger log cabin into a window, making the lower half of solid wood and the upper part of glass we had brought from St. Louis.

Old McAlilly finally moved out of the cabin he had been occupying, after grudgingly selling us what he no longer needed, including a cow that died after a few days. When he and his wife left, the name McAlilly Settlement fell into disuse. The hilltop house they had occupied was made into our main residence, and we named the place "Ruetli" [after Ruetli on the Lake of Urn]. Beds were set up for the parents, a table, chairs, and a cupboard were moved in, and a ladder was set up to provide access to the space under the roof, where we put up beds for my sister Rosa and the maid.

The lower floor serves as a community kitchen, dining, and living room, as well as a bedroom for our parents. The rest of us men sleep in John McAlilly's former cabin, the youngest in upper bunks. Our buildings certainly are badly designed, but we hope to have improved housing soon, having already made some preparation toward this end by purchasing eighty acres of land for a new building site. More of this later.

Yesterday we bought from another man 120 acres of good land containing mostly woods but also a magnificent hill. Here we performed our first bit of work, setting out our grape stock, some of which may have survived. Next spring we shall know. Please tell Dr. Troxler and extend our thanks to him.

After this we planted about eight acres of wheat, and we would have been able to do much more except that a very early frost set in. Other farmers, meanwhile, were occupied with haying, picking corn, and various other necessary work.

Every day we discover new charms in our surroundings.

There is an imposing looking hill a league or two to the southwest, and one Sunday we decided to visit it following our observance of the sabbath. For this, all of us including the servants customarily gathered in the small cabin on Sunday mornings while
someone read an appropriate chapter from the collection of devotional poetry Zschokke wrote 1810–16.

We set out for the hill, and when we climbed it we were re-
warded with a magnificient view. It is the highest elevation in this
area, and we have named it the "Rigi" after the unforgettable
mountain at home [between Lakes Lucerne and Zug]. A chain of
hills running north and south directly across from there we have
named the "Jura" [after the sub-alpine chain stretching from
southeastern France into Schaffhausen].

Toward the south and west there are almost no settlements, which
means that immigrants probably will be able for some time to get enough
land from the government. Furthermore, the land is admirably suited for
cattle raising, and while the land we own is used only for growing crops,
the vast prairies are available to everyone's herds. Moreover, a rich source
of salt in the vicinity is used by all of the livestock within a range of eight to
ten miles and adds markedly to their well-being.

Up to now we have acquired at intervals the following livestock necessary for our needs (but limited in number because of the problem of winter
feed for them): seven cows with three calves (at an average cost of $10 per
head), four draft oxen (at $40), three fairly young oxen for fattening (at
$20 to $30), four horses, one with colt, (at $80 to $120), eight sheep (at
$2.50 each), thirty hogs (at $4 to $5), six goats (at $2 each), and fifty hens
(at 4 to 5 batzen each). We have butchered one cow, an ox, a sheep, a pig,
and yesterday a deer that weighed 120 pounds after dressing. Deer are
abundant here, and last winter one farmer reportedly shot between 150
and 200 of them.

Our dogs consume more meat in a week than most families in
Switzerland eat in an entire year.

One day I went to see Joseph Howard, who lives not far from
us on a hill we have called "Sonnenberg" [after the Swiss mountain west of Aarau]. He left his place of birth in Tennessee at the

age of twelve with several older brothers and his mother and settled here in 1809. He led me to a rise several hundred feet to the
west, where the first log cabin in this area had been built at a
time when no white men were yet living to the north.

After an Indian raid at Wood River in 1814 the settlers around
Silver Creek had built a fort two miles west of St. Jacob. Three of
the eleven families that used this Fort Chilton were the Howards,
the Abraham Husers, and the Geigers, whose son William (b.
1810) was the first white child born in Saline Township.

Samuel McAlilly, Howard recounted, had first chosen this spot
to settle when he arrived from Kentucky, but then had established
the farm which he had sold to Houck before we came here. Howard, feeling that the area was becoming settled too rapidly, also
had sold his farm to Houck but had arranged to rent it for a year,
so he became our tenant when we bought it from Houck. He is
not a well-to-do man, but he seems to have no food or money
worries. A few weeks' work in his small field provides him with
gain for bread and winter feed for his livestock, his two cows provide him with milk and butter, and his hunting supplements his
meat supply. His wife makes his simple clothes, and he makes his
own shoes.

Old settlers tell me that Howard in his day shot a number of
wild boars and panthers in this region, including a nine-foot one
not far from Reynolds' place. Without ever having attended
school Howard can read and write. He concerns himself with
others' welfare, planting a sick neighbor's field and helping harvest his crops in the daytime and then attending his sickbed at
night.

Father has tried to persuade him not to leave, promising him
free rent if he will stay, but he sees the herds of grazing cattle
crowding out the deer and putting an end to his beloved hunting.
He feels that if he stays he will have to live a more regulated life
than if he goes west to the edge of civilization.

I must tell you too about another American neighbor, Squire
Thomas Chilton, who drives a big, black horse hitched to a small
red wagon with a massive seat designed to alleviate the pain his
rheumatism causes him. It is the only horse we know of that is
used to pull a wagon. The other horses to be found in such out-

lying parts of the country as ours serve well as riding horses, but are of little use as draft animals. He has refused to sell it to us for a price we feel we can afford.

Northeast of the Chilton farm is an entire section[9] held by yet another American, James East, a man of considerable wealth who arrived in this area in 1816. He divided his section of land into six parts, of which five contained a hundred acres each, and in the middle he reserved 140 acres for himself. Since the section contained about 200 acres of woods to the west and since he wanted to divide the woods equally among his six children, he had to cut the entire section, east to west, into mile-long strips.

Squire East's wife often can be seen sitting before the fireplace smoking a corncob pipe with a stem of tortoise shell, her grandchildren playing at her feet. As often as I enter the house I am sure to find a number of women at work cooking, spinning, and weaving. The men and boys of the family spend a great deal of time hunting or doing nothing, but when they do work, they leave all of us Europeans far behind. These sturdy people, who have no desire to devote all of their time to work, have adopted a mode of living which is replacing—not too abruptly—that of the original inhabitants of this land.

We decided that we could no longer put off acquiring a wagon so Suppiger and our brother Joseph set out recently on horseback for Lebanon to buy one. When they arrived at the post route from Vincennes to St. Louis they stopped for a midday meal at the post house and then succeeded in buying a wagon for $60. From now on we will use sleds for doing our hauling only when it snows.

The wagon was duly delivered, and we drove to Jarrett Dugger's sawmill six miles to the south of us to buy some lumber. His mill consists of a massive winch to which is fastened a sloping platform constructed of boards. Some oxen are induced to march on this flat part, and their weight turns the winch, setting the mill in motion. Since the incline is constantly giving way under their feet, they are forced to continue moving forward. We bought $26.47 worth of walnut and used part of it to make a sturdy door.

9. A section contains 640 acres.

After making other necessary improvements on our buildings, we set about protecting ourselves from prairie fires by burning the thick grass surrounding our cultivated land. In the fall the grass, which often attains a height of several feet in the endless prairies, is burned off, and the burned-over land provides much better forage the following year. However, these fires can be disastrous for landowners who have not taken adequate precautions to safeguard their fences and plantings.

One evening in November, only a few weeks after our arrival, after the grass of the prairie had been killed by frost, we noticed from our house that clouds of smoke were rising over the entire hill to the southwest. Somewhat frightened at the sight, all of us gathered and hurried across our field to a higher spot where ever greater columns of smoke were rising. Soon we felt warmer air, heavy smoke, fine ashes, and sometimes pieces of burning straw blown toward us by the increasing wind. A peculiar change of light came over our region. Mountains of smoke clouded the sun, and a reddish shadow moved over the plains like ghosts in flight.

Soon we had covered the short distance, the fastest far ahead, the rest following, panting heavily. Finally we all reached the top, and before us lay a scene worthy of being painted by an artist. Over the meadows so recently in bloom, now billowed heavy smoke clouds from the hills to the south, as far as one could see, and every space between them was filled with a sea of flames. Had there suddenly been a number of volcanic eruptions on this plain with lava spreading in every direction? Or was there a furious bewitched battle being fought at our feet where there had just been a peaceful meadow? We looked at this for a while before we realized its reality. There, from behind the next hill, came columns of fire like well-trained battalions waltzing along evenly laying waste to everything they touched. Another line from the south arose towards this grim enemy with rage. From a distance it appeared like a destructive musketry fire, with strange sounds of crackling and roaring rushing to the battle grounds. Soon these two were to meet; already the right wing of the one and the left of the other merged with only a small yellow triangle separating the large mass. Yet, the closer they came together, the fiercer they raged. Single bold lines pushed ahead; gradually, the whole battle field was covered with heavy clouds of smoke while some clouds moved upwards towards heaven, the fire stream beautifully illuminating the darkness. Now the two struck with eager tongues of flame from only a few feet apart, and finally pushed together. The flames rose high with hissing and crackling, and soon destruction was complete and the battle ended; all we could see was the blackened battle field with a few smoke clouds hovering about.

Yet the main battle had not ended. This was only a small part of what concerned us next. As the heavy smoke lifted somewhat, one could see hundreds of such fires miles away that seemed to be merging. This dusky reddish mountain of smoke towards the north, always moving in our direction, was our entire concern. The spell of witnessing the charm of this dramatic scene was suddenly broken. We had something more to do than watch this, for only a short time remained for us to protect our home and fields from the flames' destruction.

On the wings of fear we hurried home to find something with which to beat out the flames. We all provided ourselves with boards and hurried to our field nearest the burning prairie. On the outside of the high rail fence the cattle had made a path by going back and forth. Along this foot-wide path we took positions and stood guard over the dried-out grass with our paddles, and soon we were pleased to see that the fire was moving away from our field out into the prairie. Where the dry vegetation had been burned off there was no nourishment left for the fire to consume.

Since we had protected our field in this manner against a return of the fire, we decided to use this method to protect our woods. But as we reached the edge of our woods lying to the west, there was little time left to think of preventives. Already some smoke clouds were passing over our heads and darkening the sun; a short distance away we saw columns of flames uniting in a common attack. We could hear the hissing and roaring of the flames as we stood there feeling useless and indecisive.

In vain we looked for a path along which we could combat the fire, and finally, crowded by waves of flames pushing forward, we set the grass on fire. Yet with our greastest exertion we did not succeed in saving the woods. The burning of the prairie grass had created a slight wind which drove our own fire rapidly toward the underbrush separating the prairie from the forest. Now the flames attacked the small bushes and young trees, licking with greedy tongues until they reached their tops.

A shattering sight now met our eyes. As we moved across the black flatness covered with ashes, it was as if we were stepping on freshly fallen snow, where every footprint showed. Fire columns advanced with loud crackling and rustling; the devouring flames rushed into the masses of dead tree leaves, moved with lightning speed to the very tree tops with more noise and crackling; and tongues of flames shot still unsatisfied up into the air.

We hurried ahead of this wave of fire, which had lost much of its power after passing through the underbrush. The flames had been unable to reach the tops of the large trees, their branchless lower trunks being able to withstand them. The grass was not so thick and heavy here as on the prairie, and encouraged, we faced the flames again, battling with all our might to prevent their progress. But whenever we thought we had the fire under control with our weapons, it would start out at another point and quickly spread with renewed energy.

Meanwhile evening was approaching, and before we could notice it in our great excitement, the short twilight had passed, and night with its dark wings had spread over the earth. Our battle against the flames had taken us across several hills and ravines.

Finally after many hours of useless labor we lost courage. Physically exhausted, dripping with perspiration, our tongues parched from thirst, red-eyed, red-faced, with singed hair, scorched clothes and shoes, we sat down on a tree stump. The terrible sight of the unleashed elements around us kept us from being aware of our condition. The spreading flames, so shockingly beautiful against the dark of the night, continued to feed on the low grasses of the woods, and when it reached the underbrush it created a thousand roaring torches with flames rising heavenward. These magnificent smoke clouds now had taken on a glowing aspect, and the giant trees around whose bases the flames had licked threw frightful shadows which danced back and forth in this gruesome illumination.

Later when I had the opportunity of seeing similar scenes at night, the sight of this horrible spectacle always reappeared. It made an impression upon me so deep that it never has left me.

From our elevated position, the region as far as we could see looked like a stream of glowing lava. When we finally realized our condition, we wanted to hurry home as fast as our weary bones would take us. Yet, in what direction should we go? We had different opinions about it, but we decided that the longer we bickered about it, the less we would accomplish. Finally a reliable person was chosen as a guide, and the rest of us agreed to follow the leader.

For a long time we had been wandering away from the sooty ground where the fire passing through earlier had eaten most of the grass. The spots the fire had skipped were now slowly but surely being destroyed by the tired flames. The remains of half-rotten trees which probably had fallen a decade before were slowly being devoured by the glimmering fire and were sending up thick, acrid smoke. Dry branches and twigs which storms had broken off the oak and hickory trees blazed brightly. A number of dead trees still standing despite storms were now in flames, with arms outstretched like ghosts, covered from foot to tip with countless flames which lighted our way.

Finally, after much wandering, we came across a building on a hilltop. Encouraged by this friendly sight, we hastened to reach it, but we soon became aware that no one was living there. Hunters had built a temporary cabin which had been deserted for years, and it provided us with no hospitality.

It was now clear to all of us that we had lost our way in the dense woods. Until now none of us had advanced this far into the woods, so no one had seen this cabin. We looked about us with fear. Acrid smoke and the odor of burning filled the air in every direction of this remote forest. Hunger and thirst permitted no lingering here, so we set our course in the direction we supposed was home.

Anyone meeting these creatures wandering through the woods on this night certainly would have been frightened. The fire had taken its toll in the area we were going through, but a few trees continued smoldering for weeks. In a ravine we came upon a spring, where we quenched our thirst, and we saw two deer that stood stock still, their tongues outstretched from wide open mouths, gasping, their eyes staring, and their ears standing erect. They appeared to be greatly affected by the surrounding scene. Perhaps they had run a long distance to escape the flames and were so disturbed that they hardly noticed our presence. Only after we advanced several steps did they take flight.

We finally arrived home long after midnight, where we were anxiously awaited. With great interest we learned later that the cabin we came across that night was not more than two miles from our fields.

Different groups of Indians stopped there on their hunting trips for the purpose of driving wild animals to certain places to determine the position where to start these fires. The prevailing winds would decide the place to start the fire to obtain the best results. Many researchers want to attribute the origin of prairies in Western America to this Indian custom, holding that the white hunter learned from his red predecessor to use this destructive method of hunting.[10]

We realized at once that the natural purpose served by the prairie was to provide feed for cattle, and we proceeded as soon as possible to procure much livestock. When it became known that we would buy cattle for cash, we had someone come almost every day, eager to sell us some. We could consider these offers, for in December our work in the woods stopped for a while, so some of the men would make trips in the neighborhood to inspect the livestock being offered for sale.

Large trees bearing survey markings usually survive even a fire as intense as the one we witnessed. Their branchless lower trunks are able to withstand the fire, and of course it is forbidden by law to cut down such witness-trees. When Mr. Barnsback came with compass and measuring chain to make a new survey of our holdings—the original survey of land in this area having been made a dozen years ago—he found it much easier to locate the original measurement markings in the woods, where they had been carved on trees, than on the prairie, where stakes bearing them had rotted away. Anton Suppiger has prepared a chart of this region showing not only standard section divisions but wooded areas, prairies, and the holdings of all the farmers and their plantings as we found them when we arrived here.

Our brothers Bernard and Joseph often debate whether our

10. Salomon Koepfli devoted an entire chapter to this prairie fire in his book *Neu Schweizerland in den Jahren 1831 und 1841* (Lucerne, 1842), pp. 26–33.

move to America has improved or worsened our circumstances, but never in our parents' hearing, out of consideration for Father, who has to bear full responsibility for the move. "It certainly was carrying foolishness to the extreme," Bernard recently argued, "to live in this deserted corner of the earth where foxes and rabbits bid each other good night. Were I to weigh the facts and compare our present situation with our former life and prospects, I could only explain our entire emigration by saying that Father had a wheel too many in his head.

"His best friends, men like Dr. Steiger, Mayor Schneider, and Counselor Krauer—surely wise men—could only say, when Father announced his project: 'Old man, how is it possible that you at your age and in your good circumstances can consider such a thing? Do you wish to take this trip for your sons' sake? It would be better to provide them with the necessary money and send *them* to America.'

"If Father had followed their advice, how long would America have held us? At least I would not have tarried here. Who would want to bury himself on this desolate prairie, as if he could not find a place to live among reasonably civilized people?"

"You see only the bad side," countered Joseph. "It is true, as far as our family is concerned, that the migration's success is doubtful at present, but we are here, and I am completely satisfied with this locality, for it has all the qualities important for new settlers, and cultural conditions will improve gradually."

"By the time that happens," moaned Bernard, "we won't be able to appreciate it, for it will be long after our bones have bleached. Here in this solitude we are apart from everything that makes young people's lives enjoyable. This whole week we labored at unaccustomed work as hard as any that a hired hand in Europe or a poor Negro in the South would be asked to do. And come Sunday, what does it bring in the way of recreation? A tedious forenoon, a tedious afternoon, and a tedious evening. We have long exhausted what we could converse about, and since we don't see any other people, we have nothing new to talk about. I could take the hardships during the week, but I can't endure our Sundays, when there is nothing to do but bury one's head behind a book all day.

"When I think of my former life in Switzerland and my group

of happy friends there, I see that every stable boy at home lives a happier life than we do here. If only there were a ray of hope that we could leave sometime! More to be pitied than the rest of us is our good mother. For more than twenty years she opposed this migration project, until Father finally persuaded her that it would be best for us sons. She endured the hardship and danger of the trip here, and now she has to manage a large household in the face of the many almost insurmountable obstacles confronting her daily, even hourly!

"Then there is this house, worse than a pigpen in Switzerland, and the cooking for a hungry mob before an open fire! Without an oven she has to bake a large amount of bread every day in iron pots in the fireplace, tending the fire the while, and constantly in danger of having her clothes catch fire.

"When evening comes at last there is no rest for the poor woman, for the men return from the woods, unwashed and with torn clothes, crowding the cabin to its very corners. In addition to all of the other work she has to see that the ragged clothes are mended, and this often takes until late at night."

"Do stop your complaining," objected Joseph. "It is in our power to remove most of these inconveniences in due time. And you could well take Mother as an example. She not only bears her own burdens with patience but is always ready to cheer us up when she learns of our problems."

"What you say in praise of Mother is more than true," retorted Bernard, "but you must not believe that she finds our life here at all pleasant. Yesterday I overheard her say to Father, 'Is this the glorious life of which you dreamt in Europe? You always told me that this move was necessary for our sons' welfare. Look at your sons now! Do you still believe that it would not have been possible to give them such success at home? The older ones were mature enough to choose where they would make their life, but was it right to take the youngest son out of school to have him spend his time here driving oxen? All day long I hear this terrible "gee" and "haw," and at times I become utterly desolate when I hear this boy and consider his destiny. With what kind of eyes do you see your sons when they return bedraggled and weary from their labors every evening? I will not speak of our daughter or myself. I expected from the start what our fate would be; gladly would I make any sacrifice if good would result for our children! But what good this is to bring is not clear to me. In spite of our hard life and privation, large sums of money are being spent. Every week someone rides to St. Louis to withdraw money from the bank to make purchases. How long will it be before this money is exhausted? And what will happen then?"

"And what did Father say to this?" asked Joseph. "He stood calmly as usual before Mother, smiled, and said, 'Everything is happening just as I expected, even better than I dared hope. My heart overflows with joy when I wander through our lovely region and see the perfection spread before me. All that man needs for a successful life is here where this magnificent land has been waiting for ages to nurture a flourishing colony. For these advantages one has to practice self-denial a few years. This cannot be avoided when starting a community in a wilderness. Every year conditions will improve, and soon the worst will be behind us. As early as next year we shall build a convenient, pleasant house, and then we won't have to dread the winter. For you, especially, everything will be in better shape. Concerning the outgo of money I believe in the old maxim that he who wishes to reap must sow. As for the children, work will by no means harm them; they are remaining healthy, and they will reap the fruit of their labors'."

As I have already told you, all of us men except Father leave the main cabin to spend the night in the log cabin formerly occupied by McAlilly's son John. One evening Keller, our dairyman, was detained in the main cabin to build a shelf when the rest of us left for our quarters. We built a fire upon reaching our cabin and persuaded Suppiger to take his violin out of its case and play some cheerful music. One of the workers, a master on the clarinet, played some old Lucerne waltzes and then some lively dance music, and two of us attempted to do a dance on the rough floor.

An hour passed with lively entertainment, and still Keller had not made his appearance. Could he have lost his way and wandered out onto the prairie? It was a dark night, and we remembered how in Paris he had demonstrated a poor sense of direction, wandering about hopelessly lost an entire night. We had spotted a big, black wolf one day while working in the woods, and we began to worry about the possibility of his being attacked by wolves we had heard howling on the prairie, although they usually only attacked sheep and pigs. But aside from that possible danger, the nights were much too cold for a person to be out in the open.

We decided to sound an alarm. A man was sent over to Ruetli to find out whether Keller was still there and, if not, to bring a lantern. Meanwhile we all went outside and gave a call in unison, convinced that it could be heard in the stillness of the night for miles. The messenger returned with a lantern, which now was tied to a stick and placed high over our cabin. We were told that Keller had left the other cabin shortly after the rest of us.

We made several short trips into the prairie in various directions and continued calling. When we finally found Keller he was frightened enough. He must have walked hurriedly for some distance before becoming aware that he was lost and that he probably would not find his way back before daylight, so he continued walking because he dared not lie down. As a matter of fact it is very likely that he would have frozen to death because on this night it turned bitterly cold.

We had had a good many days when it had been uncomfortably cold, but up to now it had always been mild enough for us to do our outdoor work. Since our settlement was in the same latitude as the island of Sicily we had not expected unusually bitter weather. Now we had advanced into December, and toward midnight there was a sharp change in the weather. A strong north wind became ever more violent, crashing against the cabin with such force that it shook the beds fastened to the north wall. Our beds were becoming covered with the snow that was blowing in, and the featherbeds that had been enough to keep us warm up to now could not keep us from shivering uncontrollably.

When we ventured out after an interminable night a piercing wind penetrated our bones to the marrow and whipped blinding snow into our faces as we made our way toward Ruetli where the parents and the women slept. The dogs that usually greeted us were silent in the face of this confused weather that had made a Siberia out of a Sicily. No one in the cabin had wanted to get out of bed, Mother crying out that the cold was too severe to be endured.

We quickly built a fire, piling large logs upon one another, but the extreme cold of the room would not lessen, most of the heat going up the chimney. Sister and the maid ventured out of bed and tried to prepare breakfast as best they could, and we young men decided to see what had survived outside the house. The chickens that customarily spent the night in the trees had disappeared except for several that lay frozen stiff on the ground. The horses and sheep had sought protection in two log sheds, but the cattle were standing in knee-deep snow in the open, their lowered heads and bent backs covered with ice. When they saw us they uttered pitiful sounds, and we wanted to help them, but what could we do? We drove as many of the poor creatures as possible into the shed where the sheep were, but they fought with them, and we feared there would be casualities, so we tied a number of cows as best we could and tried to rub the ice and snow off their backs with straw. We fed them hay from the stacks and went to feed the cattle in the open before seeing to the horses. When we looked in the shed again the best cow, having fought the unaccustomed chains, stood before us with one of her horns broken off, her head covered with frozen blood, moaning pitifully.

A steaming breakfast of fried bacon, coffee, and cornbread awaiting us in the cabin helped to thaw us out, but we had to go right out into the freezing cold again to collect a large supply of wood. We needed to keep a roaring fire going day and night for the duration of the Siberian cold which kept penetrating the crude structure at innumerable points. A cord of wood per day would not begin to suffice.

Three of us took axes and went into the woods with an oxen-drawn sled, leaving the other men to take care of the livestock. The oxen strained mightily to drag the sled through the encrusted snow. As we moved slowly forward I stopped to investigate a peculiar gray pile in a thick hazel bush. As I started to bend over it, the mysterious object erupted into several dozen partridges dispersing in every direction. Huddling atop and beside one another, they had formed a ball to protect themselves from the grim cold.

When I caught up with my fellow workers they were felling a hickory, the pride of our woods. These slender, hardwood trees, forty to fifty feet tall, resemble pillars except that they are covered with scaly bark like palms. When set afire, they burn with a good deal of snapping and crackling. I found the wind in the woods much less intense, and I began to realize why the early Illinois settlers built their cabins in the shelter of the woods.

When I returned to the farm with my first load of wood, I found the men who had stayed behind to do the chores drawing water from the well, using a well-sweep standing high above it. The animals eagerly drank the fresh water and greedily devoured the hay and corn fed them.

The snowstorm raged all day and throughout the night with unabated fury. In an effort to prevent at least some of the fire's heat from going up the chimney, we pulled burning wood farther into the room, but this ignited the log along the top of the fireplace opening, and we had to quench it quickly to prevent the entire cabin from going up in flames. I'll give you an example of how cold it was in the cabin. A pail of water we had standing in the room to douse possible fires, although only a few feet from the hearth, was covered with a thick film of ice!

There was constant danger that such a roaring fire as ours would cause the clapboard roof to ignite and, if no one happened to be outside to notice it, quickly get out of control. Burning embers often shot out onto the floor, and our clothing received its share of scorched places, especially when someone rushed in from outside to warm his back in front of the fire and his pants began to scorch before he could feel any warmth.

The cold seemed especially severe to us because we had never had to spend a winter in such a miserable dwelling. And yet, many of our American neighbors live in even poorer quarters! I know of one family with small children who occupy a cabin in which a mere cloth fluttering in the wind serves as a door. But they all look sturdy and well, and these people are poorly clad, while we have plenty of warm clothing!

Like these Americans, the animals here appear able to endure this frigid weather. By the second day of the Siberian cold we decided to make the best of it. I was even happy about the snow which covered everything and had piled up so high against our six-foot-high fence that I could not see a trace of it.

But when I got home from the woods on this day I noticed that Father had opened his store of drugs, and I saw several bottles of powders, his weights and scale out on the table. It turned out that

Mother was quite ill, the wall beside her covered with blankets in an effort to protect her from the penetrating cold. There she lay with her face to the wall, and there was so little we could do for her! What if she should ask for the sacrament in which she believed and which the church considered essential, even indispensable? Our siblings seemed as worried as I, Father alone remaining calm and quiet except when he tried to cheer Mother with comforting words.

Despite the medication Mother grew constantly worse, and a number of days later Father told her that her illness had reached a critical stage and that, although he had not given up hope for her recovery, he wished to know whether she wanted one of us to ride to St. Louis to find a clergyman to come to see her.

With Sister's help Mother turned over to face him and said, "This step I do not ask, for it probably would prove a useless attempt. To calm you and the children I will say that if it is God's will that I die, I am fully prepared to do so without help from a priest. If one were readily available, it would be good, but I do not want anyone to make a long trip in this terrible weather. I am prepared to yield to the will of the heavenly Father."

You can imagine what a dark shadow our beloved mother's illness cast over us.

[Fortunately the mother recovered, and Salomon was able to write:]

Our mother is again in her element. She misses church, but the Sunday reading of religious works serves to make up for it in large part. Father could do well for himself here as a physician if he wished to devote himself to it properly. The principal ailments here are an ague which, we are told, attacks most of the new settlers. However, all of us except Suppiger are as well as or better than we were at home in Switzerland. Anton was ill with the ague for a while in St. Louis, which is known as a place where such diseases—as well as mosquitoes—are prevalent, due to its location on a river which often floods. We had experience with these pests last summer. Even more hazardous to health may well be the rapid variations in temperature, which we have not experienced to date.

Father had assembled quite an assortment of well-selected drugs while we were still in Switzerland. He kept them in a black, lacquered box fastened to the rear of our coach when we traveled to Havre. The old doctor could not be parted from his pharmacy.

Here in New Switzerland a place had to be found in the log cabin for the drugs. Curiosity about the little, old gentleman with spectacles probably prompted the first visits we received from neighbors. They had often seen him, book in hand, walking with vigorous steps through the woods and over the prairie.

When they first learned that he came from the Catholic canton of Lucerne in Switzerland they imagined him to be a Jesuit, who as such could spend as much money as he desired, for shortly before we had withdrawn several hundred dollars from New York through the Bank of the United States in St. Louis. It was said that we had brought $50,000 along from St. Louis, and we were warned about criminals in Illinoistown [East St. Louis].

When visiting neighbors found the apothecary open and saw the many bottles in it, they were happily surprised to learn that Father was a physician. The news soon spread over the entire area. One might well wonder how it was possible for news to travel so quickly. The inhabitants did not spend their free time sitting in armchairs. Their fields were small and their wants were few, and much of their time was spent hunting and visiting. Women with two or three children on a horse, or a man in the saddle, with a child on his lap and his wife sitting behind him on a piece of cloth, frequently could be seen riding about the countryside. In that way close contact was maintained among neighbors living as far as six miles apart.

A sister of Mr. Howard's was the first patient. Troubled with an old ailment, she had asked her brother, already a cherished neighbor, whether the doctor would treat her. This request could not be refused. It broke the ice, and soon others followed, some of them coming from quite a distance.

One day, at the request of old Captain Blakeman[11] of Marine Settlement, Father went there to treat the captain's wife. This in itself presented no difficulty, since he was a good rider, having served in his younger days as a regimental doctor in a campaign. But it was decided that the trip would be made by sled, it having been ascertained that our flour supply was low. Mr. Blakeman had a mill, and the trip could serve a double purpose. The two

11. Curtis Blakeman later served in the Illinois General Assembly. In 1864 he married Suppiger's widow.

most reliable oxen were selected to transport several sacks of
wheat and shelled corn on a small sled originally constructed to
haul wood.

Now the doctor in his long blue coat and in a good mood
seated himself on the sacks of grain. Since our big ox team could
not be driven, brother Joseph was chosen to lead them. It was he
who gave us a report on the outcome of the trip. They had trouble as soon as they came to cross Silver Creek. Although the
animals behaved well, the small sled threatened to fall on its side.
Father had to get off and try with all his might to keep the sacks
on the sled. On the other side of the creek the sled had to be
lifted over some tree stumps. In crossing their second stream they
could not avoid some sacks being slightly baptized.

The most difficult part was yet to come; they were nearing civilization and believed all difficulties were past, but as they
approached the Blakeman mill the ruts of the track led through
thick, young, overgrown woods. Here the beginning of a road had
been cut through the young trees, and it required an expert to
lead the oxen so that the low sled would pass exactly between the
foot-high stumps. But not all of them could be avoided. They
heard a suspicious sound, and then they saw a stripe of lovely yellow wheat on the road behind them. They stopped at once, lifted
off the upper sacks, and found that the lower sacks had been
snagged by some of the taller stumps, causing them to lose a considerable amount of their contents. Now good advice was needed;
how could the sacks be mended without thread or needle? They
were in despair until they saw a locust tree close by, full of long,
sharp thorns that offered the necessary help. The rents in the
sacks were soon closed, but now came the awkward work for the
driver, gathering up the scattered wheat with his hands and putting it into the sacks held open by the doctor.

The double purpose of the trip finally was accomplished. The
miller's wife got medical attention, and we got flour for our
larder.

As the number of patients increased the apothecary needed en-
larging, for Father added to his stocks with shipments from St.
Louis, so a board was nailed in place as a shelf to hold a row of
labeled tin boxes. But his refusal at his advanced age to learn

"gibberish," as he termed English, proved a very definite hindrance to his practice of medicine, for it meant that an interpreter needed to be present at every consultation. In the beginning Joseph Suppiger helped out, for he had picked up the language and he was usually working around the house. But then the task fell to me, who could understand only about half of what was said. My only comfort was a large dictionary I kept beside me. When the unfamiliar words were directed at me I tried to pick out one that seemed to be the key to the sentence, and then I leafed through the book until I could piece something together that seemed to make sense.

Finally when it became necessary to write directions for the use of the medicine, I took pen, ink, and paper and wrote directions in my inimitable English, which the patients must have found strange, to say the least. But to the credit of our backwoods neighbors, they always showed tact and understanding, no matter how odd the circumstances. The important thing was that Tom, Dick, and Harry use the pills and drops properly, and they must have brought about cures, for business increased, as attested to by the number of patients and the spread of the German doctor's fame.

When it became necessary for Father to make sick calls, an interpreter had to accompany him, and this gave me the opportunity to become acquainted with the people and the country for 20 miles around, and I made good use of it.

Slavery is forbidden in the state of Illinois, and every black who has reached the age of twenty is free. This is the reason we rarely have seen black faces since leaving St. Louis, and we are grateful for this. We have seen many Indians in St. Louis, mostly chieftains who were trading goods there.

There is much more I could write about, but there is so much that is new to us that I would not be able to tell you about it with a sufficient degree of certainty, so I had better desist. I hereby take leave of you again for a short while, and I will not take up room at this writing with greetings, but will refer you to my last letter. For you and yours a heartfelt farewell will suffice, for that is our most sincere wish.

Speaking for the family, your brother, Salomon

*Letter from Mr. Joseph Suppiger of
New Switzerland to the Suppiger Family
in Sursee in the Canton of Lucerne*

NEW SWITZERLAND, MARCH 19, 1832

Dear Parents and Siblings!

Thank God the winter seems to be over. The old settlers speak of it as more severe than any they have experienced. I would be happy never to have to live through such a severe one again. However, I must say that our Swiss winters are colder and longer, but the sudden changes in temperature here make one more sensitive to the cold. Furthermore, we newcomers, accustomed as we are to European heating, find the dwellings inadequately constructed for the cold **weather**.

But thank God we all remained healthy. Only old Mrs. Koepfli was ill, although never seriously, and she has completely recovered.[12] Some January and February days were so warm that we had to take off some of our outer garments when we worked outdoors, but when the north wind roared we were glad to shut ourselves in the house and sit by the fire.

The longer we live in this marvelous country the better we appreciate what Gottfried Duden wrote. What warped ideas we had about a lot of things when we were still in Switzerland! One should not come here with preconceived plans based on the European economic system. One would do better here without them, even if he were to come with the best intention of introducing something better. One will soon learn how things are done here if one does not cling stubbornly to preconceived notions of how they should be done. Some examples will show what I mean:

1. You will remember Gottfried Duden's admonition not to take along male servants from Europe and his reasons for not doing so. Now Messrs. Keller and Lutolf are with Mr. Vonarx, who is said to have promised them the same pay as Americans get, and which they cannot possibly earn at first, no matter how hard they try. Our attempt to make cheese is over. Nothing could have come of it this year, and we have had a good lesson. It would have taken too much time to milk so many cows.

12. The settlers were obviously and justifiably concerned that they would be accused, in bringing Mrs. Koepfli to America, of subjecting her to hardship and danger.

2. It is almost incredible what an American can accomplish. He splits 150 to 200 wooden fence rails a day. They are eleven feet long and three to four inches thick, and he makes them from deciduous trees which he must first fell in the woods, and of which he ordinarily can use only one or two lengths, rarely three.

He uses an axe, an iron wedge, and in the woods he makes himself some wooden mallets and wedges. At first we thought it impractical to make a zigzag fence in the American style, laying eleven-foot-long rails on the ground in a zigzag pattern, one on another, to a height of six feet. A ninth or tenth rail is placed at this height at each place of juncture at such an angle that a cross-lock is formed. Such a fence is quickly constructed if the rails have been fashioned in advance and are readily at hand. The larger the area to be enclosed, the fewer rails needed per acre. Enclosing a forty-acre square requires approximately five thousand rails. The wage per hundred rails is 62½¢ without meals, 50¢ with meals. At first we thought we could save much wood by constructing a straight fence, but the greater labor and therefore increased cost involved, caused us to hold the zigzag style.

3. It may be surprising for you to learn that an American farmer, with the help of a boy, can easily plant thirty to forty acres of corn, which is then cultivated several times to eliminate the weeds. Furthermore he considers it not at all too difficult to plant an equal number of acres in wheat. I found that one of our neighbors had eighty acres under cultivation, something that would seem incomprehensible to a European.

But what do you say to a customary annual wage of $120, approximately 432 Swiss francs, in addition to board, room and laundry? A good worker can demand $10 to $14 a month, and this probably buys more than it would in Europe. Of course he must do a substantial amount of work for this.

We would be able to lend out any amount of money at 20 percent to 25 percent interest. Often 40 percent interest is charged. Here it cannot be termed usury, for everyone can earn it, either with his work or his money. Oh, how quickly a good efficient European could earn a substantial fortune, provided he had learned the American method of working, which would permit him to earn a tidy sum of money.

To become the owner of several hundred acres of land after five to six years would be the certain fruit of his labor, and during this period he would not be termed a servant but a fellow worker. But it is too bad that most Americans take to drinking hard liquor, which leads to their physical and moral decay. Earning too much encourages extravagance, and in the case of uneducated persons the freedom and equality found here often lead to scorn for former benefactors and to a pride that elevates them beyond their actual worth. In many instances they reach a point at which they cannot maintain their equilibrium.

We have been making ready our future dwelling, and we hope to be able to move in before the end of autumn. But we have not yet experienced a summer here, and we have only a vague idea of what one is able to do in a year's time. There is sufficient wood available to fashion many thousands of rails to protect newly planted land from livestock. The plowing usually is done in June, and then after thorough harrowing of the soil, wheat is sowed, a crop which is said to yield the richest return. There is no need of fertilizer here. After having been under cultivation for twelve to fifteen years, the soil here still is producing the same yield. Rotation of crops, however, is essential. Wheat does not give a good yield in the same field two years in succession, but in fresh soil or in soil that has not been planted in wheat the preceding year, it produces better than we are accustomed to at home. One customarily uses one and a quarter bushels of seed per acre.

Our present plan, subject to change like many a previous one, is to construct a pleasant dwelling. Following this we will bring as much land as possible under cultivation. The first year's harvest should pay almost all of the expenses and the purchase price of the land. Later we will erect several log or frame dwellings for tenants, so that we can let parcels of land, and we plan never to keep more land for our own use than is necessary to provide feed for the livestock. Approximately forty acres will suffice. It is easier to find tenants than workers. A tenant usually farms thirty to forty acres and pays either a third of what he harvests or ten bushels of corn per acre. The first-named method is preferred, because with a good tenant one can look forward to receiving fifteen to eighteen bushels per acre.

After one has learned how much one's land is going to cost, how much will have to be spent for fencing, and that bringing the land under cultivation the first time will cost two to three dollars per acre, one easily can determine that the first wheat harvest will meet nearly the entire cost, since an acre can produce twenty to thirty bushels or even thirty-five to forty. The price of wheat has been fairly constant, never less than fifty cents per bushel.

Nearly everyone can succeed here in accomplishing what he sets out to do, provided that he applies himself and that his effort is adapted to prevailing conditions. There is no lack of market, but it is necessary to take into consideration in advance the fact that conditions are the opposite of those in Europe. Here land is *cheap* and labor is *expensive*. What a person does has value.

There is excellent pasture here for many hundreds of cattle. This condition will prevail for quite a few decades, and thousands of acres will be available for a long time because of the lack of wood to build fences. Not until increased population makes open grazing impossible through utilization of the prairies as farmland will there cease to be free grass for livestock. But as long as millions of acres of land in the West await settlers, there is nothing to worry about. Conditions will become ever better. Anyone can mow as much grass for hay for winter feeding as he needs. Everyone lets his cattle forage freely, paying little attention to them the year round except during the most severe winter weather when they cannot forage for themselves. The young calves, enclosed in a place near the house, call their mothers home mornings and evenings, and after some milk has been taken from the cows, the rest is left to the calves, after which the cows go back to pasture.

Cattle destined for market need only a few weeks' fattening with grain, being fatter from the grazing alone than the best livestock in Switzerland, as we have learned from experience. So anyone who begins with a few head of livestock can expect it to develop into a large herd in a few years. The cows calve without human help, and always successfully, usually in the second year, because the bull is constantly with them on the open prairie. Calving so soon, however, retards the cows' growth, and the breed here is somewhat smaller than the large Swiss cows. However, they produce as much milk as ours, rich in cream, which indicates that it lends itself to the making of excellent cheese.

The best and easiest returns are to be had from a herd of young cows, which need no care to speak of except in the last few weeks before they are sent to market, when they have to be fed grain. After four or five years such livestock will bring $14 to $20 a head, and if one does not possess the necessary cows for breeding, once can easily purchase yearlings for $2 to $3.

The breeding of hogs is just as simple, because they forage in the open for their own acorns, nuts, wild potatoes [Jerusalem artichokes?], etc. A sow produces her young in the open, often in the winter when there is snow on the ground. If hogs are fed with corn for a few weeks before being sent to market, they will bring $2.50 to $3 per hundred pounds, depending on the quality of the animal. Our neighbor butchered more than 120 hundredweight, mostly two-year-olds weighing on average 180 to 200 pounds.

During his first few years, however, every settler experiences some difficulties and disappointments, and although many real accomplishments can be achieved here, this country might well turn out to be not particularly promising to those who expect on coming here that they will be able to settle down into a way of life similar to the one they left, where they will be able to find a new home immediately without creating it for themselves. This may well be possible for persons with enough money to spend some thousands for comforts, but family heads without a great deal of money must possess a good deal of fortitude, for they must count on working hard and suffering some discomforts the first few years. Persons looking for amusements definitely should not come here. Newcomers must be prepared to face the prospect of a dearth of what properly could be termed family amusements.

But persons who with all diligence cannot support their families in Europe and cannot envisage promising futures for their children there will improve their lot immeasureably by coming here, provided of course, that they have enough money to pay their traveling costs and make the necessary purchases for the first year (until they have an income here). After two or three years here they will not wish to return home. The ease with which some of the families here manage to get along may be the main reason that so many Americans here are what we would term pauper families. They manage to lead a comfortable life, but at the end of a year they have nothing put by, for they live *from hand to mouth,* as we term it. They live a life of easygoing abundance, without a thought of providing a better future for their children. Quickly and with the least expenditure of effort the American builds himself a dwelling, and if he is unable to purchase land, he becomes a squatter on federal land, where he lives without paying for the privilege. In order not to be forced to move for as long a time as possible from land on which he has squatted, he chooses some remote place. Thousands exist in this way in Illinois.

But it would be a mistake to imagine that there is a complete lack of enterprising men here. Many make comfortable fortunes in a short time. But every method of making a living here has its own peculiarities. Artists and workers congregate in cities, where a daily market must be provided where they can buy food from the farmers who come there to barter for their necessities. In this way trade develops, and with it the development of a city and the prosperity of the surrounding area. A city like St. Louis serves an area of thirty to forty-five miles, aside from its commerce with cities as far as hundreds of miles distant.

In my opinion successful emigration will depend on the close cooperation of several families who hold together, especially during the first years. In this way much that could be disagreeable can be avoided, especially if, in addition, there is wine available! Working together would make it possible to continue to engage in pleasant European pastimes, and the wine would serve as a seasoning for the pastimes.

The Americans here abstain almost exclusively from the use of alcoholic beverages. Drunkards are despised, and excesses are less common than in Europe. Furthermore, one rarely sees liquor offered to workers, all of which helps to promote thriftiness. There are societies here whose members not only abstain themselves, but never offer alcoholic beverages to others, or even permit them to be brought into their homes. Instead, it is common to see people drinking milk, tea, etc., and eating nourishing food.

[Joseph Suppiger]

The Koepfli Family in New Switzerland to the one [of Kaspar Mauris Koepfli] in Sursee

NEW SWITZERLAND, MARCH 21, 1832

Dear Brother,

This letter will be about conditions here. This past winter has been more difficult than we could have imagined. In our poorly constructed dwellings with the impractical fireplaces we often suffered from the cold. The oldest inhabitants here have not experienced such a cold winter. In the new house we are busily preparing to build we will know how to guard against this. However, we did have many warm days in January of the kind you have in April and May, although the nights usually were cold. A few times we had a good deal of snow, which facilitated the transport of stone and wood.[13]

The rapid melting of the snow, however, caused such a quantity of water that places from which it could not run off readily became almost impassable except with horses. This was to be expected in view of the fact that the top soil is several feet deep except in a few places where there is

13. They used homemade sledges to haul materials until they acquired wagons.

exposed rock. We have several outcrops of the finest limestone in our woods. But the paths dried quickly as soon as the temperature at night no longer dropped below freezing.

Several days ago the weather started to become indescribably beautiful. Many birds, new to us, have put in an appearance, and myriads of cranes, geese, and ducks fly through our region on their way north. One pleasant day we had an especially charming sight when some brightly colored birds (emerald green with yellowish orange and red) flew over our farm. A few times they returned, as if to show off their splendor. Only a few feet above the fruit trees, they were in a position where the sun, reflected in the metallic gleam of their feathers, was virtually blinding. I judged from their size, shape, and beaks that they must belong to the parrot family. If they did indeed belong to this class of birds, they certainly outshone those that one sees in aviaries.

A certain kind of fowl is common here at all times of the year, the so-called prairie chicken (*cupido* [*Tetrao cupido,* now *Tympanuchus Americanus*]), somewhat larger and heavier than your wild ducks. Their excellent flesh and their bad habit of wanting to feed on our wheat fields make them daily targets for our hunters. This fowl came close to causing me to believe in witches. I had shot several times at the same hen but had not been able to frighten it enough to make it move from its place. Not until I ran toward it, did it take flight. Since then I have learned that I took aim at it from too great a distance in view of its mass of feathers.

Turkeys are to be seen only occasionally, and then never singly. In the winter we caught an animal that resembled a little pug dog. I believe it is the pine marten *(Didelphys opposum).* The hares here (actually wild rabbits) are quite abundant, as are several varieties of squirrels, including the flying squirrel. On one occasion we were made disagreeably aware of a skunk (*vivera putrius* [actually *Mephitis*]).

We have several workers making fence rails in our woods. A good worker can split 150 to 200 and is paid 22½ batzen [60 ¢] per hundred. We have another hired man who gets $120 a year (432 Swiss francs), and we furnish his room, board, and laundry. We are planning to fence and put under cultivation at least eighty acres this year and then continue annually at this rate while we increase our livestock holdings accordingly. (Fences, most important for effective farming, must be six to seven feet high to keep out the cattle.)

Congress has not yet designated the route the new National Highway is to take, although according to action taken in the upper house (or Chamber of Deputies [*sic*]) it is to pass through our area. There is also much talk here of a railroad (with steam engines) from St. Louis that could pass through the land we hold.

One more remark: Emigrants from Germany are beginning to make their way here via New Orleans. The ship *Boston* set sail from Havre, bound for New Orleans, the same day we left for New York, April 16, 1831 [actually June 2], loaded, as we were, with emigrants. Since then we have spoken with several persons who made the trip with the *Boston,* and they speak well of their journey (even at this dangerous time [of the year]). They experienced beautiful weather, with no storms, and they arrived in good condition in New Orleans after fifty-eight days. They paid 130 French francs to travel in the hold, with children traveling three for the price of one adult. How much more comfortable and reasonable that route must be, although Duden's advice concerning it must be taken into consideration.

Your loving brother, Salomon Koepfli

Joseph Suppiger in New Switzerland to the Suppiger Family in Sursee

NEW SWITZERLAND, SEPTEMBER 1832

Dear Parents and Siblings!

Now I usually hire workers by the month, which is very expensive, but then it is not necessary to keep them on the payroll except during the busy season. In Lucerne it is possible to get good workers for low wages. I would be glad to pay two good, faithful workers $60 for their first year before they have learned the customs and the language here, and then increase their pay later when they become familiar with their work. There may be a number of men who would like to come here. If you know of such men and are convinced of their reliability, send them to me with a letter. The journey via New Orleans should not come too high. Approximately 300 gulden will suffice for a hired man, and if he has another 200 gulden, I would advise him, in order to have maximum freedom of movement, to burden himself *at most* with an extra set of clothing. He would soon earn enough here to support himself.

But let no one indenture himself to get to America. If he does not have the price of his fare he should stay in Europe. If he can manage the fare himself he can be his own master and be as free as an American to do what he wants, without having any kind of pressure exerted on him by anyone. What he earns will be his own. He would find it demoralizing to be bound to working out his passage and might ultimately refuse to honor his obligation. How much more will be accomplished by the man who does not incur such an obligation. Let him be prepared, however, to work from sunup to sundown.

Everyone soon becomes accustomed to the food, because it is better, more nourishing, and more suitable than in Europe. The newcomer will have to resign himself, however, to doing without regular church service, and he will find no opportunity to go dancing.

I would be glad to tell more about agriculture here if I were able to do so from personal experience and not from mere hearsay. We will soon have been here a year and should shortly be in a position to tell you about some harvests. You know that we did not arrive here until October and that it took us a few weeks to buy livestock and equipment before we could get to work. This delayed us in getting our wheat planted, that is, at the proper time, for the little amount of wheat we were able to plant did not have time to get started before winter set in, and the bitter winter weather killed most of what did come up.

But several of our neighbors had fairly good crops, and next year, God willing, I will have a good yield. What we will harvest in the way of corn I do not know, but in any case this is grown only to feed livestock, and the farmer counts on no direct income from it except insofar as it can be used to fatten his cattle and hogs. Anyone here selling his cattle before the fourth or fifth year would be what we would term in Switzerland as beginning to go downhill. The best way for a farmer to make money is to grow wheat and raise cattle and hogs.

I will now attempt to tell you about agriculture here insofar as my experience permits. I may be mistaken about some aspects of it, but only slightly. Let us assume that someone buys 160 acres of virgin land from the government (and if he were to make as fortunate a choice as we did, he could be completely satisfied). If half of it were wooded, it would make quite a nice little estate. A holding definitely should contain some woods. The 160 acres would cost $200. Half of the land can be brought under cultivation at $1.50 per acre, or $120. Fencing these eighty acres will take nine thousand rails, the splitting and transport of which will come to $112.50. Erecting the fence may cost $10. Let us say that sixty acres of the holding will be planted in wheat and the rest in corn and other crops. If the land was plowed at the right time in the spring so that the grass roots were killed by lying fallow, two harrowings would suffice to prepare it for planting. To harrow sixty acres twice will cost $45. Hiring a man to plow sixty acres at the rate of one to one and a half acres a day will come at most to $20. Sowing a bushel of wheat per acre at 50¢ to 75¢ per bushel (for sixty acres) will cost $30. Mowing sixty acres of wheat costs approximately $15. Raking and bringing in the wheat may cost as much as (but I am not certain) $7.50. To complete the little estate by fencing in a courtyard with three thousand additional rails will cost $37.50. The cost of a garden and a little house will come to $200.

I would allot the rest of the land as follows:

Five acres should be devoted to growing potatoes, flax, etc., and I would plant one hundred fruit trees @ 50¢ each, which, with $2.50 for the cost of planting, would come to $12.50. Fifteen acres should be devoted to growing corn. The cost of the seed corn and preparing the soil will come to $16. The number of cattle should be in proportion to the size of the holding, but since I will speak of this later, I will simply list here: one wagon, two plows, one harrow, and some other equipment costing approximately $150. The total outlay for preparing a little estate like this [would come to] $976.

I believe the costs will be as I have listed them, perhaps even lower, barring of course misfortune and mismanagement, which are no more foreign to America than they are to Europe. But let us look at the yield that can be expected (with a fair degree of certainty) from this holding if God does not henceforth change the productive power of the soil and punish the Americans with a completely disastrous harvest:

New soil of this kind can produce 30 to 45 bushels of wheat per acre the first four years. But even with a yield of only 25 bushels per acre, there would be a harvest of 1500 bushels from sixty acres. At the customary price of 50¢ per bushel, this would come to $750.

The fifteen acres of corn should produce at least 450 to 600 bushels, and could well produce as much as 750 bushels. The price of corn, however, fluctuates drastically, sometimes increasing fourfold and even eightfold. This year it rose to 37½¢ and even 50¢, but it often has been as low as 12½¢. I believe one could count on getting $1 for every six bushels and therefore expect a total of not less than $100, because in any case it would be worth more than this if used to fatten livestock. So the farm's total yield would be $850, and under favorable conditions could be half again as much, and the farm would show this yield year after year.

Here I will stop making estimates and let you come to your own conclusions as to the profit to be derived from farming here. You can reckon the income for future years yourself, since it should be easy from the figures I have cited to reckon the future costs.

First, however, I must underline my admonition that a family be in a position to meet the expenses it will incur during the first year. These depend on the size of the family and vary according to the arrangements made on its behalf. An estimate can be made easily if one knows that wheat and potatoes cost respectively 50¢ and 20¢ per bushel, and meat 2¢ to 3½¢ per pound. Whoever buys a few cows, which cost practically nothing to feed, can expect to have plenty of milk and butter. Coffee and sugar cost the same as in Switzerland, and I cannot see that much more is needed to sustain life beyond the things I have mentioned. Chickens to supply one with eggs will cost very little. If the family maintains a garden it can save buying a good many things. The land needed for this has been included in my estimates. Feeding the livestock during the winter costs little. For $5 to $6 one can have enough hay mowed for ten head of cattle.

One more thing about raising cattle: I really am not familiar enough with this aspect of farming to be able to give specific figures, because it requires several years of experience. A Kentuckian once said: "I do not understand how tradesmen figure percentages of profit, but if I buy something for fifty cents and sell it for a dollar, I know I am making money." Cattle raising, according to experienced farmers here, is the most profitable utilization of one's land, and I can well understand this, because, except for a period of three months, one need expend no energy. I will restrict myself to making a few notes, and you can draw your own conclusions.

In our part of the country one can buy as many cattle as he can afford, and he will not have to provide even a foot of grazing land for them. I believe this situation will obtain for the next fifty to one hundred years, because many thousands of acres of prairie land are still lying fallow. They have not been bought because they lack adjacent wooded areas. Cattle are permitted to graze all summer, merely being offered some salt occasionally when they come home. Calves are kept in an enclosure, a practice that brings the cows home mornings and evenings to be milked (albeit not always at the time one might prefer), and after a part of their milk has been taken—the rest being left for the calves to suck—the cows are driven back out to pasture. This is all there is to raising cattle. In the harshest winter the cattle can be let into the harvested cornfields where they can subsist for several weeks on the leaves and stalks, and when these have been devoured, they must be fed hay, brought to them in the open daily by wagon.

The only animals that might be given shelter in a barn are horses and weak calves. Everyone can have as many hundreds of acres of hay mowed as he needs, without having to buy any land on which to grow it, for there is much unclaimed land available for this purpose. Experienced farmers, however, plant five to ten acres in hay, primarily for their horses, although this is not really necessary.

A good cow with calf is worth $10, and yearling steers cost on the average $3. If one wishes to make butter and keep a good many cows for this purpose, one can use half the milk for it and feed the other half to the calves. There is a good steady market for butter, and it brings at least 4½ batzen per pound. In St. Louis it goes up to 9 batzen in the late spring and double this in the winter. (This holds for other products also.)

If one holds on to one's yearlings, the young steers get to be worth $6 in the second year, and young cows $5 to $6. Cows usually produce calves in their second year, because the bulls are left to graze with them, and because of this it would be difficult to delay their becoming bred. On the other hand, this relieves the farmer of having to see to their being bred. In the third year the steers get to be worth $9 to $10, depending on how much they weigh, and in their fourth year $12 to $15, while in their fifth year they bring $18 to $21. There is always a ready market for cattle, and if one can fatten them well, there is even more profit. The prices I have quoted are for cattle that have been fattened on grass. Calculate your profits.

Sows cost $2.50 to $4, depending on the breed. They need no care except that for some time in the winter they need to be fed corn and potatoes. They usually have a litter two or three times a year, and there are five to six young in a litter. Usually the young pigs are permitted to run in the open for a year and a half, after which they are brought in and fattened with corn for six to eight weeks. I do not know how much corn it takes to fatten a hog. I do know that ten acres of corn are enough to fatten 100 to 150 of them.

Butchered hogs, usually weighing some two hundred pounds are sold for $3 per hundredweight. Persons farming on a large scale salt down the pork in small barrels—two hundred pounds to the barrel—and sell it, especially in the spring or summer, for $10 to $15 per barrel. Barrels for packing pork cost 75¢ each, and the salt needed to prepare a barrel costs 30¢. Salt costs much less than in Switzerland, the best kind selling for

$1.75 per hundredweight (circa 55 batzen), and one also can get salt for livestock for as little as 30 to 40 batzen per hundred pounds.

As I gain experience I shall attempt to complete these estimates where necessary, but I have observed enough to deduce that it cannot be too hard to make a living in a country where fertilizer is not needed and where raising livestock involves no expenditure of effort. If only there were enough inhabitants here so that one could find workers, even at the prevailing wages!

I will not touch on the matter of raising sheep or horses except to say that during the first year a sheep pays for its purchase price with the wool it produces, and any offspring are just that much gain. Horses, too, need little care, except that they be sheltered from the winter cold. For $50 or $60 one can buy good mares, and with luck the offspring in two years will bring what was paid for the mare. But horses require a much greater capital outlay.

[Joseph Suppiger]

PART FIVE

Advantages and Disadvantages of the Area We Chose to Settle

I am making these pages available to the public as quickly as possible because I believe the readers of the *Reisebericht* wish to know the particulars of the founding of New Switzerland, especially those who are planning to emigrate. The *Reisebericht* stressed the pleasant and the dangerous aspects of the actual journey, and these pages show the light and dark sides of life during the initial years there, written by a man who combines sound judgment with an absolute regard for the truth. All members of the Koepfli and Suppiger families are in good health. The difficult initial period of adjustment is largely behind them, and they are looking forward to a bright future in the new, free Switzerland. God grant the same to us in the fatherland.

The Editor[1]

I

The Lay of the Land in Our Vicinity, with Its Prairies and Woods. Growing Crops and Raising Livestock to Advantage

An examination of a map of western Illinois will show a good number of small streams running more or less parallel from north to south. The woods of New Switzerland lie along such streams. Between the streams lies prairie land such as covers the greatest part of the state, stretching as far north as the eye can see and as far south as the Ohio River.

The part of the prairie on which New Switzerland is located lies between Silver Creek and Sugar Creek, both of which are bordered by a band of woods. The distance between the two creeks averages two to three miles

---

1. The material comprising this part of the *Reisebericht* also was published as a 61-page monograph, *Die Licht- & Schattenseite von New Switzerland in Nordamerika* (Sursee, March 1833). The editor's note, absent from the *Reisebericht* proper, was written by Kaspar Mauris Koepfli, Dr. Kaspar Koepfli's eldest son. He, his wife Ludovika (née Schnyder), and their children remained in Sursee for eight years before joining the rest of the Koepflis in New Switzerland in 1839. He did not see fit to identify himself as editor, most likely because in introducing Salomon Koepfli's letter at the end of part 5 he identified himself beyond question when he told of having decided to include a letter of 5/13/1833 from his "brother Salomon." Kaspar Mauris Koepfli was the only one of the senior Dr. Koepfli's sons still remaining in Switzerland.

and never exceeds six miles. In our part of the state the prairie is dotted with gentle elevations ranging from 20 to 150 feet in height (drained by rivulets during the rainy season). Some of these elevations have smooth, round tops like the crystal of a watch, while others look more like bastions, but they are never steep, and they all have rich soil.

One of the elevations in this vicinity resembles those around St. Louis and surely was constructed by human hands. It looks like a pyramid with the top cut off, and on the flat top is the base for a second pyramid. It is a colossal work and in some respects resembles the Egyptian pyramids.[2] It cannot possibly have been built by the type of Indians we see today. The other elevations in the area obviously were fashioned by nature. None of the land is rugged except for some places that have been dug up by hogs, and all of it is smooth enough for the growing of crops. Tall grass covers the prairie from spring to fall, when there are also the most beautiful varieties of flowers every month.

Here and there are clusters of trees on the elevations as well as along the streams. Also to be seen are clusters of sumac, blackberry, and grape. Springs are comparatively rare on the prairie, but in the woods they are fairly numerous and often gush freely.

Most of the land in the area is elevated, but there is some that is subject to flooding at times, and this is the most luxuriant, although it is not considered arable and rarely contains settlements, because it is considered unhealthful.

Illinois has the most varied kinds of woods, some of them of very good quality. In our part of Illinois it is held that the quality of the grassland diminishes as the quality of the woods increases, but this view is not general throughout the state. Some people hold that woods in the midst of grassland gradually tend to disappear. It cannot be denied that the young tender growth at the edges of the woods is adversely affected by the burning-off of the tall, dry grass, a common practice on the prairies,

2. Kaspar Koepfli may well have confused the elevation in his vicinity with Monk's Mound in the American Bottom, about 6 miles east of St. Louis, which could more readily be described as a "colossal work." He had seen Monk's Mound when the Swiss party first came to New Switzerland from St. Louis, but there is no known record of his ever having seen the other mound, which was described later by his son Salomon as "about 80 feet high, with a flat top, still uncultivated [in 1831], so that one could see its four sharp corners distinctly from the top." On or about April 1, 1835, Johann Jacob Eggen, on a map prepared for his family in Switzerland, drew an "Indian Hill" in the SW ¼ of Section 31, St. Jacob Twp.

although in settled areas these fires easily can be kept under control. Time has shown too that considerable stands of woods have sprung up where only underbrush was growing a few years before, just as underbrush has sprung up where formerly there was grassland, all of which has caused farmers to insist that Illinois woods must gradually be increasing. Wherever this expansion is not desired, it can be prevented by the regular burning-off of the dead grass on the prairie. It is difficult to comprehend how rapidly trees grow here, unless one realizes how rich the soil is. Small scrub oaks are said to develop into large trees in thirty years.

Tree-lined Silver Creek is still too near its source here to have attained any appreciable size. In the spring its waters gain considerably in volume, but in the summer and fall it is a comparatively quiet stream. There are times when saw and grain mills on Silver Creek cannot operate, due to the lack of water. Like most streams in this part of the United States it is comparatively slow-moving at almost all times of the year. It harbors some good kinds of fish, which incidentally are fairly safe from attempts by people here to entrap them.

A valley through which a stream flows generally is termed "bottom." Trees growing on this lowland are larger than those in other woods. Some varieties are to be found only in this habitat, except for individual trees that have been transplanted. One of these is the plane tree, which impresses every newcomer from Europe by its size and beautiful shape.

The width of the woods ranges roughly from two to three miles and sometimes from as much as five to nine miles. Of course, woods are not always equally distributed on both sides of streams, and occasionally in the case of two parallel streams, woods actually extend from the one to the other, with no prairie in between.

We (that is, our family) presently own five hundred acres of woods, much of it containing a fairly heavy stand of trees. The best woods in our area are privately owned, probably because it is expected that in a comparatively short time they will increase considerably in value. The owners of plots of woods also have at their disposal the grasslands adjacent to them for livestock grazing. Without direct access to woods it probably would be impossible to establish a settlement here.

While conifers are found mostly in northern areas, there is much pine and fir lumber sold in St. Louis, where it costs almost twice as much as walnut, oak, or ash. These conifers are said to be far superior to the European varieties. Locally grown lumber one to two inches thick is available at our sawmills for five to six Swiss francs per one hundred feet.

Our own woods consist mainly of oak, walnut, varieties of elm and maple, ash, plane [probably sycamore], sassafras, and linden, as well as some wild poplar, mulberry, cherry, and plum trees. I will not attempt to list the many lesser-known shrubs and trees, because descriptions of them and other good, useful, and interesting varieties can be found in Duden's work.

Fruit trees will not be found growing wild in the woods of Illinois or Missouri except for a variety of small plum like our *Zuckerpflaum* [literally "sugarplum"] but not so sweet.

Our woodland contains excellent limestone in readily available deposits, and we have been using it as building material and for lime-burning. We also have found some inexhaustible deposits of very useable coal along the same hills. One of our neighbors dug up roughly a hundred wagonloads last summer without expending much effort. This could become a profitable business because such deposits are to be found rarely and then mostly only along our Silver Creek area.

Most of our woods are in the northwest part of our acreage. Settlers usually choose a site on grassland as close as possible to woods. It should be land that lies high enough so that it drains well and will be ready for cultivation as soon as spring comes. Most of the earliest immigrants chose level land on which to settle because they believed its soil was richer. Now more and more gentle hills are being made into farmland because it has been found that the topsoil there also produces a good yield, and it does not require drainage ditches. It may well be, of course, that the soil on the elevations will become exhausted more quickly than that on level land.

As soon as a settler has acquired his land he can begin to plow it. The usual plow leaves a furrow seventeen inches wide and, depending on the availability of good draft animals, four inches deep. Two men, using two to three pair of oxen, can plow two acres a day. One easily can have this done for seven Swiss francs an acre, and for the new arrival this undoubtedly would be the best procedure. May and June are the best months for preparing the soil because then the roots are upturned while in their most succulent stage and killed by the heat of the sun. The plowing can be done at any time of the year except when the ground is frozen, but spring is the best time because feeding the oxen at that time of the year is not an additional chore for they simply can be unyoked and left to graze overnight. Last summer we uncovered only one stone that weighed as much as a pound during the plowing of 150 acres.

Before plowing season the eleven-foot-long lengths needed for rails to use in fence making should have been split. They should be made from the largest and finest walnut or oak trees with trunks as free as possible of branches. A tree must be quite large if a hundred fence rails are to be split from it, so it is necessary to settle where enough large trees are readily available.

The felling of trees (which is done with an axe) and the rail splitting can be very exhausting work, and persons without experience in it would do well to have it done, at least at first. Americans readily can be found who will prepare rails at the rate of 22½ batzen per hundred. We used twelve thousand rails to enclose 160 acres at a cost of 270 Swiss francs. An acre contains 38,327 French square feet. Building a fence to the customary height of six feet requires eight to nine such rails laid over one another in a zigzag pattern, forming a 130° angle (as at *a* in the sketch), which means that such a zigzag fence around a field in effect takes up a four-foot-wide strip (as illustrated by *c* and *d* on the sketch).

No part of the fence described thus far needs to be sunk into the soil, which is so rich here that, even in the case of the most durable wood, any buried parts soon would rot. Such a fence, moreover, is very good for keeping hogs as well as cattle and horses out of the fields, and it is fairly inexpensive, although it is unsightly and uses up space and wood. This type of fence is widely used in the United States, which is an indication that it has its advantages. If it is constructed of good wood, it should require no major repairs for a dozen years. The cost of transporting the rails from the woods to the fields to be enclosed must be estimated. After the rails are on the spot, erecting the fence is not difficult, and 160 acres can be enclosed by two men in three weeks.

A field that has been plowed in the spring and enclosed in the summer can be planted in wheat in the fall. This can be done in either of two ways after the acreage has been harrowed several times: it can be plowed-in or harrowed-in, one bushel of seed to the acre. At harvest time a good worker using a special scythe can cut two acres a day. The wheat is sheaved on the field and threshed at home by horses, although threshing machines are beginning to be used now on larger farms. They can be purchased in St. Louis at a reasonable price (180 Swiss francs per machine).

An average yield per acre, using this method, is twenty bushels, but it is often higher. A bushel is the equivalent of 1775 French cubic inches, as compared with the Lucerne *viertel* which contains only 1733 cubic inches. A bushel of wheat always brings as much as eighteen batzen. This year the price is double that because of the bad harvest.

More wheat is grown every year, forcing an increase in the number of steam mills, to which it seems enough wheat never can be delivered to satisfy the demand for the flour they produce. The flour is packed into small barrels and shipped by steamboat up the Ohio River to the eastern states as well as down the Mississippi to New Orleans. From New Orleans it is shipped to France and England and to Mexico and South America. Salt pork and beef follow the same route.

During the European wars, it is said, all foodstuffs here increased incredibly in price, with the result that complaints frequently are voiced here about the hard times of recent years. So the more Europe suffers from want and misery as a result of war and revolutions, the more frequently the American gives thanks for good times. Apparently there is no danger here of completely lean years such as have been experienced in Switzerland.

From the above figures it should not be difficult to estimate what a comparatively small outlay of money it takes to make our savannas productive, an outlay that can be more than regained by the return from the first harvest. Wages can be estimated at thirty-six Swiss francs a month.

Swiss farmers can best come to understand the ideal conditions for agriculture here by picturing a meadow, not under cultivation for years, that now is to be used for growing wheat. It can continue to be used for growing wheat for some years with a good chance that the yield will increase in the two years immediately following and with less expenditure of effort. After two to three years of growing wheat, however, it would be well to rotate with another crop such as rye, oats, corn, etc. In this virtually inexhaustible soil, wheat produces the best yield if rotated after oats. Horses are fed some corn instead of only oats. An acre yields approximately eighteen to twenty bushels, and a bushel brings nine to twelve batzen.

Rye and wheat yields, approximately the same as oats, are sold in large part to distilleries. Barley is not grown in this area. Emigrants would be well advised to bring several glass containers of the best variety with them, for it would find a ready market, being in great demand by breweries. Maize, or Turkish corn [turkey, or squirrel corn] (called *corn* here), is grown throughout much of the United States, but it would appear to be less profitable than some other crops because of the care it requires. It usually is not exported, the farmer growing only what he needs for himself and his livestock. An average yield is fifty bushels to the acre, and it brings five to twelve batzen per bushel.

Some of our fields have been producing crops for fifteen years, and we have not been able to detect any loss of richness in the soil. Incidentally, after ground once has been plowed, it requires only one pair of oxen or horses to plow it in successive years, and only one man. One man, it should be noted, can prepare a great deal more land for planting here than in Switzerland. For keeping the weeds under control and for loosening the soil in a cornfield only one horse is needed. Fellenberg's plow for eradicating weeds could be put to good use here.[3] An emigrant would find it worth while to bring a sketch of it with him. The ordinary plows here are very light and small and have no wheels, and they cost eighteen to thirty Swiss francs.

Wagons are better built than those used in Switzerland. The wheels are like those of Swiss mail coaches except that they are narrow, having been designed for these roads and for local conditions in general. Wagon maker and smith usually work together constructing them, foundries performing much of the work that would fall to the blacksmith in Switzerland. A wagon designed for two horses costs approximately thirteen louis d'or, a heavier one up to twenty louis d'or.

For field work the farmers here generally prefer draft oxen to horses (because of their advantages). The oxen are well broken in and respond to the same commands to turn right or left as do the horses. The yoke seems well-designed, being a sort of wooden bar by which two oxen are joined at the necks for working together. It can be fashioned quickly and inexpensively. A pair of oxen, including a yoke, sells for eight to twelve louis d'or. Cows are not used as draft animals here.

Potatoes are plentiful and excellent. Sweet potatoes do well here and are a favorite of new arrivals. Both kinds of potato are popular in the St. Louis market. Like most other staples they increase drastically in price as spring approaches, and during the spring they often disappear completely from the market place. The ordinary farmer is not inclined to dig a cellar in which to preserve them until they would bring top prices.

3. Philipp Emanuel von Fellenberg (1771–1844) retired from the Swiss diplomatic service in 1794 and purchased an estate, "Hofwyl," which he set up as a model for farmers.

Other garden products such as cabbage, onions, and lettuce thrive here, onions attaining full size in one year. Pumpkins, cucumbers, melons, beans, etc. are planted in the same rows with corn, and superfluous amounts of them are produced without effort.

In this area cotton and tobacco are grown only for home use. Flax, rapeseed, and castor beans would yield a profit, for the soil is very good for growing oil-producing plants, and all oils are very expensive. But the farmers rarely grow them, seemingly satisfied with a good corn crop that will see them through, for they are not inclined to plan for the future. Now and then one can find castor beans being grown. There is a mill in the area that produces oil from these beans. It is sold in European pharmacies under the name ricinus oil. We even found substantial growths of these annuals in rich grasslands here, and although they were not enclosed, we could not see that livestock found them edible.

At this point a few words need to be added about letting renters operate one's acreage. If one feels assured that a potential renter is industrious, a third of the yield from the crops he raises on one's land can be allotted to him for his work in producing it. If the man's ability has not been demonstrated, he is asked to give the owner ten to twelve bushels of grain from every acre. Employers who furnish the necessary draft animals and farm machinery get one-half of the yield. If the renter is responsible for as many as twenty to forty acreas, he is provided housing.

Raising Livestock. The important business of raising livestock can be accomplished with much less effort than in the old country. Because of the tremendous amount of prairie land here, it can be used freely by all, for only a part of it is under cultivation, for one thing because of the lack of wood for fencing. Thus until more woods can be developed, or a type of fence can be devised that does not use much wood, only narrow stretches of land near woods will be utilized for planting, leaving the greater part of the prairie for grazing. In all probability, therefore, thousands of head of livestock will be able to forage on federally-owned prairie land for a long time to come.

Burning off the prairie grass formerly was done by hunters to drive wild game from their hiding places, but now it is done by farmers to provide new grass for grazing. If prairie grass in a particular area is set afire in the fall after it has become dry, it will speed the growth of new grass in that area in the spring. However, if one burns a selected area of prairie that was left unburned the previous fall, so that the dry grass of the previous year is still mixed with the new but already somewhat ripe stand, part of the current year's grass will be eradicated along with that left from the previous year, stimulating the growth of new grass in the middle of the summer. This procedure can be repeated somewhat later in the year on another piece of prairie, and thus one can provide fresh grass for the livestock at will.

The burning must be done carefully, however, for where the fenced areas are not separated from the prairie by lanes of some kind, the fences easily could be destroyed. To prevent this, one should plow a number of furrows around fields or wait for a favorable wind. If a large area is set afire, the six-foot-high flames can provide a terrible spectacle, especially at night.

Livestock has an abundance of grass from the middle of April until the end of November, and the animals need only to be provided with a little salt occasionally. This will encourage the young steers to come back to the farm at times. The cows are induced to stay near at hand by the fact that their calves are kept in fenced areas. If they do not come in of their own accord by milking time, it is not difficult to drive them in (especially if there are a good many of them). Some of the cows' milk is left for the calves to suck. There is enough water for the livestock in the springs and streams, so the animals can spend day and night in the open, with everything they need provided by nature, and they thrive on this kind of existence.

If someone could bring half a dozen harmonizing, bronze bells of the type worn by cows in Switzerland, he not only would be paid for them in money, but would find the recipient to be most grateful. The only bells for livestock known here are little iron goat bells.

At the beginning of August every farmer who is inclined to be the least bit provident will look for a plot in the vast prairie with a good stand of untrampled grass, which means that it will have to be some distance from his farm. This will be utilized to make hay, which will be stacked near his home and used as supplemental feed for his livestock during the winter. When there is snow, or the ground is frozen solid, the cornfields will be opened to his animals (after the harvest, of course), and they will be able to feed on the nutritious stalks. The straw left after the threshing of wheat, oats, rye, etc. also will be used as feed, for here the animals are not kept in barns, so there is no barn floor on which it can be spread to soak up their droppings. The use of manure as fertilizer is unknown here.

Ideal as conditions are for livestock in the summer, they are miserable when there is severe weather, which fortunately never lasts long. New arrivals often make plans to provide their animals with some kind of shelter from the severe cold, but such plans rarely materialize. Some type of emergency shelter for them would be desirable, but not of an indoor kind that would necessitate feeding them there all winter. If the farm animals' source of water is frozen over, it is necessary to provide well water for them.

What should be evident from all this is how effortless, inexpensive, and profitable it is to raise livestock here. And if one preserves some of the butter one churns until winter, it can be sold for nine batzen a pound at the St. Louis market. Last spring it was selling there for double that amount, and in New Orleans it is said to cost that much all year round. There is a shortage of butter in St. Louis a good part of the year, but in the summer the price drops drastically, usually to four and a half batzen per pound. It is easy to preserve butter in tubs by mixing it with salt: one-eighth of a pound for each pound of butter. It can be kept as long as desired, the salt simply washed out before it is used.

The art of making good cheese is virtually unknown here. Good cheese commands a high price, and a good cheese dairy would find a ready market for its product.

An ordinary cow with calf costs ten dollars (thirty-six Swiss francs). A cow's youngest calf usually is sold with her. Most calving occurs in March or April, and the entire process is easier here and accompanied by less worry on the farmer's part. The bull runs with the herd on the prairie.

Some people hold that fat cattle are ones that have been taken from the grassland in the fall; others maintain that to be classified as fat cattle they must have been fed with corn for a time after that. Corn also is fed draft oxen and horses in the winter, greater care being taken in feeding ears of corn to horses.

A fat steer weighing approximately seven hundred pounds can bring sixty Swiss francs. Fattened cattle either are delivered to St. Louis or driven in herds of a hundred to the Ohio River, where the meat is salted down and sent to the eastern states or to the Gulf of Mexico.

Beef is sold at two cents (seven and a half rappen) per pound, and dried cattle hides at ten cents (thirty-six rappen) per pound. The greatest profit probably is to be had by investing in young cattle. A yearling steer costs twelve francs, a two-year-old twenty, and a three-year-old thirty to forty. A yearling cow costs twelve francs, and it often produces a calf after its second year, increasing its value to thirty francs. Such early calving retards a cow's growth, but this would be difficult to prevent in view of the fact that the bull is permitted to graze with the cows at all times. In any case such young cows recover rapidly after their third year.

In addition to all of these statistics which demonstrate the desirability of cattle-raising, there is the added advantage that there is virtually no loss of any kind (cattle disease being unknown here). Families who do not have sons that are accustomed to growing crops might well prefer cattle-raising, so as not to be dependent on hired labor, which has its difficult side everywhere, but especially here.

The raising of hogs is likewise very easy. They require no man-made shelter, and only need to be fed some corn when the ground is frozen so solid that it is impossible for them to forage for the roots that are their chief source of food. In the fall they feast on the many acorns and nuts in the woods. Last year (in the fall of 1832) they needed no supplementary feed except the corn that hogs customarily are fed for a few weeks before they are slaughtered, which is usually when they are one and a half to two years old, at which time they will weigh 130 to 180 pounds. The hogs seem to be wilder than those in Switzerland, but the pork tastes the same, despite what I once seem to have read somewhere.

When butchering time comes and the owner of a sizeable number of hogs cannot find them in the vicinity of his home, he rides through woods and prairie, and when he finds ones that bear his mark, he shoots those he considers mature and heavy enough and hauls them home by wagon. (Incidentally, the farmer's cattle and sheep have their ears marked with the same kind of slit for purposes of identification.) When he gets the hogs home, he cuts them up and cleans them, packs the pieces into barrels that hold approximately 190 pounds, and ships them. Such a barrel of salt pork will bring him roughly twenty-three Swiss francs, and as a rule the price increases to thirty-six Swiss francs in the summer. Farmers buying pork from each other in the fall pay two and a half cents (nine rappen) per pound, and if it is for their own use, it often is smoked.

A good sized herd of sheep also would be a profitable investment. The breed of sheep here has especially fine wool. A medium-sized sheep costs fifty-four batzen. The meat finds a ready market in St. Louis, and the wool always can be sold for thirteen and a half batzen per pound. There are some Spanish sheep here.

Horses in Illinois are often broken in for riding. Much finer horses are to be found in the state of Ohio. Illinois horses are not so heavy as the ones in Switzerland, but they are hardier. The price is virtually the same. Breeding horses requires a greater outlay of capital and seems to be less profitable than raising cattle or hogs. Stallions always are kept in stables. There seem to be enough horse fanciers everywhere who keep them for general use.

II

Approximate Geographical Location of Our Area, Its Architecture, Drinking Water, Roads. Advantages of Prairie and Woodland Compared. The Outlook for Settlements Along the Large Streams.

Our general area is below 39° N.L., 82° W.L. (Fero).[4] It is located in western Illinois, twenty-seven English miles (approximately nine leagues) east of the well-known city of St. Louis on the Mississippi River.

Fog is rare, and rainy or snowy spells never last for more than several days at a time. The wind frequently changes direction, and there are abrupt changes in temperature, especially in the spring and fall, from beautiful warm weather to raw cold. The wind is especially noticeable on the open prairie, to the dismay of some. These winds, which often blow hard, make the winters somewhat raw, but they keep the summer heat from being as oppressive as might be expected in this latitude.

Our first winter here (1831–32), unusually cold for this latitude (roughly that of Lisbon), was much like winter in Switzerland. The spring was too wet and the following summer too dry, but the temperature never rose so high as to interfere with farm work, and it did not affect our health adversely as we had feared before leaving Europe that it might. The fall was very pleasant until well into November, when there were some cold, windy days. Then it soon turned pleasant again, and except for a few days of snow and some very cold days in February, which called for a more efficient heating system than the local fireplaces, there was no snowfall that did not melt away by noon. It froze at night throughout the winter. Old-time residents termed it in general a mild, dry winter.

During the rest of the year there was at least one thunderstorm a month, but the thunderstorms here are not so frequent or violent as one might fear, although the rains often are heavy. It rarely hails. Thawing progresses

4. Ferro, now "Hierro," westernmost Canary Island, was until the late 19th century a common prime meridian for calculating longitude.

much more rapidly than in Switzerland. In general the area may be described as healthful. Some find it more healthful here than in Switzerland. Fevers, expecially the ague,[5] occur mostly along flooding streams and woodland. Where we live there are no swamps or stagnant water.

The most common ailment is the common cold, which is aggravated by careless people through the use of poorly chosen home remedies such as calomel, which is used in alarmingly large doses. The physicians follow similar methods for the most part, helping many a patient to an early grave.

Duden claims that drinking water in Illinois contains an iron vitriol taste, but this certainly does not hold for our region, if indeed it does for any area in the state. Ours is pure and free of any unpleasant taste. The common source of drinking water here is what one would term a shallow well, which is easy to dig. After choosing a site free from surface rocks, one digs through two feet of black topsoil, after which one hits on a yellowish, clayey soil which breaks up into a fine quicksand wherever there is water underneath it. These wells vary in depth from fifteen to thirty feet. (Incidentally, in digging a well on even a good-sized hill, one often can hit water as quickly as at the foot of the hill.)

The soil is so firm that nothing need be done to shore up the walls of the well with boards, and the well will remain in serviceable condition for several years before collapsing. If one prefers a more permanent type of well, one lines it with bricks, or better, with limestone. The water in our well is clearer and fresher than that found in most springs, and it is virtually inexhaustible. During last summer's dry weather forty-six draft oxen were watered from it three times a day, and the water never failed to return to the same level. The total cost of constructing such a well would come to approximately sixty Swiss francs.

Brief mention now will be made of the architecture here. Most Americans build a log house when they first settle somewhere. They [*sic*] are constructed of tree trunks that have been adzed on two sides and grooved near each end so as to provide a good fit for the logs placed at right angles to them. The logs are placed one above the other to the desired height, and

5. Ague, variously known as "fever and ague," "bilious, or intermittent fever," and so forth, was actually malaria. It was very common in the frontier Midwest. Koepfli correctly associates it with low, wet areas. However, despite New Switzerland's relatively favorable location, some of the early settlers apparently did suffer from malaria.

the spaces between them are plastered with clay. Four-foot-long shingles are used in constructing the roof. Not until the building is up is provision made for doors and, *if desired,* windows. These structures, lacking home-like qualities, tend to serve the basic needs of newcomers. If they want to continue living on the spot they originally chose for their first dwelling, and feel up to it, they can have a better house built, using wood or brick, keeping in mind that construction involving the use of hired labor is expensive and that money invested in almost any other way would bring a far better return. Each laborer demands at least thirty-six batzen a day, plus room and board.

A brick house is more difficult to build. The layer of clay immediately below the top soil is utilized in various mixtures for the making of bricks. After it has been worked thoroughly by oxen, it is put into wooden molds, dried in the sun, and then fired. A worker can produce twenty-five hundred bricks a day if the material is readily at hand. The houses in most United States cities are built of brick.

Another style of home, more common in rural areas, is the so-called frame house. It is constructed on a wooden framework much like that of Swiss houses which are to be half-timbered. The outside of the framework here is covered with thin, narrow boards (overlapping one another like shingles on a roof), and inside, instead of straw and clay as in half-timbering, bricks are used to fill in the framework.

The framework of the roof is lightweight because it needs to bear only the weight of shingles. The exterior of these houses, including the roof, should be painted. We built a frame house last summer, using walnut wood throughout. We consider this type of construction the most sturdy, the most effective against the cold, and the most attractive.

Why did we not carry out our original plan of settling in Missouri on a navigable stream? We had come to the Mississippi Valley with the intention of farming and raising livestock, and we found after investigation that Illinois with its prairies was more suitable than Missouri. We found the prairie land of Illinois not only more practical for growing crops but better suited for raising cattle than the woodland, which first would have had to be cleared, as would have been the case in Missouri. Who would not prefer to prepare eighty acres of prairie for cultivation to twelve acres of wood-land? On such woodland, stumps and roots continue to create problems for years for they can be eradicated only with great difficulty at the very beginning.

What influenced us the most was the richness of the soil on the prairie as compared with that of land in Missouri, which is wooded, and its greater suitability for the growing of important crops like wheat. But each Swiss immigrant must decide for himself whether he would find it more desirable to live in the woods. Even if Missouri with its woodlands possessed all of the advantages of Illinois as regards *trade and the raising of crops and livestock,* the prairies of Illinois still would be preferable to the dark, somber, and definitely less healthful woodlands. To be sure, Missouri also has its savannas, but they are not so numerous or extensive, and the soil of high-lying savannas there is definitely inferior to that of the Missouri wooded land as well as that of the Illinois prairies.

We did not settle on a navigable stream, because the rivers in the Midwest do not have steep banks, and there are frequent floods. For this reason there are few farms along the Ohio, Mississippi, and Missouri rivers. The disadvantages of these river valleys (bottoms) outweigh their advantages, even in places that do not flood, for the air is filled with the harmful mists of nearby swamps or pools of stagnant water, which from spring to fall also harbor millions of mosquitoes. These pests, which lurk in the shade during the day, spend the night robbing people of sleep by biting exposed parts of their bodies so that they become swollen and even infected. These pests are not to be found on our sunny prairies.

The stories told in Europe about the difficulties of marketing one's products if one lives inland are very erroneous. If only the new arrival had enough products to sell during his first years here, he would find a ready market. Of course, if he considered it too much trouble to take the two or three days' time to load a wagon with his products and have his horses or oxen haul it to the daily market in St. Louis, where such products can be sold readily and profitably, he could find persons willing to do it, of course for pay. We have learned already how the principal products, wheat, salted meat, etc. find a ready market.

III
Purchasing Privately Owned Land Already under Cultivation. Buying Federal Land. Taxes. Indians. Slavery.

Families with some means, *and they definitely should not come without reserve funds,* would do well to buy an already established farm in a carefully selected location. This is possible because of Americans' propensity to pull up stakes and move ever farther westward. A few of the many reasons to buy such a farm can be given here.

One is that few immigrants are able right off to do all of the work that has to be done to transform a parcel of land into a producing farm. It requires practice, for example, to split as many as one hundred to two hundred rails a day, and the American has had this practice since birth. He rarely uses a saw, and he knows how to build the log houses, so practical for the initial period, quickly and inexpensively. The same holds for constructing wells. It would be foolish to restrict one's choice of a farm site to places where there are springs, with the idea in mind of sparing the expense of constructing a well, when wells are so serviceable.

In the second place, the American, when he sells, is not inclined to take into consideration all he has done to improve his farm.

Thirdly, it saves the newcomer a considerable period of paying lodging for his family while a dwelling is being built, and it keeps him from having to wait a year for his first harvest.

In the fourth place, the newcomer who insists on establishing a farm from scratch has to do without an orchard for a few years, even though trees grow more rapidly here than in Switzerland.

A 160-acre homestead that has the basic necessities presently can be bought for sixteen hundred to eighteen hundred Swiss francs. It should have eighty acres of prairie (at least half of which should be fenced) and eighty acres of woods. It should have one or more log houses, some animal shelters built of logs, a place constructed of logs in which to store one's wheat, and a good brick-lined well.

It would be good if it also had an orchard, which usually is planted in apples, of which there are several excellent, especially tart varieties, and peaches, which do so well in America and require so little care that entire hedgerows of them can be grown easily. Pear and cherry trees are rare, but they are said to do well here, and it is difficult to understand why the American farmer neglects them. It cannot be that he only wishes to have trees that bear ripe fruit, for even his apples rarely are left to ripen before he eats them unless he has quantities of them.

But to get back to the matter at hand. A newcomer should attempt to buy the already established farm before harvest time because a considerable part of the thirty to forty acres of crop land will have been seeded, possibly ten to twelve acres in wheat, some in oats, and the rest in corn, except for acreage devoted to garden produce such as potatoes, etc.

One should, of course, exercise common sense in buying land from private individuals, although in Illinois it is never so risky as leaflets circulating in Europe would make it out to be, which leaflets are published in the eastern United States. The regularized surveying of land here, which will be described later, has prevented the confusion that often occurred in the older states and also in the St. Louis area, where land titles were not in good order when the territory was acquired from Spain, with the result that often two or more persons claim ownership of the same parcel of land.

Anyone considering the purchase of land in Illinois, however, if unfamiliar with prevailing practices and unwilling to take the word of an "esquire" (a courtesy title commonly used here after the surnames of officials), can visit the federal land office to determine the status of a parcel of land, as well as the taxes due, and the encumbrances on it, if any. The last-named instance is rare.

Fraud is less common than in Europe, for here swindlers are too proud to engage in petty fraud. Naïve German immigrants are more likely to be swindled by their own compatriots here, who, while professing the utmost concern for them, relieve them of their money. A good general rule to follow would be to buy only as much land as necessary during one's first years in this country because the newcomer's first impressions of land here usually are distorted and after only two years he may well have discarded his original plans for the land and formulated new ones. If an immigrant invests everything he has right off in order to finance a particular course of action, he will have limited his freedom to alter his plans, which may well turn out to have been ill-conceived.

To understand the process involved in the sale of public lands, it is helpful to know that land here has been divided into squares by surveyors using solely a compass and a hundred-link chain. The squares, or townships, were in turn divided into thirty-six smaller squares called sections, each a mile square in size. Each township's sections are numbered consecutively, from the northeasternmost to the northwesternmost, and then back, etc., the southeasternmost being the thirty-sixth. The sections were divided into four quarters containing 160 acres each, and these in turn were divided into four 40-acre squares. Illinois presently contains fifty-five counties of varying size, and these counties' boundaries have been changed constantly, depending partly on topography and in part on the concentration of population.

Our area lies partly in Madison County,[6] which comprises thirty-five

6. Probably "our area" included Looking Glass Prairie, which extends south into St. Clair Co., and into Bond Co., which is just to the east.

[actually twenty-three] townships (as defined above). Maps of each township are available at the area land office, where there are records concerning the status of each township and its various subdivisions, and these records tell about the special signs and markings made by the surveyor. These boundary markings usually are burned into trees, while on the prairies they are to be found on marking-poles set into small mounds of earth.

New arrivals are not expected to know all about this, so when they find a parcel of land they like, they should consult someone, preferably an official surveyor, who can tell them its exact designation respecting township, section, quarter, etc. With this information in hand the buyers should go to the area land office, pay $1.25 (roughly 45 batzen) per acre, and the records will certify his ownership.

This year the law has been amended, and now the buyer, after swearing under oath that the land is for his own use, is allotted forty acres. The oath is intended to discourage land speculators.

If one has the title to the land in hand and regularly pays the annual taxes, his ownership cannot be disputed. The tax collector calls at each household semiannually. At his first call of the year he takes note of the acreage, the livestock, the luxury articles, etc. The second time he collects the tax, which can vary from ½¢ to 1¢ per acre. A cent is roughly the equivalent of 3⅗ rappen. Notable is the fact that no taxes are due the first five years on land purchased from the government.

Property other than land is taxed relatively lower. This, again, allegedly is done to ensure that absentee land owners will pay a proper share of the taxes. These taxes, however, are only for the county government. Congress ordinarily does not assess taxes on the people, operating instead on the money it receives from the sale of public land, import duties, etc. Federal funds are beginning to accumulate, and the officials have the difficult time of deciding how best to expend it. New roads and canals constantly are being built (although railroads using steam engines are becoming more popular).

The form of government in most states is quite similar, with constitutions that rigorously guarantee *freedom of religion, politics, and trade.* Any male who spends ten days in the country is subject to military service, but it is in no sense a burdensome service, being limited to three musterings a year at which *ridiculously* little is accomplished. The Americans, at least here in the West, make a poor showing in formal military drill, but in a war they probably will prove to be deadly sharpshooters. The most serious actions involving armed conflict are forays against the Indians, but enough volunteers usually can be found to take part in them for the pay is good.

To guard against farmers being molested in their fields, several companies of volunteers were enlisted last fall for the term of a year to protect the borders against wild riffraff (Indians). Most of these volunteers are stationed in Missouri. They belong to the cavalry and have to care for their own horses. They receive their keep and monthly payments totaling 1314 Swiss francs annually for privates.[7] They are unquestionably subject to many hardships. No one in our area, however, stands in fear of Indians. To get here they would have to come several hundred miles through populated areas, which for them would border on the impossible. These barbarians usually raid border areas at harvest time, never venturing to face an enemy head on, so they have to be pursued like wolves hiding in the brush.

There is always opportunity in St. Louis to see some Indians, usually walking the streets wrapped in white woolen blankets, their faces painted all over. Most of them are chieftains seeking favorable trading opportunities.

Slavery has been completely abolished in Illinois. Every black is free when he becomes twenty-one.[8] In Missouri, where slavery is permitted, we have witnessed incidents that would arouse the pity of the most hardhearted. In St. Louis one can at all times see blacks being offered for sale. Prospective buyers poke and examine them before bidding on them at auction, ridiculing them the while. It is incomprehensible that such scenes can be witnessed in a republic in which the inhabitants profess a love of freedom. We leave it to the prospective emigrant to decide whether to emigrate to a state which permits such appalling conditions to continue.

7. This would come to $368 annually, which is improbably high.

8. Apparently Koepfli was not well-informed on the true situation of blacks in Illinois at this time. While Illinois was technically a free state, Negroes commonly were held as late as the 1840s as indentured, or registered, servants, a form of involuntary servitude which, for them, differed hardly at all from slavery. Even the "free" Negroes had few rights. Probably the settlers had little opportunity to observe, in the area they settled, the harsher realities.

As late as 1845 there were no Negroes or Mulattoes free, indentured, or "French," in Highland, or in the neighboring township of Helvetia, of which Highland was a part. Saline Twp., just to the north, had two free Negroes, one male and one female (Elise M. Wasser, *1845 Census of Madison County, Illinois* [Edwardsville, Ill., 1905], p. 58).

IV
Misconceptions Commonly Held by Europeans about the Mississippi Valley. Some Customs and Usages of Americans. Hunting in This Area.

Europeans in general harbor misconceptions about the United States, which accounts for the fact that suitable persons often decide not to emigrate. By far the greater part of Swiss emigrants have not been farm workers or laborers, but students, former schoolteachers, business apprentices, frustrated speculators, or impoverished aristocrats, in short, individuals least suited for the kind of life to be found here.

No doubt they read and heard how inexpensive land was here and what a ready market there was for farm products, but they neglected to consider that land needs to be worked in order to yield. No one should come here to buy land with the intention of hiring laborers for a few batzen as in Switzerland. Hard-working individuals with few means who know English and have farming experience can acquire a farm of their own, and even if it only be undeveloped Congress land, it should not be denigrated.

However, immigrants with modest means but no farming experience and no liking for hard work usually find that unless they work harder than they did at home, they cannot succeed here, and their money soon runs out. Education and elegant manners are of little help to immigrants, especially if they do not know English. Mechanics, laborers, or farm workers will do much better. Families with children accustomed to work can improve their lot very much here, but they should be primarily moved to come here by a realization of the steadily deteriorating conditions in Europe and the growing advantages of life in America, especially in the United States.

Emigration is particularly recommended for carpenters, blacksmiths, and wagon makers, and especially for persons who combine black-smithing with wagon making. Also needed here are tailors, tanners, and harness makers. Opportunities for other workers depend on circumstances.

But to return to the matter of Europeans' misconceptions. The ocean voyage, while not free from danger and certainly not from discomfort, is not so terrible as it has been pictured, and in some respects it is a pleasant experience. Most immigrants, having found what kind of life is available here, would not hesitate to take it again. As for danger, one's life might well be in greater jeopardy on one of the miserable craft in common use on most Swiss lakes than in a seaworthy three-master on the open seas. Our own crossing was far more unpleasant than the general run of them.

Tales circulating about the prevalence of poisonous snakes and flora, wild animals, and dangerous inhabitants also are exaggerated. It is true that there are several kinds of poisonous snakes in America. We have killed many a rattlesnake, but serious mishaps because of rattlers are rarely heard of, and Americans are not reticent about such things.

Poisonous plants certainly are no more of a danger than in Switzerland. A milk disease,⁹ to which cattle in very limited areas are subject, is attributed to poisonous plants, but the stories one hears about it differ widely and would appear to be unverifiable. It would be best, of course, to avoid buying land in areas that are suspect, even if only to obviate possible resale problems.

The only rapacious animals are wolves (as they are called here). A common variety of wolf here, somewhat larger than a fox, preys on young pigs and lambs. Other small animals such as ferrets, skunks, and marsupials that eat chickens can hardly be considered dangerous to man. The subject of Indians is discussed elsewhere in this work.

What immigrants find hardest are the *first few years* here, because of unfamiliarity with the land, its *language* and customs, and its *dwellings*. During this time perseverance and adherence to one's goals are vital. Europeans gain an erroneous impression of Americans' well-being because it is not obvious. They are not inclined to accumulate displayable wealth because they prefer to live as well as possible from day to day, confident that their children will succeed on their own in a country with a future as bright as America's.

If one can speak of an American character in a country where there is such a mixture of people from all nations, the majority of whom, to be sure, find it necessary to accommodate themselves to English customs and

9. The "milk sick" was a serious disorder, both for cattle and humans who drank their milk, not infrequently resulting in death. "It was also known as sick stomach, the trembles, the slows, and puking fever. The usual symptoms were irregular respiration, cold and clammy skin, subnormal temperature, constipation, and bloated abdomen. Not until the 1920s was it discovered that its cause was certain poisonous plants, usually eaten by the cattle late in the season when other forage might be scarce in the Midwest (Madge E. Pickard and R. Carlyle Buley, *The Midwest Pioneer, His Ills, Cures, and Doctors* [New York: Schuman, 1946], pp. 20–21).

the English language, it could be as follows. They are liberal and on the whole possess a good deal of common sense and sagacity as well as a very practical nature acquired in adapting to conditions here.

Americans give the impression of bragging about themselves and others, but this impression may well be unduly heightened by the way the German-Swiss interpret their English. They have no aesthetic appreciation, as is shown by their monotonous, crude music and singing and by their preference for everything loud, bright, and unusual.

There seem to be no class distinctions, laborers and farmers, for example, being the equal of, say, clergymen and merchants. For example, the man who supervised the construction of our house is an excellent Methodist preacher who also builds houses and plasters them, makes boots and shoes, makes and lays bricks, and owns land and cattle.

Americans customarily greet one another politely, but are not particularly inclined to tip their hats. The males are especially deferential to women. Fathers expend more care on the training of their daughters than on their sons. They seem very much at ease in social gatherings without being at all crude. They do appear to be competing with one another as to who can slump in his chair in the most relaxed manner.

The males chew their tobacco, and only the females venture to smoke pipes. Americans eat well, The *average* farmer expects to be served two kinds of meat at every meal of the day, but soup is rarely served. Fresh bread for every meal is baked in iron pans. Corn bread, very popular with Americans, has come to be a favorite of the Swiss, who could not bear it at first. Butter and usually also honey are found at every meal, at least during the summer.

Beverages are coffee or tea in the morning and evening and milk at noon. Many a Swiss remembers fondly the glass of wine he used to be served at mealtime in Switzerland, especially when a cup of insipid tea is set before him. Various kinds of strong wine can be purchased in St. Louis at prices ranging from twenty-seven to thirty-six batzen per gallon (roughly 2¼ Lucerne maas),[10] which makes them no more expensive for Americans than wine in Switzerland is for the Swiss. There are various kinds of hard liquor, made from wheat, rye, apples, and even peaches, but they are not favorites of the Europeans. The local beer does not compare with that in Switzerland, just as the apple wine cannot match Swiss pear wine.

---

10. Dictionaries define *maas* variously as a quart, a pot, a pint, a mug, or a stein, usually adding "especially of beer."

Although there is good hunting, we buy most of our venison, one of our favorite meats. We see deer at all times of the year, often even in our fields. In the winter they are to be seen in groups of ten to thirty, but in the summer they usually appear in small groups or singly. Most of them are a small kind, rarely weighing more than 100 to 120 pounds. They cost thirty-six batzen per head, including the hide, which always can be sold for eighteen batzen.

The rifles brought by the immigrants are not suitable for hunting most of the local wild game. Double-barreled guns seem unknown here. What is needed for fowl such as turkeys is a long, "duck-barrel" [gun] as it is called here. Perhaps more suitable would be a kind of field-*stutzer* using shot weighing roughly seventy to eighty to a pound.[11] With this *stutzer,* which costs thirty-six to sixty Swiss francs, one can shoot incredibly accurately from a distance of a hundred feet.

Local farmers often hold small shoots with a head of livestock etc. as a prize. This sort of affair easily could become a kind of sharpshooting event on a larger scale.[12]

The only open market is the daily one in St. Louis. It might prove profitable to hold an occasional exchange and livestock market in our area, advertising by means of leaflets.

V

Advice to Emigrants, Based on Our Experience, as to What to Bring with Them, What Route to Take to Get Here, and How Best to Cope with Certain Problems They are Likely to Encounter

Given the detailed information that has been provided in this writing, the prospective emigrant can, after due deliberation, decide for himself whether this is an area that would provide what he is seeking in the way of a place to live.

11. Grimm defines *stutzer* as a short weapon, as does Muret-Sanders, adding that formerly it was called "musketoon," which the current Webster's unabridged defines as a "short musket with a large bore."

12. In 1863 Salomon and Joseph Koepfli donated a 31-acre tract of land for use by area sharpshooters, and a big shoot was held on July 4 of that year. A year later the

We have outlined both the advantages and disadvantages of this area. Whether or not an immigrant finds the kind of life here he hoped for will depend primarily on himself. As has been indicated, it is not a place for persons who are happy only when taking part in a continual round of social activities such as parties, dances, bees, weddings, christenings, concerts, and fancy dress balls. Anyone wishing such activities must bring his own social-minded company with him or not come here at all.

Most English- and American-born persons here apparently frown on such frivolity. Many of them would feel more comfortable at a fanatical gathering at which all worldly pleasures are foresworn. Excepted are the so called Yankees, or the settlers from the eastern states or New England, who seem to take a greater interest in social life.

Swiss, then, who after due deliberation have decided to emigrate, should bring the following articles with them:

1. These foodstuffs for the voyage (if it is planned to embark at Havre where it is practically impossible to find things of this kind): a good supply of Swiss cheese which will stand them in good stead); some dried fruit (especially of an acid variety such as prunes); some well-smoked meat, ham, tongue, and sausages (but not salted meat, there being too little fresh water aboard to wash out the salt, so it can only be thrown overboard).

2. The following articles that will be found to be especially useful here: enough [good] linen for several years, especially shirts, for only flax and cotton products are usually available here; [other] clothes, [such as] overcoats with cowls (of good sturdy material instead of the fashionable French clothes in vogue here, especially if farming is to be engaged in); good, coarse linen garments practical for summer wear; sturdy reinforced shoes and boots of good leather (for local leather is poorly worked, probably having been tanned too rapidly) and hobnails (the local ones being unsuitable); bedding, especially for the voyage, consisting of good, small mattresses, simple but well-filled featherbeds and pillows, and woolen blankets; seeds of various kinds, including turnips (especially of the large variety, suitable for hog feed) all enclosed in well-stoppered bottles to protect them from the sea air; flowers (for example carnations) of the simple Swiss varieties so admired here; oil-producing plants like rape, together with haircloth for oil-pressing, and canvas; some plum, cherry, pear, and possibly grape pits (the seedlings and stock we brought having died from neglect and from having been out of the soil too long);

---

national American Sharpshooters Society was organized in Highland, and it held its first festival in May 1865.

and fir and pine cones (on the chance that they might be grown here to line future avenues).

3. The following items from Havre: a good supply of butter (which is excellent there), flour, eggs, sugar, coffee, potatoes, noodles (which can be prepared easily aboard ship), a sort of twice-baked bread (which can be baked to order in quantity for one if ordered in advance, and which should be taken instead of zwieback, which is so hard to chew that we left untouched the huge amount we had dragged aboard), red wine, which, if any is left over, can be taken up the Mississippi easily (but no white wine, for that available in Havre does not keep well on the ocean), and cream, mixed with sugar, heated, and bottled, which is likely to keep during most of the voyage. As for vinegar the minimum amount one can take is specified by law.

A surplus amount of all foodstuffs should be taken on the chance that the voyage will be longer than expected. Chests for transporting one's goods should be flat-topped and lightweight but reinforced with iron bands and small enough to be carried by two men when fully packed. No merchandise should be taken for trading purposes, since profits from this type of operation can be made only by persons familiar with markets here.

Ordinary farm tools, harness, and saddles can be bought in St. Louis fairly inexpensively, and iron products are lower in price there than in Switzerland, and they are not enough higher than in seacoast cities to warrant laying out money for them before they actually are going to be used, especially in view of the prevailing rates of interest. An exception would be flax combs, both fine and coarse.

Drafts are the best medium of exchange, that is, drafts on reputable banks in United States seaports. The Iselin Brothers in Basel can be relied upon to transmit drafts to their brother in New York. These bills of exchange can be cashed everywhere by the United States Bank, but first they must be sent to New York for approval, the answer being forwarded to us via St. Louis, the entire procedure taking only four weeks. Any money one does not need to draw can be left on deposit to earn good interest. We had only the most satisfactory dealings with the Iselin Brothers in Basel and New York, and we have found them to have their clients' best interests at heart.

Emigrants should be sure to take enough money to cover travel expenses. Spanish or French money also is used, French five-livre taler being exchanged here in St. Louis for 93 ¾ cents, or roughly 33 batzen, 7 rappen. Old French, Swiss, or German money is unknown here.

Havre is the best port of departure for Swiss because it can be reached most quickly and inexpensively by stagecoach. Travelers who wish to economize as much as possible should take along food rather than eat in the expensive post houses. It will be necessary, however, to have one's bottles refilled with some kind of fruit drink from time to time.

The steamboat transportation between Paris and Havre is not to be recommended unless it has improved in the past year or more. Excess baggage (not permitted on the stagecoach) should be taken to St. Louis near Basel or to Muehlhausen, whichever is closer or more convenient, several weeks beforehand. Such baggage can be sent from either place well-insured but inexpensively to Havre. Wagons loaded with cotton and other material are always arriving there and usually returning to Havre empty. Best of all would be to write to the Swiss firm of Wanner, Langer, and Company in Havre. These dependable men will be able and willing to give the most reliable and up-to-date information concerning the cheapest way of sending excess baggage through France as well as to report what ships will be sailing to New Orleans at particular times.

Traveling to the Mississippi Valley via New Orleans is far preferable to coming by way of New York, as is evident from our short account of our journey. Provided that travel during the hottest weather is avoided, there is no more danger in traveling by way of New Orleans than via New York. Passage should be arranged with the captain of the ship rather than with commission agents. A warning is hereby issued to avoid a man by the name of Barbe, who preys on many an unwary emigrant. Wanner, Langer, and Company, on the other hand, are highly recommended as being helpful to inexperienced Swiss.

It might be a good idea to check with the captain well before departure to ensure that enough good water in sufficient quantities has been brought aboard to permit everyone to receive his specified daily allotment. Furthermore, it should be specified in writing that the captain pay the sick bay fee (one dollar per person, I believe), which charge may be affected by whether or not a physician is aboard.

Sea crossings vary in length from forty to seventy days, depending in large part on the weather. Seasickness is induced by the constant rocking of the ship, and when this becomes excessive, the traveler is likely to experience an unpleasant nausea, much like the sensation one experiences during a storm on a lake craft that is being tossed about like a cork. If the sea is rough when the voyage begins, vomiting will become general within a few hours. In a violent storm the rocking motion often becomes so pronounced that more and more travelers are forced to vomit.

The closer one is to the center of the ship, the less one is subjected to rocking. It is advisable to force oneself to stay on deck as much as possible and to lie down only during the most severe attacks of seasickness. Persons who lie on their bunks continually during the first few days often become too weak to get up later on. No members of our family experienced severe seasickness, and some were spared completely. Preventive medication is ineffective, but vomiting possibly could be eased by taking effervescent powder (*Sal. essent. tart* with magnesia).

One should refrain from giving importunate sailors too much to drink, to prevent the likelihood of disorderly conduct. One's worst clothes should be worn during the voyage. Only the clothes one leaves packed away withstand the destructive effects of salt water.

Passengers arriving in New Orleans may report to Theodor Nicolet, the Swiss commercial consul, who is reputedly a pleasant man. Several steamboats leave New Orleans for St. Louis each week except in the winter. The trip costs cabin passengers about ten dollars; deck passengers pay four to five dollars. By helping carry firewood aboard one can cut the cost of passage a dollar, but this might prove to be somewhat onerous work. The trip usually lasts from six to ten days.

Much French is spoken in New Orleans, less in St. Louis, although there are still many French there. On arriving in the United States one must make use of an English dictionary. English is not difficult for a German to learn, especially if he knows Latin or French. Books and tutors can prove a help with the written language. No language requires more practice in speaking than English. One should possess a grammar book as well as a dictionary.

Much effort has been expended in Germany during the past few years on the planning of joint or cooperative settlements. There was talk of a Wuerttemberg venture and then of a Swiss one. In the case of the former, the advantages of close cooperation were described in lofty terms, but the good people did not take into consideration what would be involved to hold such a group *together* when the members began to feel that too much was being asked of them for the good of the group and they took it into their individual heads to try their luck on their own.

Most cooperative attempts of this kind have failed. Many persons of means have lost everything they had through their well-meant efforts to make such ventures succeed. The sad experience of a Hanoverian may be cited as a case in point. This well-intentioned man laid out the travel money for a group of poor people from his neighborhood. In addition he spent a good deal of money buying everything that was thought necessary to establish a successful colony. The party [of about thirty families] left Europe (on a leased ship) in 1819. After they arrived in this country the man selected some not particularly suitable land [near Vandalia, Illinois], saw to its fencing and plowing, and to the erection of buildings. When it came to assigning each person his plot, so that planting could be undertaken, no one wanted to lift a finger for the common good, and each of them began looking elsewhere for something better. Poor [Ferdinand] Ernst could not meet his financial obligations and died of grief. He had left Europe with a fortune of roughly a hundred thousand francs, but his family was left destitute.[13]

The only successful cooperative venture of this kind was that of the clergyman [Johann Georg] Rapp, but the members of his group were held together by his fantastic sermons and by sectarian religious principles. But now the members have separated into two groups, and the end of the venture cannot be far away.[14]

The benefits to be derived from a cooperative settlement of German immigrants could be tremendous, but with too much insistence on cooperative effort such a project would be doomed in advance. At most the transport of baggage through France and the chartering of passage on a ship could be arranged cooperatively.

Written agreements made outside the country are not valid in the United States. Thus one would be well advised not to take along workers from Europe in the expectation of benefiting thereby in the fabulous new

13. Ernst was the first German to write at length about Illinois. He had toured the state the year before the publication of his book in 1820, visiting the Sangamon country, and Vandalia; he decided to settle the last-named place. Fever killed many of the families. His book: *Bemerkungen auf einer Reise durch das Innere der Vereinigten Staaten von Nord Amerika im Jahre 1819* (Hildesheim: J. D. Gerstenberg, 1820). The part of Ernst's work dealing with Illinois was translated by E. P. Baker and published as "Travels in Illinois in 1819," *Illinois Historical Society, Transactions,* 1903, pp. 155–65.

14. Rapp's New Harmony colony is described in *A Documentary History of the Harmony Society in the Indiana Decade, 1814–1824* (Indianapolis: Indiana Historical Society, 1975), by Karl J. R. Arndt. Selling their New Harmony property to Robert Owen in 1825, Rapp and his followers established a very successful communal settlement at Economy, Pa.

country. Such workers, on arriving in this country, become so entranced by the seductive visions of freedom and equality that even the most devoted of them are likely to succumb and desert families they have served for many years.

When public lands were opened to individuals, a certain man called Schmidt from Boston bought fifteen hundred acres of land, half of it covered with a stand of good trees. It lies roughly nine miles to the northwest of us and appears to be good land, although its location leaves something to be desired. He is prepared to sell the land for the same price he paid the government for it, but the buyer must take the entire holding. This land might well provide a good living for several families. Eight to twelve farms could be established on it. At present the land is still completely undeveloped, but the good virgin forest must be taken into account.

It is necessary to bring this monograph to a close. Our original intention was to say more with fewer words, but even so we believe we have omitted much verbiage. All that is written here is concurred in by every member of our family.

Written in March 1833

                    Kaspar Koepfli [Sr.], physician

At this point I find it necessary to share with the public an excerpt of a letter I received on June 28, written by my brother Salomon on May 13, 1833. Although many of my efforts and many a beautiful hope of mine have come to nothing, I cannot withhold from the public these well-meant, and doubtless well-founded, warnings expressed by my dear brother, for from day to day I am more convinced of the truth of what he writes me.

The Editor [Kaspar Koepfli, Jr.]

Dear Brother,

We could not read without misgivings your recent letters which dealt so enthusiastically with the question of joint emigration and settlements and which extolled the central issue of Swiss emigration, the beckoning star of the emigrants, New Switzerland. But we had pictured things the same way and formed the same unrealistic ideas before we left Old Switzerland. We, too, dreamed of large group emigrations of the cream of Switzerland hither, building cities, designing community schools and churches, and even holding property in common.

But we ask ourselves: "What has become of all this?" Only too clearly we are beginning to see that realization of such a commune is something bordering on the impossible. Only our experience and arrival here make it possible to understand this. Such joint ventures usually are already completely disintegrating, and the initial goals rejected by most of the members long before they land in this country.

At this point I must reiterate: "*In such a society, the greater the insistence on cooperative activity, the greater the rapidity of its demise.*" It is considered a kindness to shelter naïve persons from swindle during their journey, to tell them in carefully worded correspondence the best time to leave their fatherland, to give them good advice as to the kind of ships on which to sail, and to counsel them as to the best route to take through France. But to let them travel in a completely cooperative manner is like burdening them with the devil. Arguments, quarelling and disunity usually follow in a few days.

Whoever has been elected to manage the group's affairs has the worst and sorriest role. He sows effort and accommodation and reaps rank ingratitude. This one claims that he is being deceived, that one insists he has been cheated, and soon there is total dissolution, which results in such enmity that when the group arrives in America most of its members fervently long to settle as far from their faithless, selfish, thievish traveling companions as possible. The leader of such a group usually has his character blackened so badly that his reputation suffers for an indefinite period. The picture I have just drawn is not one I have made up out of thin air. Unfortunately we witnessed it all too often.

Whoever wishes to emigrate may well do so as a member of a group, but without sharing expenses or holding provisions in common, etc. Let the more experienced lead the others but never attempt to serve as guardian, or ingratitude will be his lot, and the greatest honesty on his part will never enable him to lay low the suspicion that he is acting entirely in his own interest.

It is best that the emigrants not hold too fantastic a picture of the new country, or they will find the first years here harder to bear. They would save themselves many disappointments if they harbored more modest expectations than the ordinary emigrants. Above all it is necessary to dispel the somewhat overly favorable picture of this country which the usual reader has formed from Duden's book, without any fault on his part.

You may accept as *valid* anything we have written, but *do not pass lightly* over what we have described as *difficult,* for it would be unfortunate if you were to imagine conditions to be *any more favorable* than we actually have described them.

On your entire journey you will seek in vain the picturesque landscapes in which Switzerland abounds (especially entering the United States via New Orleans). New Orleans has a very unhealthful location, surrounded by swamps. In fact, the bed of the Mississippi actually lies higher than the city. For this reason, only speculators, mostly Frenchmen, are to be found there. They remain for a few years in order to be able to make enough money in business to take back and spend in the motherland.

Having experienced a rude awakening in New Orleans with his first look at America, the immigrant proceeds up the Mississippi in a steamboat. From it he sees nothing but vast woods as far as the eye can reach, except for some country stores and dwellings at intervals, grandly bearing the names of world famous cities. There are few settlements, for the reasons touched upon in general at the end of chapter 2 [of part 5] of our little account.

St. Louis is an important place, comparing favorably in size with many a Swiss city, and it is growing constantly in the facilities it has to offer. In the summer there are often twelve to eighteen steamboats on the river front. Incidentally, the steam engine appears to be more common in the United States than elsewhere.

Our locality cannot compare with magnificent regions in Switzerland, but in our opinion it surpasses all places we have seen here in the West. Nature has outdone herself here, where beauty is combined with utility, needing only the hand of man to make it an ideal settlement. We are twenty-six miles from the Mississippi, not so near as you seemed to think.

You asked in your last letter whether Illinois really was preferable to Missouri. I refer you to our last communication, and at this point I will add that we can only recommend Illinois to our Swiss compatriots. Illinois has so many advantages that it certainly will surpass most of its sister states. The advantages in general surpass those of other states, and for anyone interested in owning land, there is no place where the quality of the soil is better.

It only serves the interest of St. Louis to demean this state. Between our state and St. Louis, Missouri, flows the Mississippi, which at this point is more than a mile and a half wide. Most of the foodstuffs for this city come from Illinois, but the Illinois farmer is by no means solely dependent on the St. Louis market. Efforts are being made to develop Alton, an Illinois town above St. Louis, near the mouth of the Missouri River.

In the winter it sometimes happens that ice interrupts the steamboat service connecting us with St. Louis, causing a significant rise in prices of commodities there because the Missouri side cannot yet supply the city's needs. Now St. Louis is trying to influence all settlers to proceed up the Missouri River by discrediting Illinois, primarily by pointing to the Mississippi [American] Bottom as swampy and unhealthful. Such propaganda can sway credulous persons and keep them from investigating properly on their own. Far be it from me to attempt to lure anyone to our area to serve our own interests.

I have written you these truths as a well-meant warning. Equally true is the fact that we are doing very well. The first difficult years are behind us, our hopes have been fulfilled, and we are looking to a bright future. In short, we are feeling more at home all the time, and gradually we are beginning to develop some aptitude in the language, which seemed so difficult to us at first. There is always more than enough work for everyone, which leaves little time for getting bored.

Occasionally we buy another piece of land, and then we are faced with the pleasant problem of how to put it to the best use. Already we are farming on a fairly large scale. We have a hundred cattle, forty draft oxen, and a good many horses. A few weeks ago we tried cheese-making, and after a number of failures, we succeeded in producing something that could be termed Swiss cheese.

As you probably have guessed, we spend many an evening discussing conditions in Switzerland and weighing the prospects of improvement in those conditions. We are happiest of all to be able to report that we are all in the best of health. The climate here appears to agree with us. The weather has been ideal up to now, and everyone is expecting a good harvest.

Joseph Suppiger's father and his traveling companions arrived here without mishap.[15]

Fare you well, and give our best wishes to all who cherish freedom and justice and who continue to be our friends.

New Switzerland in Illinois, May 13, 1833

> With regards from your family, Your brother Salomon

15. The traveling companions of Suppiger's father (Jacob *Joseph* Aloys) were Suppiger's half brother Melchior, his uncle Johann, and his cousins Xaver, Bernhardt, Johanna, and Regina. Suppiger's father was the first Swiss to die in the new colony, only three months after his arrival.

Epilogue
Appendix
Bibliography
Index

EPILOGUE

By the end of the 1830s about two dozen new Swiss surnames, coming from many cantons in addition to Lucerne, had been added to New Switzerland and environs. In 1837 a town site of about a hundred acres was laid out and divided into over five hundred lots. Significantly, in order to promote development of the town as more than just a Swiss community, the town's citizens were dissuaded from naming it Helvetia and agreed to call it Highland, the name it bears today. Two streets were named Zschokke and Troxler, a third after the great Swiss educator, Pestalozzi, and three after Washington, Franklin, and Jefferson. By 1845 Highland had grown to 409 inhabitants, 243 male and 166 female, and "greater" New Switzerland was at least twice as large. However, though the Swiss may have been in the majority, the native American element was also substantial.[1]

Although Highland has been credited by John Paul von Grueningen as being by 1870 "the largest rural Swiss colony in the United States," and by Metraux as probably being "at one time . . . the largest Swiss rural community outside Switzerland itself,"[2] it was never, even in the beginning, exclusively Swiss. The new town quickly established itself as the center of commerce and small industry for the surrounding area. Thus, slowly and inevitably, Highland became Americanized. But its Swiss heritage is still proudly remembered and vestiges of its Swiss background survive and still make for distinctive differences.

It remains now to tell very briefly what became of the original party of Koepflis and Suppigers.

Near the end of their first decade in New Switzerland, Dr. Koepfli, or "Father" Koepfli as he was commonly called, announced: "Now just ten years have gone by since we emigrated from the old country in 1831; at that time I made a promise to my friends to visit them in ten years, and since it seems to be fitting just now, let us leave here toward the end of March." Thus all of the six Koepflis who arrived in 1831 returned to Switzerland in 1841. Bernard, who never liked his new environment, remained in Switzerland, where he died in 1882. Salomon and Joseph returned to Highland in the summer of 1843, sometime after the death of their mother, who had died May 31, 1843, until the last steadfast in her adherance to the

1. See Elise M. Wasser, *1845 Census of Madison County, Illinois* (Edwardsville, Ill., 1905).
2. John Paul von Grueningen, ed., *The Swiss in the United States* (Madison, Wis., 1940), p. 24; Guy Serge Metraux, "Social and Cultural Aspects of Swiss Immigration into the United States in the Nineteenth Century" (Ph.D. dissertation, Yale Univ., 1949).

Catholic faith. Dr. Koepfli and Rosa, who had married Jacob Eggen in 1836, remained in Switzerland until their return to Highland in 1849, Rosa dying of cholera within a few weeks after her arrival. Dr. Koepfli, while in Switzerland, had tried to publish his reputedly voluminous political writings but had been informed that they would have to be censored. The only work of this period which we know to have been published was his *Spiegel von Amerika,* a guide to those considering emigration. He died in Highland on December 11, 1854, at the age of eighty, twenty-three years after his arrival in New Switzerland. On New Year's Day 1855 a funeral procession more than a quarter of a mile long, including more than eighty vehicles followed to his grave site.

Joseph and Salomon Koepfli remained closely associated, living together and working for the development of Highland until Salomon's death in 1869 at the age of fifty-five. Joseph, who never married, died in 1874. In 1848, Salomon Koepfli married Elisa Gysin, by whom he had one son, Eugene, who lived most of his life in Geneva. After his first wife's death, Salomon married Rosalie Brodtbeck in 1865. Their only child was Joseph Otto (1866–1942), the father of Dr. Joseph Blake Koepfli.

About Anton Suppiger the records are scanty. He suffered from malaria as early as the fall of 1831, before the family moved from St. Louis to New Switzerland. For a time he carried the mail weekly between Highland and St. Jacob. He is the presumed author, "A. S.", of a long article in the *Highland Herald* of December 1, 1888, describing conditions in Switzerland which led to the emigration of the Koepflis and Suppigers in 1831. He married Monica Wickenhauser on April 14, 1842, and died September 20, 1900.

Though the Koepflis played an important role in establishing Highland as a town in 1837, it was Joseph Suppiger who took the principal initiative in having it platted and whose enterprise contributed most greatly to its subsequent development.[3] He worked tirelessly and effectively to advance the interests of the community. The esteem in which he was held is indicated by the publication following his death on April 24, 1861, in the *Highland Bote* of his obituary consisting of two full columns in each of three successive issues.

---

3. He married Mary Thorp on March 22, 1837, and they moved into the first house built in the newly established town.

A P P E N D I X

Batz(en): 10 rappen (centimes) or ¹⁄₁₀ of a Swiss franc or roughly 2¾ cents
Brabant taler: *See* Taler, Brabant
Centime (or rappen): ¹⁄₁₀ of a batz or ¹⁄₁₀₀ of a Swiss franc (3.6 centimes or
    rappen equal 1 cent)
Florin (gulden): Approximately 40 cents
Franc de France (livre): 100 centimes or 20 sols (sous) or 19 cents
Franc (Swiss): 10 batzen or 100 rappen or 28 cents
Gulden: *See* Florin
Livre. *See* Franc de France)
Louis d'or: Replaced by the 20-franc piece with the introduction of the franc
    currency in 1803 France
Napoleon: A 20-franc piece
"Pitt" [bit]: A Spanish real or 12½ cents
Rappen. *See* Centime
"Shilling": A term formerly used in New York for the Spanish real (12½
    cents)
Sol (sou): 5 French centimes or ¹⁄₂₀ of a franc de France
Sou: *See* Sol
Taler, Brabant: 36 batzen and 6½ rappen or approximately 1 dollar
Taler, French 5-franc (French 5-livre): 94 cents
Taler, French 5-livre: *See* Taler, French 5-franc
Taler, Mexican or Spanish: Equal to a U.S. dollar, according to Suppiger
Taler, Spanish-⅛: 1 real or 1 "pitt" or 12½ cents

Are: 100 square meters
Aune de France: Roughly 2 yards (although Suppiger defined a yard as ¾ of
    an aune, which would make it 1.413 meters instead of .9144 meter)
French inch: *See* Inch, French

See Suppiger's explanation of units of currency, measure, and weight at the end of
part 3.

Hektar: 100 ares (10,000 square meters) or 2.471 acres

Inch, French: 11¼ to an American foot or 33¾ to an American yard

Joch: 57.55 ares or 1.422 acres

Jucharte: 36 ares or ⁹⁄₁₀ of an acre

Klaster: Shorter but higher than an American (4′ x 4′ x 8′) cord

Maas (masz): Customarily a 1½-liter measure (although according to Dr. Koepfli a Lucerne maas was 2 liters)

Masz: *See* Maas

Morgen: 25.532 ares or almost ⅔ of an acre

Poststunde (land league): 4.83 kilometers or roughly 3 American miles

Stunde: Roughly 3 English or American miles

Viertel (Sursee): Roughly ⅔ of a bushel

Loth: ½ ounce (although 9% heavier, according to Suppiger)

BIBLIOGRAPHY

The following list represents only those sources of direct relevance to the *Reisebericht,* which deals with a limited time period. Much fuller bibliographies and descriptions of sources are appended to *The Swiss on Looking Glass Prairie* (Betty Coats, compiler) and Max Schweizer's *Neu-Schweizerland: Planung, Gruendung und Entwicklung,* described more fully below. A useful recent selective bibliography on the Swiss in America is Leo Schelbert's *Swiss in North America,* published as no. 3 of the Balch Institute Reading Lists (Philadelphia, 1974). The most comprehensive source of information regarding research on the Swiss in America is contained in the *Newsletter* of the Swiss American Historical Society, published since 1965, currently edited by Heinz K. Meier, Old Dominion University, Norfolk, Virginia.

PUBLICATIONS

Abbott, John C.
For his introductions to translations of books by early nineteenth-century Swiss settlers see entries under Spahn, Betty A., and Spahn, Raymond J., eds., *New Switzerland in Illinois;* and Koepfli, Salomon, *The Story of the Settling of Highland.*
Coats, Betty Spindler, comp. *The Swiss on Looking Glass Prairie: A Century and a Half, 1831–1981.* Edited by Raymond J. Spahn. Foreword by Joseph Blake Koepfli. Edwardsville, Ill.: Friends of Lovejoy Library and the Highland Historical Society, 1983.
For translations of German-language writings made under Coats's auspices see entries under Zschokke, Rolf, "Beitrag;" and Koepfli, Kaspar, *Licht- & Schattenseite.*
Driesner, Manfred Hartwin.
For his translation of writings about early nineteenth-century Swiss settlers see entry under Eggen, Jacob, "Chronicles of Early Highland."
Duden, Gottfried. *Bericht ueber eine Reise nach den westlichen Staaten Nord-Amerika's und einen mehrjaehrigen Aufenthalt am Missouri (in den Jahren 1824, '25, '26, und 1827) in Bezug auf Auswanderung und Ueber-voelkerung.* Elberfeld, 1829.
In the foreword to his 2d ed. (Bonn, 1834) Duden refuted reports that Suppiger and the Koepflis had attacked his work.

————. *Report on a Journey to the Western States of North America and a Stay of Several Years along the Missouri (during the Years 1824, '25, '26, and 1827).* Edited and Translated by George H. Kellner, Elsa Nagel, Adolf E. Schroeder, and W. M. Senner. Concerning Emigration and Overpopulation and Its Significance for the Domestic and Political Situation of the Europeans, edited by James W. Goodrich. Columbia: The State Historical Society of Missouri and University of Missouri Press, 1980.

Eggen, Jacob. *Aufzeichnungen aus Highlands Gruendungszeit zum fuenfzigjaehrigen Jublilaeum.* Highland, Ill., 1888.

————. "Aufzeichnungen von Jacob Eggen." *Deutsch-Amerikanische Geschichtsblaetter,* 5 (1905): Heft 1, 52–55; Heft 2, 13–54; Heft 3, 1–36. Contains material expurgated from Eggen's 1888 *Aufzeichnungen.*

————. "Chronicles of Early Highland." A translation by Manfred Hartwin Driesner of Eggen's 1888 *Aufzeichnungen* and other previously untranslated writings. Comprises book 2 of *New Switzerland in Illinois,* edited by Betty A. Spahn and Raymond J. Spahn.

Der Eidgenosse. Sursee, January 31, March 21, May 30, August 1, and September 16, 1833. These five issues carry Suppiger advertisements and correspondence.

Der Eidgenosse. Lucerne, February 9, 1855. Contains the only known obituary of the senior Dr. Kaspar Koepfli.

Gerke, Heinrich Christian. *Der Nordamerikanische Rathgeber, nebst den in den Jahren 1831 und 1832 in der Union gemachten Reisebeobachtungen.* Hamburg, 1833.

Grueningen, John Paul von, ed. *The Swiss in the United States.* Madison, Wis., 1940.

Huber, Heinrich. *Bericht ueber das Auswandern nach Amerika.* Ragatz, 1845. Pages 16–21 concern Highland, which Huber treats favorably.

Kaeser, Jennie Latzer. For her translations of books by the founders of New Switzerland see entries under Koepfli, Kaspar, "Mirror of America"; and Koepfli, Salomon, *The Story of the Settling of Highland.*

Koepfli, Joseph Blake. *Koepfli: A Partial History of the Family.* Privately printed, 1981. See entry under Coats, Betty Spindler, comp., *The Swiss on Looking Glass Prairie* for his foreword regarding events preceding his forebears' emigration.

Koepfli, Kaspar. *Die Licht- & Schattenseite von New Switzerland in Nordamerika.* Sursee, 1833.

This work also was published (with slightly altered title) as part 5 of the *Reisebericht*, 2d ed., where it lacks the introductory paragraph by the editor, the junior Dr. Koepfli. A translation of this work under the auspices of Betty Spindler Coats appeared serially as "The Light and Dark Side of New Switzerland in America" in the *Highland News Leader*, November 6, 1974–January 8, 1975.

———. *Spiegel von Amerika: Praktische Grundsaetze, Belehrungen und Warnungen fuer Auswanderer nach Amerika: Nebst zwei Reiseberichten, einer Ansicht der Stadt Highland und Plan seiner Umgebung.* Lucerne, 1849.

———. "Mirror of America: Practical Principles, Advice and Warnings for Emigrants to America."

A translation by Jennie Latzer Kaeser of Kaspar Koepfli's *Spiegel von Amerika,* comprises book 1 of *New Switzerland in Illinois,* edited by Betty A. Spahn and Raymond J. Spahn.

Koepfli, Salomon. *Geschichte der Ansiedlung von Highland.* Highland, Ill., 1859.

This work was reprinted serially in *Deutsch-Amerikanische Geschichtsblaetter,* 5 (1905): Heft 1, 53–59; Heft 2, 13–54; and Heft 3, 1–6. It appeared serially also as "Beitraege zur Geschichte unserer Ansiedlung" in the *Highland Bote,* ?/?/1859–July 27, 1860.

———. *The Story of the Settling of Highland.* Translated by Jennie Latzer Kaeser. Edited by Raymond J. Spahn. Introduction by John C. Abbott. Privately printed, 1970.

Kaeser's translation of Koepfli's *Geschichte* also appeared serially in the *Highland News Leader,* beginning October 13, 1971.

———. *Neu-Schweizerland in den Jahren 1831 und 1841.* Lucerne, 1842.

Metraux, Guy Serge. "Social and Cultural Aspects of Swiss Immigration into the United States in the nineteenth Century." Ph.D. diss., Yale University, 1949.

Der Nordamerikaner.

A St. Gallen weekly, the issue for July 3, 1833, contains a letter from Giovanni Paoli Zoya and "A. M." in Hickory Grove (Pocahontas, Illinois) to "dear Mother and Sister" in Switzerland, written March 16, 1833. It tells of buying land "nine miles from Dr. Koepfli, in conjunction with Mr. Tscharner," after staying more than a month in New Switzerland (pp. 146–51). The issue for December 13, 1833, contains excerpts from a letter by "Tscharner Brothers" (recipient not named). Dated St. Louis, April 18, 1833, it tells of buying a hundred acres of land "on Shoal Creek, nine miles north of New Switzerland" (pp. 57–58).

Peck, John Mason. *A Gazetteer of Illinois.* Jacksonville, Ill., 1834.

A second edition was published in Philadephia in 1837.

Schelbert, Leo. "On Becoming an Emigrant: A Structural View of Eighteenth-

and Nineteenth-Century Swiss Data." *Perspectives in American History.* 7 (1973): 441–95.

Schweizer, Max. *Bilder aus Neu-Schweizerland, 1831–1900: Werden und Wachstum einer Schweizerischen Einwanderersiedlung in den Vereinigten Staaten von Nordamerika (Madison County, Illinois).* Zug, 1978.

———. *A Portrait of New Switzerland, 1831–1900: Origin and Development of a Swiss Settlement in the United States of North America (Madison County, Illinois).* Translated by Harold Schweizer and Lynn Schweizer. Zug, 1979.

———. *Neu-Schweizerland, 1831–1880: Genese und Funktion einer Schweizerischen Einwanderer Siedlung in den USA.* Diss., Universitaet Zurich, 1980.

———. *Neu-Schweizerland: Planing, Gruendung und Entwicklung einer Schweizerischen Einwanderersied lung in den Vereinigten Staaten von Nordamerika (Madison County, Illinois).* Zug, 1980.

Schweizerbote, Der aufrichtige und erfahrene, no. 35, 1833, *passim.*
Heinrich Zschokke edited this Aarau weekly 1804–42.

"Schweizerische Auswanderungsgesellschaft." *Der Nordamerikaner.* No. 8, May 26, 1933, p. 29.

Shelley, Jane, and Wasser, Elise M. *Naturalization and Intentions of Madison County, Illinois: An Index, 1816–1900.* Edwardsville, Ill., 1983.

Spahn, Betty A., and Spahn Raymond J., eds. *New Switzerland in Illinois as Described by Two Early Swiss Settlers, Kaspar Koepfli, in Spiegel von Amerika, and Johann Jacob Eggen, in Aufzeichnungen aus Highlands Gruendungzeit.* Translated by Jennie Latzer Kaeser and Mansfred H. Driesner. Foreword, "The Pioneer Writings about Highland," by John C. Abbott. Edwardsville, Ill: Friends of Lovejoy Library, 1977.
"Mirror of America," Kaeser's translation of Koepfli's *Spiegel von Amerika,* comprises book 1; Driesner's translation of Eggen's *Aufzeichnungen,* under the title "Chronicles of Early Highland," comprises book 2.

Spahn, Raymond J. "German Accounts of Early Nineteenth Century Life in Illinois." *Papers on Language and Literature,* 14, no. 4 (Fall 1978): 473–88.
Pages 485–86 concern Highland.
For Spahn's role in editing works by nineteenth-century Swiss settlers see entries under Coats, Betty Spindler, comp., *The Swiss on Looking Glass Prairie;* and Koepfli, Salomon, *The Story of the Settling of Highland.*

Spencer, Amos Patrick. *Centennial History of Highland, Illinois, 1837–1937.* Highland: Highland Centennial Association, 1937.
Spencer's book, parts of which had appeared in the *Highland News Leader,* was reprinted in 1978 by the Highland Historical Society. The

reprint contained an index by Carolyn Werder, a preface by Russell Hoffman, and a foreword by William J. Tudor.

————, ed. "History of Highland." *Highland News Leader,* January 24, 1933–January 25, 1935.

This history contained some excerpts from Eggen's *Aufzeichnungen* as translated by the Rev. Charles E. Miche; the first few installments (January 14 to June 20, 1933) appeared as "Eggen's History of Highland."

Spindler, Julius J. "Our Town, a History of Unrecorded Highland." A weekly column, *Highland News Leader.*

Parts 1–3 of the *Reisebericht,* translated by Spindler and Emilie Abendroth, appeared under this masthead October 28, 1947–April 12, 1949.

Staffelbach, Georg. "Wie d'Surseer z'Amerika aene d'Stadt Highland (Illinois) gruendet und drin e Laebtig gha hend." Offprint, *Luzerner Landbote.* Lucerne, 1952.

————. "Das Luzerner Zofingertrio Doctores medicinae Kaspar Koepfli sen. et Jun. und Luzerner Kolonie Neu-Schweizerland oder Highland im Staate Illinois im Jahre 1831." Offprint, *150 Jahre Zofinger Luzern 1820–1970.* Immensee, 1970.

————. "Surseer Korporationsbuerger, die in Amerika einen neuen Wohnsitz suchten, 1831–68." *Der Schweizer Familien-Forscher* (Bern) 15, no. 3–4, (1948): 18–22.

————. "125 Jahre Neu-Sursee oder Highland, Illinois, USA." In *700 Jahre Stadt Sursee, 1256–1956.* Sursee, 1956, pp. 279–90.

Steinach, Severin Adelrich. *Geschichte und Leben der Schweizer Kolonien in den Vereinigten Staaten von Nord Amerika.* New York: Steiger-Bund, 1899.

"A. S." [Suppiger, Anton?]. *Highland Herald,* December 1, 1881.

This article discusses the conditions in Switzerland leading to the 1831 emigration of the Koepflis and Suppigers.

Suppiger, Joseph. "Ansicht ueber Kolonizations- Gesellschaften." *Der Nordamerikaner,* no. 19, August 10, 1933, pp. 73–74.

[Suppiger, Joseph, and Koepfli, Salomon.] *Reisebericht der Familie Koepfli & Suppiger nach St. Louis am Mississippi und Gruendung von New Switzerland im Staate Illinois.* Sursee, 1833.

This edition contained four parts.

[Suppiger, Joseph; Koepfli, Salomon; and Koepfli, Kasper.] *Reisebericht der Familie Koepfli & Suppiger nach St. Louis am Mississippi und Gruendung von new Switzerland im Staate Illinois.* 2d ed. Sursee, 1833.

This edition contained a part 5, Kaspar Koepfli's "Licht-& Schattenseite der Gegend, die wir zu unserm Aufenthalt auserkohren," with a letter by Salomon Koepfli to his brother Kaspar-Mauris in Sursee, who edited and saw to the publishing of the *Reisebericht*. Reprinted Bern, 1973. Also reprinted serially in the *Luzerner Neueste Nachrichten,* July 17–October 5, 1976.

Translations of portions of the *Reisebericht* were published in the United States: the first three parts by Julius J. Spindler and Emilie Abendroth, *Highland News Leader,* October 28, 1947–April 12, 1949; a portion of part 3 (the Swiss group's trip through Ohio, August 10–22, 1831) by Leo Titus, *Bulletin of the Historical and Philosophical Society of Ohio,* no. 3, July 1956, pp. 167–85; and part 4, also by Titus, *Journal of the Illinois State Historical Society,* winter 1956, pp. 431–44. (Lovejoy Library's Suppiger Collection also has a typescript translation by Titus of parts 1–3.

Copies of the five-part *Reisebericht* are known to be held by only five libraries: Library of Congress; New York Public Library; Zentralbibliothek, Lucerne; Belleville, Illinois, Public Library; and Newberry Library, Chicago.

Titus, Leo G.

For his translations of portions of the *Reisebericht* see entry under [Suppiger, Joseph; Koepfli, Salomon; and Koepfli, Kaspar].

Wasser, Elise M. *1845 Census of Madison County, Illinois.* Edwardsville, Ill., 1985.

Widmer, Max, and Lauer, Hans E. *Ignaz Paul Vital Troxler.* Zug, 1980.
Pages 147 and 168 concern Kaspar Koepfli.

Zschokke, E. "Kaspar und Salomon Koepfli und die Gruendung der Schweizerkolonie 'Highland' in Illinois." *Der Deutsche Pionier* II (1879): 43–50, 97–104.

Zschokke, Heinrich. "Die Gruendung von Maryland" (The Founding of Maryland). In *Gesammelte Schriften.* Aarau, 1851.
Cited by Kaspar Koepfli in his "Farewell Letter," this series of twenty-three fictitious letters can now be found in Zschokke's *Werke,* ed. Hans Bodmer, 12 vols. (Berlin: Bong, n.d.), 8:115–93.

———. *Stunden der Andacht zur Befoerderung wahren Christentums und haeuslicher Gottesverehrung.* Aarau, 1825.
This devotional work, which appeared weekly 1808–18, was cited by Salomon Koepfli in his *Geschichte.*

Zschokke, Rolf. "Beitrag zur Gruendungsgeschichte der City of Highland, Madison County, Illinois, USA." In *Festschrift Karl Schib*, pp. 420–58. Schaffhauser Beitraege zur vaterlaendischen Geschichte, no. 45. Thayngen, 1968. A translation prepared under the auspices of Betty Spindler Coats in 1970 is in Lovejoy Library's Suppiger Collection.

UNPUBLISHED MATERIAL

Articles of Association, or "Hauptbuch ueber Soll und Haben der Company Koepfli und Suppiger vom Oktober 1831." Koepfli Collection.
Agreement between five Koepflis and two Suppigers to buy and hold property in common.
Brodtbeck, Susette (née Gysin). Two German-language copybooks containing (1) a diary begun in 1815 by Susette Brodtbeck's mother, Anna (née Seiler, 1797–1846; (2) a diary kept by Susette's sister Liseli (1824–62), who became the first wife of Salomon Koepfli. Koepfli Collection.
Eggen, Jacob. Letter to Jh. Jc. Eggen [Sr.] in Aarau. New Switzerland, April 5–May 3, 1835. Photocopy. Suppiger Collection.
A map of "Neu Schweizerland" enclosed in Eggen's 1835 letter shows Saline, Helvetia, St. Jacob, and Marine townships, with holdings of individuals indicated, as well as woods, prairies, streams, and the hills "Rigi" and "Jura."
Journal der Company Koepfli & Suppiger, 1831–32. Koepfli Collection.
Begun October 1, 1831, this journal includes an inventory of the items held in common, listing of expenses incurred by the company and by Suppigers and Koepflis individually, a listing of Dr. Koepfli's patients and the amounts charged them. It comprises 46 pages of a ledger, the last 246 pages of which contains records of transactions with various individuals.
Koepfli, Kaspar. Farewell Letter. Koepfli Collection.
The multilithed copy used for our translation has a hand-written notation giving the day of the Swiss group's departure from Sursee as April 22, 1831, though the actual date was April 21.
Land Records involving the first tract (E½, NE¼, Section 31, 4N, R4W) settled by the Swiss colonists. Photocopies. History Collection, Louis Latzer Memorial Public Library.
The records include the grant to Joseph Howard November 16, 1816, its transfer by Howard to Ross Houck December 31, 1830, and its sale by warranty deed to Kaspar Koepfli, Joseph Suppiger, and Joseph Vonarx October 5, 1831.
Records and Accounts of the Koepflis' financial dealings with various persons and firms. Koepfli Collection.
Comprising 1676 pages, the records contain entries from October 4, 1831, through July 2, 1869.
Schweizer, Max "Koepfli's Neu-Schweizerland 1831–50," Diplomarbeit, Geographisches Institut, Universitaet Zurich, 1978. Typescript.

Available at Elijah P. Lovejoy Memorial Library, Southern Illinois University–Edwardsville, unless otherwise indicated.

Suppiger, Joseph. Journals. Widener Library, Harvard University.
    Suppiger's class notes, kept as a student at the *Lehrverein* in Aarau,
    1824–25, were donated March 30, 1945, Leo Ammann to Widener Lib-
    rary, where they are listed as "Journals."

COLLECTIONS IN ILLINOIS LIBRARIES CONTAINING CATALOGED MATERIAL ON NEW SWITZERLAND

Historical Collection, Louis Latzer Memorial Public Library, Highland, Ill.
    Contains an extensive collection of documents, correspondence, microfilms,
    genealogy, books, reprints, and illustrative material pertaining to Highland.
Koepfli Collection, Lovejoy Library, Southern Illinois University–Edwardsville.
    Contains thirty-six packets of documents, letters, manuscripts, certificates,
    diaries, warranty and mortgage deeds, indentures, contracts, land transfers,
    nineteenth-century newspapers, and rare books. Donated by Joseph Blake
    Koepfli, great–grandson of the Swiss colony's founder.
Suppiger Collection, Lovejoy Library, Southern Illinois University–Edwardsville.
    Contains several steel files of documents, correspondence, manuscripts, illus-
    trative material, translations, certificates, deeds, land grants and transfers,
    rare books, and nineteenth-century newspapers. Donated by Betty Spindler
    Coats, whose forebears helped found New Switzerland.
Highland Collection, Lovejoy Library, Southern Illionois University–Ed-
    wardsville.
    Contains research material—other than that in the Koepfli and Suppiger
    Collections—consisting of rare books, maps and atlases, and documents.
Illinois Historical Survey Library, University of Illinois, Urbana.
    Houses an extensive collection of material concerning the Swiss in Illinois.

Family histories in these collections are listed in Betty Spindler Coats, comp., *The
Swiss on Looking Glass Prairie,* ed. Raymond J. Spahn (Edwardsville, Ill.: Friends
of Lovejoy Library and the Highland Historical Society, 1983), pp. 113–15.

INDEX

Aarau, Educational Institute at, xi
Agio, defined, 8
Ague, in Illinois, 156, 187
Akron, Ohio: canal lock at, 112; description of, 113
Albany, N.Y.: arrival in, 96; coach shipped to, 73, 93; description of, 96; elevation of, 102; steamboat trip to, 73, 92, 94–96. *See also Henry Eckford*
Albany and New York Line (steamboats), 111
Albion, N.Y., 107
Alexander's Bridge, N.Y., aqueduct at, 98
Alton, Ill., development of, 206
Ambuel, Abraham, 25
America. *See* United States of America
Amsterdam, N.Y., 99
André Guillot & Company. *See* Guillot, André, & Company
Anthony's Nose, observed, 94
Antonin (two-master), departure of, 46
Architecture, 99, 187–88
Ashtabula, Ohio, 111
Athens, N.Y., 95
Aufzeichnungen aus Highlands Gruendungszeit (Eggen, 1888), xii, xv, xvii, xviii
Azores: hurricanes in, 51; not observed, 61

Ballast: function explained, 52–53; reserve water as, 65
Bank notes, American use of, 91

Banks, American: daily operations of, 90–91; organization of, 91–92; services available at, 92. *See also* United States Bank
Barbe, Mr. J., 33–34, 40–41, 46, 49; warning against, 200
Barley, 180
Barnsback, George, 136n.3
Barnsback, Julius L., 136, 138, 139, 149
Barriere la Chapelle St. Denis (Paris), arrival at, 17
Bar-sur-Aaube: distance to, 10; passage through, 14
Baylett, Thomas (captain of *Emigrant*), 121
Bear Mountain, observed, 94
Beaver hats, 88
Bedlow (Bedloe's) Island, 71
Belfort: distance to, 9; passage through, 11–12
Blacks, in Illinois, 159, 193
Blakeman, Curtis, 157–58
Blanc, X., 122
Bolivar, Ohio, 114
Boston, from Havre to New Orleans, 167
"Bottom," defined, 177, 189
Bourglibre, France, 9. *See also* St. Louis, France
Brak, Mr., 115
Brockport, N.Y., 105–6
Buehlmann, Mr., 14
Buffalo, N.Y.: arrival at, 108; booked passage to, 96; canal near, 102; description of, 109; elevation of, 102. *See also New Philadelphia*

Butter: canned, 77; sale of, 171, 184

Calomel, use of, 187
Canada, observed from Lake Erie, 109
Canajoharie, N.Y., 100
Canal travel, 97–108, 111–14, 122, 125
Canastota, N.Y., 103
Canton, N.Y., 103
Canton, Ohio: German tanner from, 113
Cape Girardeau, Mo., 127
Capen, Timothy (captain of *Citizen*), 112
Carlists: departure from Paris, 19–20, 22; collaboration with Napoleonists, 23
Carondolet, Mo., 128
Champlain Canal, 108
Charles X, 6n.2, 22, 23. *See also* Carlists; France, revolution in 1830
Chaumont-en-Bassigny: distance to, 10; passage through, 13
Chavanne-sur-l'Étang: distance to, 9; documents sent from, 10
Cheese-making: attempted, 160, 206; market for, 184; milk for, 163
Chilton, Thomas, 143–44
Chronicles of Early Highland (trans. Dreisner, 1977), xii, xvii, xviii
Cincinnati, Ohio: arrival at, 121; bishop at, 123; cost of trip to, 119; departure from, 124; description of, 122; future of, 124; steamboat trip to, 119–20; ways to approach, 114, 115
Citizen (canalboat), 112. *See also* Ohio and Erie Canal, booked passage on
Clarkson, N.Y., 106
Cleveland, Ohio: arrival at, 111;

booked passage to, 109; departure from, 112; description of, 112; lock at, 112
Climate. *See* Weather
Clyde, N.Y., 101, 102, 104
Coats, Betty Spindler, xii, xviii
Collinsville, Ill., 137n.5
Combeau-Fontaine: arrival in, 13; distance to, 9
Communes, impracticality of, xx–xxi, 201–2, 204–5
"Company Acts of the Family Koepfli and Suppiger Brothers" (1831), xx n.7
Cooperative colonist ventures. *See* Communes
Corn: for hogs, 168; yields of, 169, 180–81
Courtage, defined, 8
Cows: cost of, 99, 171, 184; fattened, 184; return on, 163, 168, 170, 184–85; upkeep of, 106, 163, 170–71; uses of, 106
Cumberland (steamboat), 124, 125
Cumberland Road, 137n.5. *See also* National Highway

Dancing, lack of, 168
Das illustrirte Mississippithal (Lewis, 1854–58), xvii
Dayton, Ohio, 114, 122
Deck, Michael, 138
Democrats, in France, 23
DeRham, Henry Casimir, 8, 90n.3
DeRham, Iselin and Moore: New York bills of exchange payable at, 8, 9, 90
Die Licht- & Schattenseite von New Switzerland in Nordamerika (K. Koepfli, 1833), xvi, xvii, 175n.1
Dommann, Jakob, Sr., 8
Dresden, Ohio: arrival at, 114;

booked passage to, 112; description of, 114; travel to Zanesville from, 118

Driesner, Manfred, xii

Drinking, American habits of, 161, 165

Duden, Gottfried: in Dutzow, Mo., 129n.16; on Illinois prairies, 139; impressions of USA from, 205; influence of, on Koepfli family, xxix; on male servants, 160; reference to, in *Reisebericht*, xxii, 50, 53, 74, 80, 110, 119, 120, 122, 123, 124, 129; on traveling via New Orleans, 167; trees listed in, 178; on water in Illinois, 139n.8, 187; writing of, xv, xix

Dugger, Jarrett, sawmill of, 144

Dutzow, Mo., 129n.16

East, James, 144

East St. Louis. *See* Illinois Town, Ill.

Edwardsville, Ill., federal land office at, 137

Eggen Johann Jacob, xii, xv, 176n.2, 212

Eggen, Rosa Koepfli (Mrs. Jacob Eggen): bedroom of, 141: birth of (1810), xxvi; death of (1849), 212; emigration of (1831), xxx; health of, 74; marriage of (1836), xv; during sea voyage, 53; trip to Switzerland (1841–49), 211–12

Emigrant (steamboat), 121. *See also* Ohio River, steamboat trip on

Emigration (general): character of other emigrants observed, 18–19, 24–25; difficulties of, xx–xxii, 1, 164, 195, 205; disappointment of, 205; encouraged, xix, 162–63; exploitation of, 33, 34, 94, 123, 191;

indentured, 167–68; money needed for, 168–70, 180, 199; requirements for, 164; scenario for future of, through France, 26–27, 200; and servants, 202–3; success of, 164–65, 194; suggestions for, 198–201; through France, 6, 11, 18, 200; treatment aboard ships, 32–33

Emigration, by Koepfli and Suppiger family: accommodations during, 13, 14, 15, 17, 41, 45–46, 94, 96, 98, 103, 110, 115, 117, 118–19; arrival in New York, 68, 69, 70–73; composition of initial party, xxx, 2, 119n.11; costs of, 26, 42, 44, 80–83, 94, 101, 106, 108, 109, 115, 116, 119, 124, 125; decision made by Kaspar (1831), xxix, xxxii; departure from Sursee, 5; first considered (1817), xxv; good treatment in New York, 94; inconveniences of, 13; preparations for sea voyage, 24, 45–46; provisions used during, 82–83; reasons for, xii, xxv, xxviii, xxx, xxxii; sale of horses during, 18, 19, 20–21; steamboat trip from Paris to Havre, 18, 19; suspicions cast on, 39; treatment during, 15–16; wagon repairs during, 6, 7–8, 14–15. *See also* Sea voyage to New York

Enclyde (steamboat), 125

England, coast described, 47

English (language): K. Koepfli's refusal to learn, 158–59; use of, 201, 206

Engoville, near Havre, 32

Enterprise (steamboat), 112. *See also* Lake Erie, steamboat passage over

Erie, Pa., 110

Erie Canal: architecture seen from, 99; bridges over, 101, 103; canalboat accommodations, 98, 103; canalboat size, 102; construction of, 98, 100, 102; cost of land along, 99, 105; cost of travel on, 101, 106, 108; diagram of, 101–2; entry into, 97; length of, 97, 101–2; locks of, 99–100, 101, 102–3; ownership of, 97; passing boats on, 101; repairs to, 106, 107; tolls on, 97, 106; traffic on, 100; travel on, 98; weigh house on, 97. *See also names of individual towns along*; *New Philadelphia*

Ernst, Ferdinand, commune of, 202

Faehnrich family, 48–49, 58; travel diary by son, 49, 53, 71, 79

"Farewell Letter" (K. Koepfli, 1831), xxix, xxx–xxxiv

Farmers Line (canalboats), 112

Farming: arable land for, 178; cost of, 168–70; profit from, 170

Fellenberg, Philipp Emanuel von, 181

Fencing, American-style, 161, 168, 178–79, 183

Food. *See* Provisions

Fort Chilton, 143

Fort Lafayette, passage near, 71

Fort Richmond, passage near, 71

France: border crossing into, 5–6, 9; coast described, 46; emigrant party's impressions of, 11, 12, 24; farming in, 11; late eighteenth-century domination of Switzerland by, xxvi–xxvii; law on freight wagons in, 6–8; passage of other emigrants through, 6, 11, 18; political factions in, 22–23; post regulations in, 10–11; revolution in 1830, xxix, 6n.2; roads described, 12, 16; road tolls (*droit de poste*)

in, 5, 10, 12–13; royal hunting lodge observed, 17; scenario for future travel through, 26–27, 200

Francois I (mail ship), 32, 36, 37

Fraud, 191

Freemason, Kaspar Koepfli as, xxvii

French (language), use of, 201

Fritz, Captain (of *Henriette*), 35, 36, 39, 45; and arrival in New York, 69, 71–72; gift to, 44

Funk, Captain (of *La France*), 40, 47, 56, 63, 68, 69

Galant, 89

Gallipolis, Ohio, 120

Geiger, William, 143

Geiger family, 143

Geisshuesler, Moritz: emigration of (1831), 2; in Havre, 25; in Paris, 19; sea voyage on *Henriette*, 44; steamboat trip to Havre, 21; and wagon repairs, 14; as watchman, 15; in Zanesville, 115

Genesee River, 104

German emigrants: in Illinois, 167; in New York State, 105; in Ohio, 113, 114, 122–23

Geschichte der Ansiedlung von Highland (S. Koepfli, 1859), xii, xvii, 129n.16

Government, local, 192

Grantfork, Ill., 137n.5

Gruenenwald, N., 123

Grueningen, John Paul von, 211

Guillot, André, 36

Guillot, André, & Company, 35, 36, 39, 43

Gulf Stream, effect on rough seas, 61

Gutmann, Mr., accompanying party to Albany, 93–94

Hares, 166

Hauenstein Mountains, 5

Havre: accommodations in, 24, 25; arrival at, 24; departure from, 24; description of, 31, 32; meals while staying in, 31–32; recommended to other emigrants, 200; by stagecoach from Paris, 22, 23–24; by steamboat from Paris, 18, 19, 200; tides observed at, 31; travel distances to, 9–10

Haymaking, 183

Helfenstein, Kaspar: in argument at Pont-sur-Saône, 12; emigration of (1831), 2; in Havre, 25; lost in Paris, 19; sea voyage on *Henriette*, 44; settlement in Albany, 115; steamboat trip to Havre, 21

Helvetia township, blacks in, 193n.8

Henderson, Ky., 126

Henriette: accommodations aboard, 37, 38; arrival in New York 69, 72; booked for passage, 36–37; contract for, 36–37, 43; departure of, 45; inspection of, 35; number of passengers on, 37–38, 39, 41–42; preparations made aboard, 38–39; registration of passengers aboard, 40, 41–42; water casks for, 39; withdrawal from travel on, 41, 44. *See also* Sea voyage to New York

Henry Eckford (steamboat), 111. *See also* Albany, N.Y., steamboat trip to

Herbster, Mr., 109

Herculaneum, Mo., 127, 128

Herkimer, N.Y., 101

Highland, Ill.: Americanization of, 211; blacks in township, 193n.8; growth of, 211; naming of, 211; site laid out, 211. *See also* New Switzerland

Hitz, Anna, 25

Hitz, Christina, 25

Hitz, Hans: assistance of, 24, 25, 36, 37, 42, 45; health of, 75; reasons for emigrating, 49; during sea voyage, 53; settling in Hoboken, 93

Hitz, Johann, 25, 49

Hoboken, N.J., settlement in, 93

Hogs: breeding, 163–64, 168, 171, 185; butchering, 171–72, 184

Holzhuete, 88

Horses: cost of, 99, 172, 185; in Illinois, 185; in New York City, 89; in Ohio, 117, 185; sale of, in Paris, 18, 19, 20–21; shipping of, 111; upkeep of, 171, 172, 184–85

Houck, Ross: land purchased from, 135, 137; and land purchased from McAlilly, 143

Howard, Joseph, 138, 142–43; sister of, 157

Howes, Wright, xvi

Hudson, N.Y., 95

Hudson Canal, 108

Hudson River: description of, 95; falls on, 100; traffic on, 96

Hudson River valley, description of, 94–95

Huger, Catherine: bedroom of, 141; in initial party, xxx, 119n.11; in Havre, 25

Hunting, wildlife for, 166

Huser, Abraham, 143

Illinois: decision to settle in, xxix, 1, 135–37, 188–89, 206; discredited in St. Louis, 206; land survey in, 191; move to, 138–40; woods in, 176–77, 178; unhealthy areas in, 176, 187, 206

Illinois Town, Ill., 138, 157

Indentured emigration, 167–68

Indiana, wine from, 114, 123

Indian Hill, St. Jacob Twp., 176n.2

Indians: near New Switzerland, 143, 149; pyramids of, 176; in St. Louis, 159, 193; volunteer military against, 193

Ireland, passage near, 48, 50

Irish emigrant: dislike for, 99, 116

Iselin, Isaac: in Albany, N.Y., 96; bid farewell by, 94; correspondence with, 135; letter of recommendation from, 43; money managed by, 90. *See also* DeRham, Iselin and Moore

Iselin Brothers, Basel and New York: money-changing at, 8; postage care of, 9; reliability of, 199

Jacobson, John, 114, 115

Jefferson Barracks, Mo., 128

Jenny, Mr., 24, 45

Jews, money-changing by, 8

Joller, Mr.: assistance from, 35, 36; payment demanded by, 42, 43

Jordan, N.Y., 103

Joy, Mr., 109

Jura, naming of, 142

Kaeser, Jennie Latzer, xii, xvi, xvii

Kappeler, Alois: emigration of (1831), 2; in Havre, 25; joined initial party, 8; sea voyage on *Henriette*, 44; and wagon repairs, 14; in Zanesville, 115

Keelboat, described, 117

Keller, Sebastian: beds made by, 140; in initial party, xxx, 2, 119n.11; in Havre, 25; lost in New Switzerland, 152–53; lost in Paris, 19, 20; with news of broken wagon wheel, 14; in New York, 73; and sea voyage on *Henriette*, 44; and steamboat trip to Havre, 21; wages for, 160

Kill Van Kull, 71n.9

Koepfli, Bernard (founder's son): birth of (1804), xxvi; death of (1882), 211; debate with Joseph, 149–52; emigration of (1831), xxx; health of, 74, 75; land inspected by, 135, 136; return to Switzerland (1841), 211

Koepfli, David (founder's son), death of (1819), xxvi

Koepfli, Elisa Gysin (Mrs. Salomon Koepfli), 212

Koepfli, Elisabeth Widmer (Mrs. Kaspar Koepfli): cheerful countenance of,151; death of (1843), 211; emigration of (1831), xxx, 2; illness of, xxii, 10, 74, 155–56, 160; marriage of (1798), xxvii; opposition to emigration, 151–52; return to Switzerland (1841), 211

Koepfli, Eugene (Salomon's eldest son), 212

Koepfli, Johannes Sebastian *Kaspar* (one of colony's founders): birth of (1774), xxvi; death of (1854), 212; education of, xxvi; on elements of successful emigrant, xxi–xxii; as emigration leader (1831), xi, xxv, xxx, 2; health of, 74; illness of, 13, 15, 16, 17; land inspected by, 135, 136; marriage of (1798), xxvii; move to Sursee by (1821), xxviii; as physician in Illinois, 157–59; pleased with move to Illinois, 152; political views of, xxvii–xxviii, xxix; religious views of, xxvii; reasons for emigrating, xii, xxv, xxviii, xxxi–xxxiv; during sea voyage, 53; as signer of *Henriette* contract, 37; trip to Switzerland (1841–49), 211–12; writings of, xv, xvi, xvii, xxix, xxx–xxxiv, 212

Koepfli, Joseph (founder's son): arranging canalboat, 111; birth of

(1804), xxvi; death of (1874), 212;
debate with Bernard, 149–52;
emigration of (1831), xxx; health
of, 75; sale of horses by, 19, 21–
22; sightseeing in Paris, 22;
stagecoach trip to Havre, 21, 23–
24; trip to Switzerland (1841–43),
211; wagon purchased by, 144
Koepfli, Joseph Blake (founder's
great-grandson), xvii, xviii, xxv
n.1, 212
Koepfli, Joseph Otto (Salomon's son)
(1866–1942), 212
Koepfli, Joseph *Salomon* Julian
(founder's youngest son): birth of
(1814), xxvi; caution of xx–xxi;
on cooperative colony of emigrants, xx–xxi; death of (1869),
212; education of, xi; emigration
of (1831), xxx; health of, 74; as
interpreter, 159; trip to Switzerland (1841–43), 211; wives of,
212; writings of, xv, xvi
Koepfli, Kaspar Mauris (founder's
eldest son): birth of (1799), xxvi;
caution of, xx; education of, xxvi,
xxviii; emigration of (1839), xi,
xxx; family of, xxx; foreword to
Reisebericht, xix, 1–2; as recipient
of letters, xi; writing of, xvi, xvii,
175n.1
Koepfli, Katharina (founder's sister).
See Suppiger, Katharina Koepfli
Koepfli, Ludovika Schnyder (Mrs.
Kaspar Mauris Koepfli), 175n.1
Koepfli, Rosa (founder's daughter).
See Eggen, Rosa Koepfli
Koepfli, Rosalie Brodtbeck (Mrs.
Salomon Koepfli), 212
Koepfli: A Partial Family History (J.
B. Koepfli, 1981), xxv n.1
Koepfli travel party: composition of,
xxx, 2, 119n.11; financial means

of, 157; respect accorded to, 55–
56; return to Switzerland (1841),
211. *See also* Emigration, of
Koepfli and Suppiger family

Laborers, in USA. *See* Wages, in USA
Lacroix, Paul, 122
La Doele, stove from, 76
La-Forge-Foret: breakfast in, 24; distance to, 10
La France (packet): accommodations
aboard, 41, 45–46, 47, 56, 59–60;
arrival in Havre, 40; arrival in
New York, 68, 69, 70–73; cooking
aboard, 54–55, 75–76; cost of
travel on, 44; crew of, 47–48, 57,
59, 68, 69–70; decision to travel
aboard, 41; departure from Havre,
46; description of, 52–53; greeted
by press boats, 68, 69; health inspection of, 72; passengers described, 48; preparations aboard,
45–46; storage aboard, 45, 47, 57,
63; storm damage to, 58, 68;
stowaway aboard, 46; unloading
of gear from, 87. *See also* Sea
voyage to New York
Lake Erie, steamboat passage over,
109–11
La maison rouge: accommodations
at, 17; distance to, 10
Lancaster, Pa., emigrants headed for,
48
Land speculation, discouraged, 192
Land survey: markers for, 149; and
ownership claims, 191, 192; process of, 191
Langres: arrival in, 13; distance to, 9
Lebanon, Ill., wagon purchased at,
144
Le Havre. *See* Havre
Les Granges: accommodations in, 17;
distance to, 10

Les Grez: chalk stable at, 17; dis-
   tance to, 10
Lewis, Henry, xvii
Little Falls, N.Y., 100
Livestock: acquired at New Switzer-
   land, 142, 149; identification of,
   185; observed in New York City,
   89–90; pasture for, 163, 182–83;
   shelter for, 183–84. *See also* Cows;
   Hogs; Horses; Oxen
Livingston, N.Y., stop near, 95
Lockport, N.Y., 102, 107–8
Log houses, construction of, 187–88
Long Island: described, 71; land
   sighted, 67, 68
Looking Glass Prairie, description of,
   139; location of, 191; size of, 139.
   See also New Switzerland
Louis Philippe I (king of France):
   celebration for, 13–14; followers
   of, 22; palace of, 21; reign of, 23
Louisville, Ky.: booked passage to,
   122; description of, 126; travel to,
   124
Lucerne, Lake of, compared to up-
   state New York, 94
Luethy, Dr., 25, 53
Lure: arrival in, 12; distance to, 9
Lutolf, Mr., wages for, 160
Lyons, N.Y., 104

McAlilly, John, 138, 140, 141
McAlilly, Samuel, 138, 140, 141, 143
McAlilly's Settlement, 138, 140. *See
   also* New Switzerland
McConnelsville, Ohio, 117
McCoy, Ralph, xvi
Madison County, Ill., 191–92
Maize. *See* Corn
Malaria, 187n.5. *See also* Ague
Mandrot de Luze, B., 43
Marietta, Ohio: arrival at, 119; dif-

ficulty reaching, 115; flatboat trip
   to, 115–16, 117–18
Marine Settlement, Ill., 137n.5, 138
Martiniquaise (three-master), 46
Massillon, Ohio, 113
Maysville, Ky., 121
Medicine: available, 155, 156–57;
   plants, growing wild, 100; use of,
   187
Medina, N.Y., 107
Metraux, Guy Serge, xvi, xx n.7, 211
Meuli, Mr. and Mrs. 25, 42, 43
Miami Canal, 122
Miami River, 122
Michigan, emigrants headed for, 111
Midletowe, N.Y., aqueduct near, 98
Military service, for Americans, 192–
   93
"Milk sick," 195n.9
"Mirror of America" (trans. Kaeser,
   1977), xii, xviii
Mississippi River: arrival at, 127; de-
   scription of, 127–28; navigation
   of, 127
Missouri: cost of land in, xxxiv; den-
   igration of, 123; intent to settle in,
   xxix, xxxiv; reasons for not set-
   tling in, 129n.16, 188–89
Mohawk River valley, description of,
   98, 99, 100, 101, 103
Money-changing, 8–9, 90, 199
Money-lending, in USA, 161
Monk's Mound, 176n.2
Montezuma, N.Y., 104
Mueller, Johann, 123
Mullanphy, John, 129n.16
Muskingum River, description of,
   114, 116, 117, 118, 119

Napoleon, veneration of, 23
Napoleonists, 22–23

National Highway, route of, 116, 137, 166

Neuenkirch (canton of Lucerne), xxvi–xxviii

Neu-Schweizerland, 1831–1880: Genese und Funktion einer Schweizerischen Siedlung in den USA (Schweizer, 1980), xx n.7

Neu-Schweizerland in den Jahren 1831 und 1841 (S. Koepfli, 1842), xvi

Newfoundland Banks: arrival at, 62, 63; passage near, 61; weather near 66

New Jersey, near coast of, 65

New Orleans, emigration via, 167, 200, 205

New Orleans (three-master), departure of, 45

New Philadelphia (canalboat), 112. *See also* Erie Canal, canalboat accommodations; Erie Canal, canalboat size

News, spread among neighbors, 157

New Switzerland: blacks in, 193n.8; buildings at, 138, 145, 152, 162, 165, cheese-making at, 160, 163, 206; crops at, 141, 162, 166, 168, 181–82; description of, 142, 205–6; drinking water of, 139n.8, 187; emigration to, xix; fencing at, 161, 166; growth of, 211; hunting at, 166, 197; lack of interest in, xv–xvi; land preparation at, 141, 168; livestock at, 142, 149; location of, 135, 175–76, 186; move to, 138–40; naming of, 1, 138; purchase of land for, 135–38, 141, 177, 206; settling into, 140–41, 145; shoots at, 197; soil of, 187; survey of, 149; tenants for, 162, 182; town site in, 211; trees at, 138, 149,

176, 177, 178; vineyard at, 141; writings about, xv–xviii. *See also* Highland; Looking Glass Prairie

New Switzerland in Illinois (ed. Spahn and Spahn, 1977), xii, xviii, xxiii

New York City: architecture of, 72, 88–89; arrival at, 67, 68, 69, 70–73; climate of, 87, 92; farm houses in, 90; fires in, 71, 87–88; good treatment in, 94; harbor described, 71, 72; map of, 87; prices in, 88; shops in, 89; streets in, 87, 89; uses of land in, 88

New York State: description of, 94–95, 109–10

Niagara Falls, N.Y., 108

Nicolet, Theodor, 201

Oats, cultivation of, 180

Ohio, description of, 114, 117, 119, 120, 124

Ohio and Erie Canal: booked passage on, 112; cost of travel on, 112; description of, 112; inspection of goods on, 112, land along, 114; location of, 110n.7; route of, 114n.9; travel on, 113

Ohio River: description of, 126, 127; size of, 119, 120; steamboat trip on, 119–21, 124, 126

Overpopulation, as problem in Europe, xxxiii

Owen, Robert, 202n.14

Oxen, 181

Painesville, Ohio, 111

Palmyra, N.Y., 104

Paris: accommodations in, 17–18; arrival at, 17; Carlist departure from, 19–20, 22; confusion in, 87, 89; depressed economy of, 20; dis-

Paris *(continued)*
tance to, 10; inspection avoided at,
17; paved roads in, 16; paved
roads to, 16; port of St. Nicholas,
18; sale of horses in, 18, 19, 20–
21; sightseeing in, 21, 22; transit
through, 18
Passports and visas, for emigration,
40
Pestalozzi, Johann Heinrich, 211
Philadelphia, emigrants headed to, 48
Piccoli, Mr. *See* Picoli, Mr.
Picoli, Mr.: assistance of, 19, 35, 36,
37; payment to, 44; quarrels with,
73; suit brought by, 42, 43–44
Pilot Line (canalboats), 112
Pine marten (*Didelphys opposum*),
166
Pittsford, N.Y., 104
Pleasant Point, Ohio, 120
Plows, 181
Pocahontas, Ill., 137n.5
Politics, treatment of in *Reisebericht*,
xxii
Pont-sur-Saône: distance to, 9; pas-
sage through, 12
Postage, care of Iselin Brothers,
Basel, 9
Potatoes, cultivation of, 181
Prairie: description of, 139; fires on,
145–49, 182–83
Prairie chickens (*Tympanuchus
Americanus*), 166
Press boats, 68, 69
Provisions: costs of, 80–83, 99; sug-
gested, 76–80, 198, 199; in USA,
168; used by Koepfli party, 82–83

Rabbits, wild, 166
Railroads: popularity of, 192; from
St. Louis, 167
Rapp, Johann Georg, 202

Reichstadt, duke of, 22, 23
Reilly, M., 122
Reisebericht: editions of, xvi–xvii,
xix–xx, xxiii; publication of
(1833), xi, xix; purpose of, xix,
xxii, 1; references to Duden in,
xxii, xxix, 50, 53, 74, 80, 110
Religion: treatment of, in
Reisebericht, xxii, 122, 123; in
USA, 168
*Report on a Journey to the Western
States of North America* (Duden,
1829), xv, xix, xxii, xxix
Reynolds, James, 139, 141
Ricinus oil, 182
Rigi, naming of, 142
Rindisbacher, Peter, 129n.16
River travel, 19, 115–29
Rochester, N.Y., 102, 104–5
Rome, N.Y., 101
Rouen: description of, 24; distance
to, 10
Rousseau, Jean Jacques, influence on
Kaspar Koepfli, xxvii
Ruetli, naming of, 141
Rye, cultivation of, 180

St. Louis (formerly Bourglibre),
France: arrival at, 5; customs
charges at, 26; departure from, 9,
10; distance to Havre, 9; inspection at, 5–6
St. Louis, Mo.: bishop at, 123; first
impression of, 128, 205; steamboats to, 122, 124–25, 201
Salem, Pa., 111
Saline township: blacks in, 193n.8;
first white baby in, 143
Salt meat: regulation governing
amount of, aboard ship, 54; provisioning of, 76, 78, 198
Salt pork: marketing, 180; prepara-

tion of, 171–72, 185; profit from, 185

Sandy Hook, lighthouse observed, 70

Schenectady, N.Y., 98

Schmidt, Mr., land for sale by, 203

Schweizer, Max, xx n.7

Schweizerbote (weekly newspaper), received in USA, 135

Seasickness: cause of, 109, 200–201; during Lake Erie voyage, 109, 110; during sea voyage, 47, 48, 50, 51, 53, 56, 59, 74–75; relief for, 78, 80, 201

Sea voyage to New York: activities during, 52, 61, 63; anticipating end of, 66, 67, 68; best timing for, 73; changes in arrangements for, 33–39; cost of, 24, 33, 34, 44; dangers of, 73–74, 194–95; fishing during, 63–64; length of, 46, 61, 64, 67, 73, 200; maneuvering during, 52; meals and provisions for, 54–55, 75–83; papers for, 40; passage booked for, 24, 41; preparations for, 24, 39–46, 75, 77–80, 82–83; proper clothing for, 74, 201; seasickness during, 47, 48, 50, 51, 53, 56, 59, 74–75; ships for, 31, 73; ships passed during, 47, 50, 51, 56, 57, 59, 60, 61, 62–63, 64, 65, 66, 67, 68, 71; treatment of emigrants during, 32–33; weather during, 46–47, 48, 50, 51–52, 53, 54, 55, 56, 57, 59, 60, 61, 62, 63, 64, 65–66, 66–67, 68; wildlife observed, 47, 50, 51, 60, 61, 62, 63, 64, 65, 66. *See also Henriette; La France*

Settlement: cost of, 168–70, 180, 199; land selection for, 178, 189–90, 192

Sheep, breeding, 172, 185

Shippingport, Ky., 124, 125

Silver Creek, 138, 139, 175, 177

Sissach (canton of Basel), arrival at, 5

Skunk (*vivera putrius,* actually *Methitis*), 166

Slavery, prohibited in Illinois, 159, 193

Smallpox, among emigrants, 42

Smith, Mr., 115, 116

"Social and Cultural Aspects of Swiss Immigration into the United States in the Nineteenth Century" (Metraux, 1949), xvi, xx n.7

Soller, Mr. *See* Joller, Mr.

Sonnenberg, naming of, 142

Spahn, Raymond Jurgen, xviii

Spiegel von Amerika (K. Koepfli, 1849), xii, xvii, 212

Spindler, Julius, xii

Squirrels, 166

Staten Island: lighthouses on, 70; quarantine station on, 71

Statue of Liberty, 71n.9

Steamboats: construction of, 118, 121; repairs on, 126; rivalry between, 124–25

Storm, at sea, 56–60

Story of the Settling of Highland (trans. Kaeser, 1970), xii, xvii, xxiii

Strohmann, Captain (of Erie canalboat), 109

Sugar Creek, 139, 175

Suppiger, Anton (founder's halfbrother): death of (1900), 212; during sea voyage, 53; in initial party, xxx, 2, 119n.11; health of, 74, 156, 212; map by, 149; writings of, xxv n.1, 212

Suppiger, Bernhardt (founder's cousin), emigration of (1833), 207

Suppiger, Franziska (founder's daughter), 212

Suppiger, Jacob *Joseph* Aloys, Sr. (1770–1833) (founder's father): death of (1833), xxx, 207n.15; emigration of (1833), xix, xxx, 207; marriage of (1804), xxvii

Suppiger, Johann (founder's uncle): emigration of (1833), xxx, 207; family of, xxx

Suppiger, Johanna (founder's cousin), emigration of (1833), 207

Suppiger, Johannes (1730–1805) (founder's grandfather), attack on, xxvii

Suppiger, *Joseph* Kaspar Thomas, Jr. (one of colony's founders): ability to speak English, 159; arranging canalboat, 111; birth of (1804), xxvii; as business manager, 36; construction work by, 140, 141; death of (1861), 212; as diary keeper, xi, xix, 2; education of, xi, xxviii; health of, 75; importance of, 212; in initial party, xxx, 2, 119n.11; "Journal" of, xi; land inspected by, 135, 136; lodgings in New York, 72; as paymaster, 17; reasons for emigrating, xxx; sale of horses by, 19, 21–22; sightseeing in Paris, 22; as signer of *Henriette* contract, 37; stagecoach trip to Havre, 21, 23–24; and wagon wheel repairs, 14; wagon purchased by, 144; writings of, xv

Suppiger, Katharina Koepfli (1772–1806) (Mrs. Joseph Suppiger, Sr.), marriage of (1804), xxvii

Suppiger, Mary Thorp (Mrs. Joseph Suppiger, Jr.), 212n.3

Suppiger, Melchior (founder's half-brother), emigration of (1833), xxx, 207

Suppiger, Monica Wickenhauser (Mrs. Anton Suppiger), 212

Suppiger, Regina (founder's cousin), emigration of (1833), 207

Suppiger, Xaver (founder's cousin), emigration of (1833), 207

Sursee: departure from, 5; family left in, 175n.1; family move to (1821), xxviii

Suzenecourt: distance to, 10; passage through, 13

Sweet potatoes, cultivation of, 181

Swiss Emigrants Society, 1

Swiss on Looking Glass Prairie: A Century and a Half, 1831–1981 (comp. Coats, 1983), xii, xviii, xxiii

Switzerland: conservative backlash in, xxix; consul in Havre, 43; liberal reform in, xii, xxvi–xxvii, xxix; news of events in, 135; problems in, xxxiii, xxxiv; road tolls in, 5

Syracuse, N.Y., 103

Talisman (steamboat), 125. *See also* St. Louis, Mo., steamboats to

Tannery, in Canton, Ohio, 113

Tenant farming, in New Switzerland, 162, 182

Tensier & Frère, lodgings with, 72

Tobel, 113

Toes, Sebastian, 123

Toscan (Toscar), the Italian, 25, 42, 43

"Tossing around" (game), 52

Troxler, Ignaz Paul Vital (1780–1866): emigrants' visit with, 9; grape vines from, 141; influence on Kaspar Koepfli, xxvii; influence on Joseph Suppiger, xi; political activity of, xxvii–xxviii, xxix; street in Highland named for, 211

Troy, Ill., 137n.5

Troy, N.Y., 97
Troyes: accommodations near, 15; arrival in, 16; distance to, 10; treatment of emigrants near, 15–16
Turkeys, 166

United States Bank, 90, 91, 92, 199. *See also* Banks, American
United States of America: accommodations in, 118–19; architecture of, 160, 187–88; birds in, 166; character of, 195–96; cost of settling in, 168–70; currency in, 130; dangers in, 195; drinking habits in, 161, 165; excessive cleanliness in, 59; farm equipment in, 181, 199; fencing in, 161, 168, 178–79; food in, 168, 196; honesty in, 191; hunting in, 166, 197; lack of dancing in, 168; land sighted, 67; maps of, 88, 114; meals in, 110; misconceptions about, 194–95; price of land in, 99, 105, 111, 124, 135, 138, 168, 190–91; religion in, 122–23, 168; soils in, 119, 126, 127, 165, success in, 161, 164–65, 169, 172, 180; Swiss admiration for, xxviii; trees in, 94–95, 120, 126–27, 177; wages in, 123; weights and measures in, 130–31, 137, 138, 180; wildlife of, 166, 195; work load in, 161, 198
USiana (Wright), xvi
Utica, N.Y., 101, 102

Valley of the Mississippi Illustrated (trans. Poatgieter; ed. Heilbron, 1967), xvii n.5
Vandalia, Ill.: cooperative near, 202; land near, 136
Vandeuvre: accommodations in, 14; distance to, 10; wagon repairs at, 14

Vevay, Ind., 124
Vevay vines, 123
Visas and passports, for emigration, 40
Vonarx, Joseph: in initial party, xxx, 2, 8, 119n.11; in Havre, 25; health of, 75; as paymaster, 17; wages for, 160; as watchman, 15

Wages, in USA, 123, 161, 162, 166, 167, 172
Wagons, American, 181
Wanner, Mr.: assistance of, 43, 45; as correspondent, 46; letters of introduction from, 46, 122
Wanner, Langer & Company, 42, 200
Washington, George, as a model, xxiii, xxx–xxxi, 211
Washington (steamboat), 125
Weapons, 197
Weather: during sea voyage, 46–47, 48, 50, 51–52, 53, 54, 55, 56, 57, 59, 60, 61, 62, 63, 64, 65–66, 66–67, 68; in USA, 114, 153–55, 160, 163–64, 180, 206
Weibel, Franz, 123
Weinmueller, Mr.: accommodations of, 48; accompanying party to Albany, 93–94; opinion of Barbe, 56
West Point, passage near, 94
Wheat: amount planted, 161, 162, 168, 169; market for, 180; price of, 169; sowing of, 179; yields of, 169, 179–80
Wilson, Mr., 115
Wine: made in Indiana, 114, 123; needed for sea voyage, 79–80, 199; prices of, 80–81, 196
Wine vinegar: required, 79, 199
Witness-trees, 149
Wuest, N., 18, 22

Zanesville, Ohio: accommodations
  in, 115, 117; arrival at, 115; described, 116; passage to, 112, 115,
  118
Zinc, manufacture of, 49–50
Zoar, Ohio, 114
Zschokke, Johann Heinrich Daniel
  (1771–1848): influence on Kaspar

Koepfli, xxvii, xxxi–xxxii; influence on Joseph Suppiger, xi;
  references to, in *Reisebericht*, 99;
  street in Highland named for, 211;
  writings of, xxviii, 99n.6, 142
Zwieback: regulation governing
  amount of, aboard ship, 54; provisioning of, 76, 77, 81, 83, 199